FOOTBALL IN THE DIGITAL AGE
Whose Game Is it Anyway?

EDITED BY
Sean Hamil, Jonathan Michie,
Christine Oughton and Steven Warby

FOREWORD BY JOHAN CRUYFF

MAINSTREAM
PUBLISHING
EDINBURGH AND LONDON

First published in Great Britain in 2000 by
MAINSTREAM PUBLISHING COMPANY (EDINBURGH) LTD
7 Albany Street
Edinburgh EH1 3UG

ISBN 1 84018 329 2

A catalogue record for this book
is available from the British Library

Typeset in Stone Serif
Printed and bound in Great Britain by Butler & Tanner Ltd

Contents

Foreword

JOHAN CRUYFF

Whose game is it anyway? Money appears increasingly to be the driving force in football, with media contracts not far behind. But anyone who knows anything about the game knows that nothing can be taken for granted. Anything can happen. And when it comes to the future ownership and direction of football, it is up to us, those with an interest in the good of the game itself, to make sure that the right decisions are made and that the right things happen.

The first goal of football must be the quality of the game. The role of money in today's game is important, of course, and cannot be ignored. But the huge flow of funds into the game from TV deals will only continue if the quality of the game is good enough to keep delivering the audiences. And, in terms of today's broadcasting arrangements, that means an audience that is not only attracted to watch the matches on TV but also to pay for the privilege, whether on a match-by-match basis through pay-per-view or by paying for a cable subscription or a satellite dish. Without an attractive product, there is nothing to sell.

Football has been described as 'the people's game'. Many of those in and around the 'business' today just do not think in these terms. They think not of the people but of the 'customers', the 'product', the 'branding' and the 'audience'. But in the long term these business opportunities will only be sustainable if the sport can remain just that – a sport. It is and must remain the people's game. If football does continue to serve the people, audiences and money will certainly follow. If the aim instead is just to exploit and make money, football itself will suffer and so too will the profitability of the 'business'. You cannot make money for long by selling a second-rate product. But by then of course the broadcasters would have moved onto some other entertainment 'content' with which to attract viewers, advertisers and subscribers. There is a real danger that commercial interests outside the game will kill the goose that lays the golden egg.

I write this not as someone who harks back to some 'golden age'. I do understand the modern game, including the commercial pressures and opportunities. Indeed, I have spent all my life in the service of football – first as a player, then as a coach. I think that I do have just as good an understanding of the 'business' of football as do those who are now moving in to use the game in the interests of rival broadcasting empires. The contributors to this book, myself included, are not advocating a return to the past. On the contrary, we need to move forward to ensure a greater degree of participation from fans than has generally been achieved so far.

We are not against progress. Nor are we against good management practices or increased commercial revenues. For my own part, I have been well rewarded for my efforts within the game, and that is as it should be. If football is pursued as a sporting spectacle, money will flow in, those involved can be properly rewarded, and the game can serve an important sporting, cultural and social role. Sporting success will lead to financial success. That is quite different, though, from wanting to use the game simply to make money.

In the book *A Game of Two Halves?* my friend Sir Alex Ferguson wrote:

> Certainly, football is big business. But it also plays an important role in the country's social and cultural life. Some may see it as just about money. I see it as much more important than that.

I would endorse these sentiments wholeheartedly. Sir Alex has been responsible for Manchester United becoming the wealthiest club in the world. But he knows that the real wealth lies in the devotion of the fans to their club, and in what football can bring to the lives of millions of people. That goes far beyond what can be accounted for in the balance-sheets.

And I would make one further point about Manchester United. As with all clubs, they have signed players from abroad and many of these players have been hugely successful, including with the fans of the club. But at the heart of the team is a group of local players who were brought up through the club's youth system. And that, too, is how it should be. Football clubs must remain precisely that – clubs. What does this mean? Well, a club must have responsibilities not just to the investors. A club must have a responsibility to its fans and to its local community. It should be involved in the life of the local community. And an important aspect of this is to encourage and train young players from the local schools, to bring them through the club's youth system and into the first team.

This might sound strange coming from the pen of someone who was signed as a foreign 'star' by Barcelona. But FC Barcelona have always played an important social and cultural role in the community. This is discussed in Chapter 15 by the L'Elefant Blau, the supporters' group that is defending the great traditions of FC Barcelona. One of these traditions has been to bring local players into the team to play alongside those who come from other clubs. Local involvement and responsibility are vital.

These sporting traditions are under threat across the world in all sorts of ways from commercial exploitation. Control has too often passed from people concerned with the good of the game to business people with their own agendas. For example, the stars are signed up for commercial promotions and activities. More and more competitions are dreamt up for TV broadcasters, with players required to play an impossible number of games. You can end up with a top international player being paid huge sums to promote some brand of football boot, for example, who, as a result of the increased number of games, is then repeatedly injured. Hardly a great promotion – more like the golden goose being strangled.

These are important issues that need to be analysed and discussed. It is therefore an extremely welcome development that alongside this increased commercialism over the past few years we have witnessed the growth of supporters' organisations such as L'Elefant Blau in Barcelona and seen a growth of serious policy analysis, such as this book. Clearly solutions to the new problems *are* emerging. There *is* a better way to proceed than the headlong rush into commercial exploitation. Football *can* be developed as a sporting, social and cultural institution at the same time as being well run and even profitable. Indeed, it is the sporting success that underlies the commercial opportunities. Forget that and you can forget everything.

For many in the game today, money seems to come first, with football a poor second. This, though, is a short-term and ultimately self-defeating attitude. The priorities need to be reversed. Football has to be enjoyed – by the players and the fans. That was always my attitude as a player and as a coach. The same attitude is needed from those who run the game today – the clubs, the football authorities and governments. Each country needs to find its own way of ensuring that those who are running football clubs cannot exploit the fans for their own personal or financial benefit. It is the people's game or it is nothing.

Johan Cruyff

Preface and acknowledgements

SEAN HAMIL, JONATHAN MICHIE, CHRISTINE OUGHTON AND
STEVEN WARBY

In our previous book, *A Game of Two Halves?,*[1] we attempted to do two things. First, to document that there are indeed growing problems within the business of football which, if not tackled now, threaten the long-term future of the business – quite apart from the game on which that business relies. Pre-publication copies of that book were provided to all delegates at a major international conference held at Birkbeck College in July 1999 attended by representatives of all the key footballing bodies and leading industry analysts. This first point gained widespread consensus – that there are indeed problems deserving of serious analysis and action.

The second aim of that book was to put forward our own views as to the best way forward. These issues are discussed in more detail in Chapter 1 below, but here we should acknowledge our gratitude to our co-authors of *A Game of Two Halves?* for those ideas; and to all those who attended the July 1999 conference to participate in what was an extremely well-informed and constructive event. The present volume came out of the July 1999 conference. As can be seen from the chapters that follow, differences emerged as to the most appropriate forms of policy action. But here we simply want to thank the various authors for the positive way in which they have engaged with the issues.

This volume aims to follow up *A Game of Two Halves?* by providing what we hope is the most comprehensive account yet produced – from the leading 'players' in football – of where the game is heading. For the first time ever, the views of the FA, the Premier League, the Football League, UEFA, the government, the Football Task Force, the Professional Football Association, the Coalition of Football Supporters and others have been brought together to take stock not only of where the industry is today but where it is going and what needs to be done to ensure that it develops positively in the future.

In addition to this cast from the footballing industry, the book includes the exclusive story from a member of the Monopolies and Mergers Commission panel for the BSkyB/Manchester United case on their decision to block BSkyB's moves. With this route blocked, BSkyB embarked on their 'plan B', as documented in this volume by Adam Brown. The chapters that follow likewise include reports from some of the key players in the Office of Fair Trading's case before the Restrictive Practices Court.

Bringing together as it does the leading football analysts and commentators with representatives of the main football and regulatory bodies to report on the latest developments and to reflect on future prospects, this book will, we believe, become the authoritative guide against which future developments can be assessed. The various authors provide unique insights into the key debates within the industry today. The text will therefore serve, we hope, as an essential 'one-stop' work of reference for all journalists, academics, lawyers, accountants and financial advisers, club administrators and regulatory and government officials with an interest in policy developments in the game.

For the fan we aim to offer a comprehensive and up-to-date account of the key issues facing football. This is the first book to analyse the implications of the 1999 Restrictive Practices Court ruling on the collective sale of football broadcasting rights; the implications of the UK government blocking of BSkyB's attempted takeover of Manchester United – and of BSkyB's subsequent attempts to buy into other Premier League clubs; the October 1999 policy proposals from the government to establish supporter-shareholder trusts and for a levy on the Premiership television deal to fund the grass-roots of the game; and the deliberations of the Football Task Force.

Our main debt of gratitude goes to all the authors for having provided their chapters under such tight deadlines and for having responded so fully and efficiently to all requests. As mentioned above, the authors presented their initial thoughts on their respective topics at a conference at Birkbeck College in July 1999 and we are grateful to the sponsors of that conference, the Co-operative Insurance Society (CIS), the Chartered Institute of Management Accountants (CIMA), FT$port, Soccer Investor, Waterstone's Bookshop, the Royal Economic Society and Birkbeck College itself. We are also grateful for assistance from Gerry Boon of Deloitte & Touche and Peter Hunt, General Secretary of the Co-operative Party. Many others assisted in making that conference the huge success that it was and our thanks go to Andy Burnham, Josie Charlton, Vivek Chaudury, David Conn, Neil Conway, Jenny Cook, Simon Deakin, Carolyn Downs, Duncan Drasdo, Ray Eccersely, Julia Elias, Dave Fenton, Michael Flaherty, Andrew Gamble, Laurence Harris, Patrick Harverson, Moira Hunter, Ricky King, Michael Kitson, Marianne Knight, Simon Lee, Yang Lin, Mark Longden, Jacqueline Mitchell, Roland Muri, Steven Parrott, Simon Roberts, Huw Richards, Nicola Richards, Simon Rundle, Lee Shailer, Peter Trim, Shraddha Verma, Andy Walsh, Charlie Whelan, Jim White, Shonagh

Wilkie and Paul Windridge for their assistance and participation.

We are grateful to Mainstream Publishing for their professional work in producing this book. As with *A Game of Two Halves?*, the staff at Mainstream turned the manuscript round with speed and efficiency and we are particularly grateful to Sharon Atherton, Bill Campbell, Judy Diamond, Sarah Edwards, Andrea Fraile and Elaine Scott.

The work that has gone into this book has led to two hugely encouraging developments. Firstly, a broad consensus has emerged across fans' organisations, players' and managers' representatives, officials from the footballing bodies, government and others with an active interest in the health of football, for tackling the problems of the game in a positive fashion. Those who say that nothing can be done, or that nothing *should* be done, have been well and truly left behind, as have those who are clearly pursuing their own financial, business or egotistical agendas.

Secondly this consensus has spread internationally, not only in consultation with the international organisations but also with the active participation of fans from European clubs. This is particularly important since one of the stock responses from those who wish to head off any interventionary measures is to say that nothing can be done since it would have to be done at an international, or at least European, level. To this the growing answer that is emerging is: yes, fine, let's take action collectively, at the European and international levels. Here our colleagues from FC Barcelona , organised through L'Elefant Blau (the Blue Elephant), have been truly inspirational. Particular thanks go to Armand Carabén and Joan Laporta.

Sir Alex Ferguson contributed an important foreword to *A Game of Two Halves?* in which he warned of the unsustainable pressures emerging in the game and called for action very much along the lines of the growing international consensus just referred to. In view of this growing coalition of forces it is particularly pleasing and appropriate that the foreword to this book should have been contributed by one of the greatest players of all time, and someone who is known for his genuine love and knowledge of the game – Johan Cruyff.

In *A Game of Two Halves?*, we advocated the increased involvement of supporters in their clubs, including through share-ownership and even the mutualisation of clubs. It was therefore fantastically exciting for all involved in the game in Britain when the Secretary of State for Culture, Media and Sport, the Rt Hon Chris Smith MP, announced at the Labour Party conference in October 1999 that the government were to give assistance to such efforts by fans. We are grateful, of course, to Chris Smith for his vision and courage in making this commitment, and also to his

Special Advisor Andy Burnham for his work in translating this political commitment into practical action through the establishment of a national unit to provide legal and other advice to such supporter groups. Great work is also being done on this by the Football Trust, and the gratitude of all football fans should go to Alastair Bennett, Philip French, Peter Lee and Tom Pendry, and likewise to Brian Lomax, Trevor Watkins and others who have been working unpaid to make a success of this initiative.

Key to the success of this project is of course the work being carried out by football fans across the country at various clubs, and Jonathan Michie is particularly grateful to his colleagues in the supporter-shareholder organisation Shareholders United, especially Ernie Battey, Monica Brady, Roger Brierley, Michael Crick, Eric Downs, Sarah Downs, Oliver Houston, Richard Hytner, Alastair Lees, Stewart Matthews and Sue Simpson. Jonathan is also grateful to various officials at Manchester United, including those on the plc board for their constructive and positive attitude. Thanks also go for valuable advice and assistance to David Dunn of the Co-operative Bank, Neil Harding of stockbroker Wise Speke and Kevin Jaquiss of Cobbetts Solicitors.

The authors are collaborating with supporters at numerous clubs to try to put these democratic principles into practice, and in addition to Brian Lomax, special thanks for assistance goes to Jeanette Findlay and Kevin Miles.

Finally, a special thanks from Jonathan Michie goes with love to Carolyn, Alex and Duncan.

Sean Hamil, Jonathan Michie,
Christine Oughton and Steven Warby

1. Whose game is it anyway?

SEAN HAMIL, JONATHAN MICHIE, CHRISTINE OUGHTON AND
STEVEN WARBY

The background to and purpose of this book is indicated in our preface above. The purpose of this introductory chapter is to place the various events referred to in that preface, and the substantive analyses of the following chapters, within an overall context.

INTRODUCTION: THE BUSINESS OF FOOTBALL

There has long been a keen interest in all things football – as a cultural and sporting activity in Britain. The business and regulation of professional sports has failed to arouse the same passion, however. This is in contrast to the United States where sport has attracted serious attention from business, financial and academic analysts, and where there is a large literature on these issues. This, however, is changing rapidly – the business of football has been transformed in Britain over the past few years and so has interest in all aspects of the game, including the money, the power and the corporate battles. Over the last five years the growing importance of televised football as the key software in the expansion of non-terrestrial television services, the flotation of clubs listed on the stock exchange under 'Leisure, Entertainment and Hotels', and the tensions between this new commercialism and football's cultural purpose, has seen interest explode into the financial and political spheres of public life, sparking significant debate over the future of the football and media industries in the UK, Europe and globally.

As a result, the governance of the game has assumed growing importance. It is seen as an issue on which government has to have a positive policy agenda. It is crucially important for competition policy (with particular reference to public-interest concerns) and the concentration of media power. Media companies are taking stakes in the leading clubs (most recently in the UK with Granada in Liverpool FC, NTL in Newcastle and BSkyB in Leeds Sporting, Manchester City and Sunderland FC to add to their continued stake in Manchester United). These issues are acquiring growing importance in the run-up to the renegotiation of the Premier League's broadcasting rights in 2001 (see Chapter 8, 'Sneaking in through the back door? Media company interests and dual ownership of clubs' by Adam Brown).

The speed with which this transformation has taken place has created a highly fluid and confused situation. Increasingly the regulation of, and strategic planning for, the sector is being undertaken not in the head-quarters of the traditional regulatory bodies of the Football Association and the Football League, but in the boardrooms of international media companies, and in regulatory arenas such as the government's Football Task Force; the Monopolies and Mergers Commission (MMC)[1] (with its enquiry into BSkyB's bid for Manchester United); the Office of Fair Trading (OFT) and Restrictive Practices Court (RPC) (with the OFT challenging the Premier League's collective sale of television rights in the RPC and losing a case for the first time in history); and the European Commission and other European institutions.[2]

This same period has seen the emergence of independent supporters associations, the explosion of fanzine culture and organisation, the establishment of the Football Supporters Association, and in 1999 the founding of the Coalition of Football Supporters, bringing the various supporters' groups, including the National Federation of Football Supporters Clubs, together in a single national organisation. Alongside this have emerged serious attempts by supporters to take ownership stakes in their clubs and create democratic structures to allow the supporters to have a voice. This development was welcomed in 1999 by the Football Task Force and officially endorsed by the government with the announcement in October 1999 by the Secretary of State for Culture, Media and Sport of a new unit to be established within the Football Trust[3] to assist supporter-shareholder groups. The supporter-shareholder movement received a major boost earlier in 1999 with the organisation of Manchester United shareholders against their own board's attempt to sell out to BSkyB, and the subsequent founding of Shareholders United, holding a block of shares in the club, to ensure that all interests of supporters, including emotional, are taken properly into account by the board of the plc.[4]

These same issues are being faced across Europe, as demonstrated by the international contributors to this volume. But despite the pervasiveness of this change within the game, the debate about how the challenges raised should be addressed has been characterised by often confused com-mentaries. This is perhaps best demonstrated by the widespread surprise expressed on the business pages of the main broadsheet newspapers at the MMC's decision to recommend rejection of BSkyB's bid for Manchester United.[5] Of course, as any reading of the MMC's report into the bid will confirm, this decision was entirely logical and predictable when judged against the most conventional anti-trust criteria, leaving aside any wider public-interest considerations. Perhaps it is the peculiar economics of successful sports leagues, where a key requirement is to maintain and nurture healthy competition rather than eliminate competitors as in conventional marketplaces, which has served to inhibit a true understanding of the dynamics of the football marketplace. Whatever the reason, there is certainly a need for more penetrating analyses as to the true nature of the challenges facing football. And that is what we have tried to provide in this volume by bringing together such a wide range of commentators to present their views on where the game is going. The succeeding chapters seek to place the key challenges in context under nine headings, each addressing a key issue facing the game.

PART I: ANOTHER FINE MESS
In the first and introductory section the scene is set for the analyses which follow. Four contributions present an overview of where the game is now and where it may be heading. Firstly Gerry Boon, in Chapter 2, 'Football finances: too much money?', reviews the scale of change in the finances of football over the recent past in the UK, Europe and globally, drawing on data from Deloitte & Touche's authoritative *Annual Review of Football Finance* series.[6] He urges that the new global developments be appreciated, not as something inevitable that has to be accepted fatalistically, but rather as presenting opportunities that, if properly grasped, could be harnessed for the good of the game. In Chapter 3, 'Reforming football's boardrooms', Professor Tom Cannon and Sean Hamil reflect on the tensions that the use of plc status by clubs to float on the stock exchange has created with traditional fan-bases, and bemoan the incompetent management prevalent in much of the game, across plcs and non-plcs alike. 'The players' perspective' is given in Chapter 4 by Gordon Taylor, chief executive of the Professional Footballers Association, discussing recent changes in the game, making particular reference to the impact of the Bosman ruling, the outcry over spiralling players' wages, and the argument that more effective regulation of the game is required. In Chapter 5, 'Why football needs a regulator', Rogan Taylor, a member of the Football Task Force, considers the current state of the regulation of the game by the Football Association and argues that it is the FA's abandonment of its traditional regulatory role and its unwillingness to engage with supporters that has led to the widespread call for an independent regulator. This is a call which the author supports and is returned to in the final part of this book.

PART II: IMPLICATIONS OF THE BSKYB/MANCHESTER UNITED CASE
The government's blocking of BSkyB's attempted takeover of Manchester United in 1999 – on the recommendation of the MMC – raised crucial

questions about the relationship between football clubs and media companies. The MMC report blocked the proposed merger for two main reasons. Firstly, that it would have distorted competition in the broadcasting market by allowing BSkyB to sit on both sides of the negotiating table, and secondly that it would have adversely affected the quality of football, particularly if it had triggered a series of similar takeovers, by widening the gap between the richest and poorest clubs and by allowing BSkyB a say in organisational aspects of the game. This ruling had the initial effect of discouraging other media companies from attempting to take over football clubs. For example, the cable TV company NTL decided not to pursue its intended takeover of Newcastle United plc after the MMC's ruling and the announcement that the Competition Commission (formerly the MMC) were to turn their attention to the NTL-Newcastle deal.[7]

Peter Crowther, consultant to Rosenblatt Solicitors, outlines the background to the case in Chapter 6, 'The attempted takeover of Manchester United by BSkyB', and sets out the competition and broader public-interest arguments against the attempted takeover that were made in the submission to the MMC by the organisation Shareholders United Against Murdoch, for whom Dr Crowther acted in this case. Nicholas Finney, a member of the MMC panel for the BSkyB/Manchester United enquiry, explains in Chapter 7, 'The MMC's inquiry into BSkyB's merger with Manchester United PLC', how the panel reached their decision to recommend that the bid be blocked, and the implications both for future mergers between media companies and for the future regulation of football.

In response to the MMC decision, BSkyB have bought into Leeds Sporting (owners of Leeds United FC), Manchester City and Sunderland FC, while retaining what is the largest single shareholding in Manchester United.[8] NTL have retained the shareholding that they took in Newcastle United at the time that they were contemplating a wholesale takeover, and Granada TV have bought a stake in Liverpool FC. These developments are analysed by Dr Adam Brown in Chapter 8, 'Sneaking in through the back door? Media company interests and dual ownership of clubs', highlighting the dangers that these developments pose for football if allowed to proceed unchecked.

PART III: THE NEW COMMERCIALISM AND PLCS

Critics argue that football is losing its social purpose as supporters are exploited by exorbitant ticket and merchandise prices, with many traditional supporters being priced out of grounds. On the other hand, the game has never been so popular and has opened up to a new audience as it has modernised. These developments are discussed in Chapter 9, 'The changing face of football: a case for national regulation?' by John Williams, who also outlines possible ways forward.

Mark Goyder, of Tomorrow's Company, outlines in Chapter 10, 'Tomorrow's football club: an inclusive approach to governance', how plc status can incorporate a social-responsibility dimension, developing themes from the Royal Society of the Arts' *Tomorrow's Company Report*. In Chapter 11, 'Football, fans and fat cats: whose football club is it anyway?', Kevin Jaquiss discusses the sort of issues posed in any attempt to make a football club more responsive to its supporters and local community.

PART IV: INTERNATIONAL DEVELOPMENTS

The attempt to organise a breakaway super league from existing UEFA structures demonstrates that recent developments in Britain are not unique, just more advanced. Part IV analyses these developments and the likely response to them from football's governing bodies. In Chapter 12, 'International developments and European clubs', Andy Walsh of the Independent Manchester United Supporters Association provides an overview to these developments and of the other contributions to this section, and calls for supporters to link up internationally to counter what are after all international threats and challenges. Alasdair Bell reports in Chapter 13, 'Sport and the law: the influence of European Union competition policy on the traditional league structures of European football', on the UEFA perspective on how football might best be regulated internationally and how the international bodies such as UEFA can best work with national governments to ensure that international and European developments can be compatible with healthy national leagues and national teams.

Representatives from supporters groups in Germany and Spain outline how moves toward plc status have changed the game in their countries, and the consequences of these developments and of supporter resistance to them. In Chapter 14, 'Commercialisation and fan participation in Germany', Stuart Dykes represents the fans' organisation for German club Schalke 04 and reports on efforts there to secure greater fan representation in the running of the club. L'Elefant Blau is an association of Barcelona fans established in 1997 with the aim of democratising the running of the club and preserving its original and still current status as a non-profit sports association. They report in Chapter 15, 'The struggle for democracy at FC Barcelona and the case for a European independent regulator of professional football', on their work, and support the call for more co-operation by such supporter groups across countries, especially at a European level.

PART V: FINANCING AND ACCOUNTING FOR CLUBS

Supporters of plc status have argued that this is the only effective structure for clubs that wish to finance stadium reconstruction, and that it offers a real vehicle for supporter ownership of their club. Critics argue that there are alternative means of raising money, and that plc status has often been used as little more than a mechanism for incumbent owners to cash in at the expense of fans' loyalty. The issue of plcs is discussed in this section, as is the more general issue of the difficulty facing football clubs of balancing the financial performance of the club with performance on the field, as these two areas of a club's activity may conflict. An introductory note by City of London fund manager Nigel Hawkins assesses the performance of football club shares as financial investments and highlights the idiosyncratic nature of this investment market (Chapter 16, 'The financial performance of football stocks').

In Chapter 17, 'Playing in a different league', Tony Dart provides an overview of management accounting issues in the football industry, outlining the past record of generally poor financial management, the difficulties facing lower-division clubs, and the various challenges that football clubs face, such as asset-stripping developers seeking to purchase clubs to use the grounds for property development (for example at Brighton). Lee Manning, of corporate insolvency experts Buchler Phillips, explains the practical consequences of football clubs' traditionally unsophisticated approach to accounting and financial management drawing on his firm's experience as receiver at, amongst others, Millwall FC (Chapter 18, 'Football club balance-sheets: fact or fantasy?'). In Chapter 19, 'Business management issues', Robert Matusiewicz, consultant to a number of football clubs and also a FIFA agent, discusses how recent trends have affected the quality of business management at football clubs and speculates on likely future developments in this area. Stephen Morrow discusses in Chapter 20, 'Achieving best practice', how football clubs present particular problems in terms of valuation of their balance-sheets and considers the tensions thrown up between small, and institutional and incumbent-dominant, shareholders by the flotation of football clubs.

PART VI: THE RESTRICTIVE PRACTICES COURT CASE AND LEAGUE BALANCE

Organised sport has traditionally sold its TV rights collectively on a league basis. In the United States, sports leagues are specifically excluded from anti-trust legislation. The OFT's case against the Premier League at the Restrictive Practices Court (RPC) threatened this principle in the UK but was rejected on the grounds that the league brings substantial benefits to the game such as the promotion of competitive balance by redistributing income from leading to lagging clubs and redistribution from the Premier to the Football League. In Chapter 21, 'The Restrictive Practices Court case, broadcasting revenues and league balance', Professor Peter Sloane presents an overview of the economics of professional sports leagues, making particular reference to the outcome of the RPC case and the implications of the advent of pay-per-view televised games. Professor Martin Cave outlines the background to the OFT's decision to bring the case against the Premier League in Chapter 22, 'Football rights and competition in broadcasting'. Dr Stefan Szymanski, an expert witness on behalf of the OFT in the RPC case, presents the arguments against collective selling in Chapter 23, 'Hearts, minds and the Restrictive Practices Court case'.

Richard Scudamore, an expert witness on behalf of the defence and at the time of writing chief executive of the Football League argues that the collectivity and exclusivity of the existing contract is essential not only for redistribution within and between the Premier League and Football League, but also to ensure that the market for live televised football is not flooded and attendance at grounds diminished. The potential for inequality to emerge if the current collective agreement were to end is illustrated by the fact that matches featuring the top five Premiership clubs account for over 70% of all of BSkyB's viewers. It is notable that this was the first time the OFT has ever lost a case in the Restrictive Practices Court. This outcome appears to have been largely as a result of a lack of appreciation on the part of the OFT of the positive benefits that come from league collectivity. Also central to the case is the role of match-going fans. In Chapter 24, 'The Restrictive Practices Court case: implications for the Football League', Scudamore reports the case made before the court. He stresses in particular that the role of match-going fans is crucial to the long-term health of the game, not only because of the revenue collected directly, but also because all other revenues, including broadcasting revenues, depends ultimately on match-going fans sustaining the game.

PART VII: NURTURING THE GRASS-ROOTS: LOCAL CLUBS AND COMMUNITY INVOLVEMENT

The role of the Football Trust and local councils as partners in stadium development and, in the case of the latter, in the provision of wider sports facilities, is critical for the health of the game at the grass-roots level. In Chapter 25, 'Partners for progress', Tom Pendry, chairman of the Football Trust and also of the House of Commons All-Party Sports Group, presents his vision for the future of the game. This is best secured, he argues, by a structure that recognises that the professional game is only the apex of a much larger and deeper movement stretching into local communities and grass-roots football.

Local councils have also played an important role in many clubs' attempts to address the problems of racism and hooliganism which have afflicted the game. Piara Power outlines in Chapter 26, 'Kick racism out of football', the work of the anti-racist 'Kick it Out' campaign, and describes how clubs, local authorities and fans can work together to improve the game by combating racism and thus ensuring that 'community involvement' really does involve the whole community. Tony Clarke reports in Chapter 27, 'The future of football: safe in whose hands?' on the experience at Northampton Town FC where an active partnership between an independent supporters' group and Northampton Council secured the financial future of the club. In Chapter 28, 'The Football Task Force and the grass-roots', Task Force member Chris Heinitz draws on his experience in promoting local government sporting and leisure activity, and outlines practical strategies for nurturing football's grass-roots through local government partnerships.

PART VIII: THE FOOTBALL TASK FORCE

The Football Task Force was asked by the government to develop a blueprint for how a game, perceived to be in crisis, might move forward. Key figures from the Task Force, and the Department of Culture, Media and Sport (DCMS) discuss the extent to which it has met its objectives. Andy Burnham presents an overview of DCMS policy on football in Chapter 29, 'The Task Force and the future regulation of football', with particular reference to the work of the Task Force itself. Nic Coward, of the FA, reports on the FA's views of the Task Force's work, and on what role the FA might play in securing the various aims as set out in the Task Force's published reports (Chapter 30, 'Facing football's future: the Task Force and beyond'). In Chapter 31, 'The Football Task Force: a Premier League view', Mike Lee gives the FA Premier League's response to the Task Force's work and reports in particular on the joint report submitted to the Task Force by the FA, the Premier League and the Football League. This joint document opposes the establishment of an independent regulator but does propose two other measures. First, that best-practice guidelines be established in key areas such as ticketing and merchandising, and secondly that an Independent Scrutiny Panel be established to conduct a regular health check, or audit, of governance in the game.

Dr Adam Brown, a member of the Task Force, discusses the work of the Task Force in the context of the regulation of football, and makes two essential points which fit well with the book's concluding chapter from

Brian Lomax. First, that the great debate over whether there should be an independent regulator or not should not allow us to be deflected from the key point, that what is required is proper and appropriate regulation and governance. How this is brought about is a secondary, albeit important, question. And secondly that the two issues of regulation or governance on the one hand, and increased supporter involvement (including through ownership) on the other, should not be seen in isolation from each other, and far less should they be seen as alternatives as some have done. On the contrary, the two should be seen as complementary and self-reinforcing. To improve the degree of supporter ownership and involvement will require regulatory intervention. And good regulation of the game will depend crucially on increased supporter involvement in the game at all levels. (Chapter 32, 'The Football Task Force and the "regulator debate"'). These are conclusions with which the editors of this book, and the authors of this chapter, would endorse wholeheartedly.

PART IX: DO WE NEED AN OFFOOT?
Finally, then, Part IX of the book considers the question explicitly of what sort of regulation is required. In a period of extraordinary change should football be left to regulate itself when what happens in the game now has implications that go beyond the football pitch to the heart of the emerging media industries so central to the government's project to modernise Britain? Or does it need government regulation to protect the cultural distinctiveness of the game, and to guide its development in the twenty-first century? The three chapters in this section reflect on what sort of regulation and governance is required.

In Chapter 33, 'Why football needs an independent regulator', Gerry Sutcliffe MP explains the reasons behind his ten-minute Bill in the House of Commons proposing that football should have an independent regulator. The independent fanzine movement, and the emergence of the Football Supporters Association after the Hillsborough disaster, have been important manifestations of the desire of supporters to play a more active role in the development of the industry. The Independent Manchester United Supporters Association and Shareholders United Against Murdoch played an important part in opposing BSkyB's attempted takeover of Manchester United. Around the country independent fan organisations are now promoting the concept of the mutualisation of football clubs to make them truly accountable to fans. Alison Pilling, chair of the Football Supporters Association and a leading light in the formation of the Coalition of Football Supporters, outlines the new initiative to construct a single body representing all football fans and discusses the likely view of this body on regulatory issues in Chapter 34, 'Uniting the fans'. And Brian Lomax in Chapter 35, 'Self-regulation or regulation?', discusses how the appropriate regulation and governance of the game should best be pursued. Regarding the question of whether an independent regulator is required or whether instead the FA remains the appropriate body, the author reports his experience as a probation officer where the appropriate decision might be to allow the FA just one more chance.

CONCLUSION

As indicated above and also in *A Game of Two Halves?*, in our view there are serious threats to the game of football in Britain and Europe generally – threats from increased commercialism, the move to plc status by football clubs, the attempts by broadcasters to use football to sell subscription television, and the inflation in ticket prices. However, there are also some encouraging signs. Amongst these we would list the 1999 defeat of BSkyB's attempt to take over Manchester United and the defeat, also in 1999, of the OFT's attempt to break up the Premier League's collective selling of TV rights. Added to these, the work of the Football Task Force has been a hugely positive development.[9] The October 1999 announcements by Culture Secretary Chris Smith were extremely welcome, firstly regarding the intended redistribution of money from the Premiership TV contract to the game's grass-roots and secondly regarding government support for supporter-shareholder groups and the trust holding of shares by fans.

We would totally reject any fatalistic view that the game has changed and that nothing can be done about it. In our view there is just as much scope for action now as there ever was. Indeed, as many of the authors of the present volume demonstrate, there are perhaps greater opportunities for democratising the game today than there have ever been. While the floating of clubs as plcs has had a number of negative implications that do certainly need to be tackled, it has at least weakened the grip of the old owners who in many cases were a major part of the problem. We do *not* want to go back to the good old days. As the following chapters demonstrate, there are new opportunities opening up which, if properly grasped, could lead to a greater degree of democratic involvement and accountability than was ever witnessed in the past. We hope that the present book will play some positive part in those opportunities being taken rather than squandered.

PART I

ANOTHER FINE MESS

2. Football finances: too much money?
GERRY BOON

It is important to note that the English game, when looked at from the European mainland and indeed the rest of the world, has in recent years achieved a number of major successes. This is particularly so in terms of the way it has modernised its business organisation, for which it is rightly admired. I am thinking of issues such as the safe and efficient management of stadiums, its league organisation, merchandising and business structure. I believe it is right that those of us with an interest in the industry should criticise it constructively. But this criticism should be balanced. The industry has a lot to be proud of, and is certainly not in crisis as some would have us believe.

THE CURRENT FINANCIAL STATE OF THE GAME
First of all in this chapter I present a financial profile of the English game. It is important to note that football is no longer just a series of local markets. It is now a European and global marketplace for playing talent, for TV rights and for merchandising. English football has to operate within the reality of this framework. Technology, largely related to broadcasting, has made this possible over the last ten years. Off the pitch English football is considered very successful; the rest of Europe really does envy our financial performance.[1] For example, looking at the Premier League, between the 1991–92 season and the 1997–98 season the compound annual turnover growth of the clubs in the Premier League was 23.2%. In other words, in six years the Premier League has grown to become 3.5 times larger than the old First Division. This is a fantastic performance by anyone's standards.

In the 1997–98 season Premier League clubs spent over £190 million on players' wages. They spent a further £171 million on transfers, of which 45% went on players from outside the UK. Operating profits in 1997–98 were over £100 million – a record. Seventeen of the 20 clubs are profitable on the basis of their day-to-day activities.

If you put the Premier League in a European perspective, it is bigger in financial terms than Italy's Serie A by 20%, than Germany's Bundesliga and Spain's Primera Liga by approximately 25%, and France's First Division by 175%. France is a country which did very well to win the World Cup, but in my view is excessively domestically focused in the way it looks at the management of its game. And that has put their clubs, as opposed to the national team, at a severe disadvantage when competing in Europe. Indeed, I believe there is a direct trade-off between prioritising domestic success and European competition success.

In 1997–98 the total revenue of the Premier League was £569 million, of which £203 million (36%) was match-day receipts, £152 million (26%) was TV receipts, and £214 million (38%) was from merchandising and other commercial income. What this illustrates is that, while TV money is an increasingly important part of the revenue pie, paying customers through the turnstiles remain essential to the financial success of the game. Attendances have continued to grow. This is despite the fact that match-day tickets in the Premier League (and the First Division before it) have risen by four times the rate of inflation over the last ten years whilst cinema tickets, for example, have only risen by the rate of inflation. This is a very important point. What the market is saying is that more people want to watch English football and they are prepared to pay more money to do so, both in the Premier League and the Football League. People like the product. That is a pretty powerful endorsement. But let's put all this financial expansion in some sort of business context. Enterprise Oil has an annual turnover very similar to that of the Premier League's £569 million. But it is ranked only number 124 in terms of market capitalisation on the stock exchange. So it is important to realise that Premier League football is only a medium-sized enterprise by comparison with the real giants of British industry, despite its considerable recent financial success.

FOOTBALL'S STAKEHOLDERS: WHO ARE THEY?

If football clubs are to be successful, they need to build mutually beneficial relationships with a range of what I would term 'stakeholders'. The three main groups of stakeholders are outlined in Figure 1 overleaf.

I am unhappy when the choices in football are presented as two opposites: a commercialised future where traditional fans have no place and financial imperatives rule; or a return to some form of idealised sporting model where financial issues are completely subservient to the sporting ethos of the game. We need to adopt a balanced approach. Clearly we need to retain the strengths that football's deep roots of tradition give it in people's affections. But we must also remember that football is a business, and we do not have the option of choosing between a 'sporting' model of the industry and a 'business' model. Business practices, and influences from other business sectors such as television, are having a huge influence on football. That is reality and therefore we have to deal with it. We must not lose tradition and the other good things that go with it. But

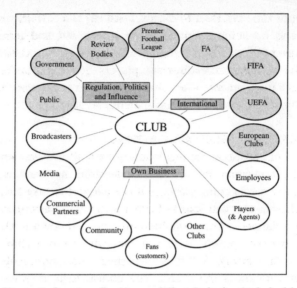

Figure 1: Sport or Business – What Role for Stakeholders?

the marketplace for football is global. Do you want to compete? That is the key question. Any industry has international, national and local 'players'; football is no different. Good policies and good practices are good for business whatever industrial sector you are in.

By way of example, we have a saying at Deloitte & Touche: 'no fans equals no value'. It is bad news for the business not to look after the fans; looking after fans and running an efficient and profitable business are not mutually exclusive. Both objectives can be put into operation simultaneously, and already are at the best clubs. For years we – as fans – complained about the lack of proper business practices in football clubs, how badly run they were, how poorly they treated the fans and so on, and now there are proper business structures we complain that they are too 'business-like' or 'commercial'.

Football's business continues to develop apace – some welcome that and work to channel that dynamic force into business efficiency which creates profitable activity and generates cash for investment in players, stadiums, training facilities and complementary activities to the core football club. Others bemoan the passing of a more egalitarian age when 'market forces' was an irrelevant concept. Whatever their point of view, what is undeniable is that the Pandora's box of business structure and market competition has been opened in the football industry and cannot now be closed. Clubs and governing bodies need to choose between embracing that dynamism with attitudes and structures designed for the modern business age; or they can react to events, resist the forces (rather than ride them) and end up being swept along in a reluctant and introspective mode. Whatever the strategy, the high profile of the game and its principal players (clubs, chairmen and directors, players, governing bodies – even government), now mean that there is an ever-present need for accountability, responsibility and transparency in dealings.

MEDIA OWNERSHIP OF CLUBS: A RED HERRING?

A major point of debate on the regulation of football between what might be termed the 'traditionalists' and the 'modernisers' has been around the issue of whether media companies should be allowed to take over football clubs and whether this will lead to further polarity in performance. I feel that there is a danger of the game becoming bogged down in this debate as it misses two key points. First, it is not who owns a club which is important, as fans always feel they own their club emotionally anyway regardless of who owns the shares. The critical issue is how clubs are managed as a business, and the extent to which they satisfactorily address the concerns of their various stakeholders. Secondly, polarisation of 'football power' has always existed. We at Deloittes believe that properly structured commercial development enhances competitive balance. Dramatic intervention by government or regulatory bodies is not what is required here.

What really is important is that clubs organise themselves on a professional basis, recruit and retain competent and imaginative managers with the skills and experience to manage a growing business in a dynamic marketplace. A lot of people get very irate about the stockmarket flotation of clubs and complain that this has distanced them from their supporters. I do not accept that this has in fact happened; clubs have always been private limited companies owned by private investors. Fundamentally, I think the focus on how football club ownership has changed as more and more clubs have floated on the stock exchange reflects a nostalgia by many who enjoyed far greater influence over the game in its, it has to be said, inefficiently managed, traditional, established, order. This group have much less influence in the market-orientated, media-floodlit football industry of today, and I am afraid many of them have not adapted to these changes in the game, to the extent that they are blinded to its genuine successes.

PLAYERS' WAGE DEMANDS: WHO DECIDES?

The players' wages, and in particular the way in which they have dramatically increased in recent years, have become a major talking point within the game. Between 1996–97 and 1997–98 alone the total players' wage bill in the Premiership rose by around 40%. Since the Premiership's inception in 1992–93, compound annual growth in players' wages has been 26%. The concern is that the spiralling wages will effectively bankrupt many clubs, and that they need to be curbed.

The views of Gordon Taylor, chief executive of the Professional Footballers Association, are reported elsewhere in this volume (Chapter 4). As far as I am concerned, the key question that should be asked is: who should be responsible for deciding players' wages? Who should be accountable? The player, the agent, the PFA, the manager, the coach, the sponsors, the league? I actually do not think any of these should be. They all have the right to do their best for their client or their interest but the people who are actually responsible are the chairman and the board of directors. All our clubs have been limited companies for roughly a hundred years and the limited company structure places responsibility for employee wages firmly with the chairman and the board.

We very often hear football club chairmen and directors bemoaning their lot. What they don't say (but in effect mean) is: 'Please help us to help ourselves. We need to be protected from our own weaknesses.' I think, though this may sound a little cynical, that this attitude represents a failure to accept responsibility and is a negation of duty. Clubs must acknowledge and take responsibility for managing their own players' wage bills.

A number of centrally organised remedies have been proposed to deal with wage inflation. Some sort of centrally administered salary cap is one, but I think this is extremely unlikely to happen. To be successful it would have to be organised on at least a European basis so there would be problems in co-ordinating such an initiative, particularly where clubs have such a strong incentive to secure competitive advantage by bypassing such a stricture. It would also be open to challenge in the employment courts in the same way as the Bosman case.

Another option is to have more redistribution of income within the leagues to help shore up the finances of lower-division clubs in particular. A variation of this scheme operates in English cricket. However, again, I think this kind of intervention is extremely unlikely to happen given the current structure of the football industry in England. And as I have also stated in the latest Deloitte & Touche *Annual Review of Football Finance*,[2] there is a strongly held point of view that those who do not control costs with firmness should not be entitled to look to others for handouts.

It is clear that some action must be taken by clubs, particularly in the lower divisions, if they are to survive. The Premier League clubs may be able to sustain higher wages, albeit increasing at a lower rate, provided they can improve the quality and size of their revenue streams from other sources and be more disciplined in their negotiating with top players. But in the lower divisions some tough decisions will need to made – either individually at club level or prompted by initiatives at divisional, or Football League, level. An excellent precedent is set by rugby league's 'Super League'. The intention is to pay players' performance-related pay out of merit awards (for final position) rather than the game's guaranteed payments for appearance money as at present. Football, perhaps starting from Division Three and working upwards, would do well to follow suit. There are, though, prerequisites – unanimity from the clubs, a clear rule and strict enforcement.

FOOTBALL'S HIERARCHY OF POWER: A BIGGER SAY FOR CLUBS?

If one were asked to list an established pecking order of where power lies within football, a conventional and traditional response would be to start with FIFA, the world governing body, work your way down to UEFA, the European governing body, proceed to the FA and then to the individual clubs. But I would pose the question: how entrenched and established is this order? Critically, Manchester United's decision not to enter the FA Cup in 1999–2000, and the FA's decision to allow them not to compete in order to permit them to participate in FIFA's World Club championship in Brazil in January 2000, has thrown this question into some relief.

In my view the clubs have the real power in football. They just have not yet learned how to use it properly. The birth of the 'super league' concept, of which the FA Premier League was the first incarnation, was the initial manifestation of this power in a negotiating context. It represented an attempt by the bigger clubs to have a larger say in how the game was run, the future direction it would take, and the distribution of the financial rewards. Now the major Scottish clubs have followed suit and set up their own Scottish Premier League. The attempted setting up of a European super league outside the existing FIFA and UEFA structures in 1998 was the most aggressive manifestation of this trend. It forced UEFA to overhaul its competitions and establish a 'new' Champions League more in tune with the demands of the major European clubs.

Clubs have started to recognise their own power and have begun to use it. And power follows control of the commercial properties in the game: image rights, TV rights and so on. So it is all about a battle for control of those commercial properties. We can look at the music industry as an example: there, power has actually passed from the traditional seat of power – the recording companies – to the individual entertainers. I do not think that will happen with football, certainly not fully, because we are dealing with a team game here. But power will certainly continue to move from football's current governing bodies, associations and leagues, to the clubs.

The battleground on which clubs will fight for influence with the industry's current governing bodies is illustrated in Figure 2 below. Clubs have a critical source of power in that they provide the players to all competitions, at whatever level. Currently clubs' power can be measured as increasing the further they are removed from the international competitions (north to south on the right-hand axis in Figure 2). But even at the level of national country team competitions clubs have some potential leverage because of their control over the supply of players.

The power of the game's administrative bodies is currently strongest the further you move away from the domestic leagues (west to east on the

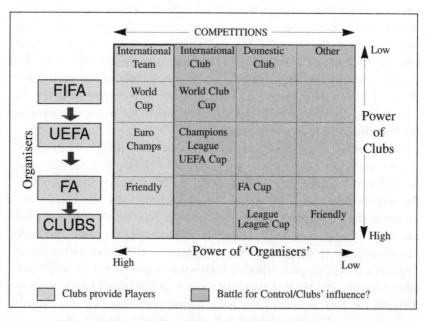

Figure 2: Priorities/Tensions – International v. Domestic

horizontal axis). Correspondingly, the power of the clubs is obviously high where they organise their own league, such as the Premier League, which is managed by the 20 clubs concerned. Essentially, there is a battle for power going on between football's governing bodies and the clubs. If you drew a line from top right to bottom left across Figure 2 dividing football into two spheres of dominant influence, with the governing bodies on the left and the clubs on the right, each side is trying to push that line in the opposite direction to expand their sphere of influence. And obviously that struggle is the source of many well-publicised tensions.

I do not have the answers to all of the questions raised by this struggle for power. But I do have some views on them. Critically, I believe this struggle is all about who controls the game and its many competitions. The player and squad numbers will provide the upper limits on capacity for both the total number of games it is possible to play and competitions it is possible to compete in seriously. The decision by Manchester United to withdraw from the FA Cup to participate in the World Club championship is not a one-off problem, despite what people say, but simply the manifestation of what will be a growing problem as the possibilities expand for more lucrative and attractive international competitions. This raises key questions: where do the clubs want to draw the line in terms of deciding which competitions to compete in? Would they prefer that their governing bodies make those decisions for them? Or should they make these decisions themselves? And if the clubs are being forced to make those choices, they have to be given the real authority to actually make the choices and not be the ping-pong ball in the middle as has been Manchester United's experience over their decision to withdraw from the FA Cup. Giving them this authority, or them seizing it, has major implications for how the game is currently organised.

Essentially the problem is a scheduling issue. Why do we not have one overall authority to schedule all games and competitions? Why can football not organise itself so that all these power groups do not conflict the way they do now? I am not giving a view personally either way, but I do think the furore over Manchester United's decision to withdraw from the FA Cup raises a critical question for fans of English clubs. Domestic audiences need to decide whether they support the global ambitions of England's largest clubs or whether they want to put domestic issues first. Does choosing the latter demonstrate a lack of ambition? We do need to preserve the best aspects of the game's long traditions, but the football marketplace is changing and we in England cannot suddenly slow down the market.

In conclusion, the number of games and the size of divisions are actually a function of scheduling and agreed priorities. Conventional business organisations would find that difficult but they would sit down and sort it out using business processes. Football needs to address this issue in the same pragmatic and businesslike way. We have a unique challenge here. Regrettably, football's stakeholders do not have an exemplary record when it comes to resolving such issues – but (as you would expect from an Oldham Athletic fan) there's always hope!

3. Reforming football's boardrooms

TOM CANNON AND SEAN HAMIL

Issues of governance and regulation are fundamental to the future of our national game. The structure of governance that has stood for most of the twentieth century is collapsing under a series of pressures. Some of these pressures result from internal changes in an increasingly international sport, where the gap between the grass-root supporters, the players and administrators is widening. Alongside this, there is a massive shift in the financial basis of a sport that is becoming, willingly or not, part of a complex leisure industry. These shifts are provoking a major debate about the ownership, control and future of clubs, leagues and the game itself.

At the heart of this debate are the extraordinary and complex changes that are occurring in the environment of a game which is fundamentally simple and which has a support base that is relatively conservative. The question to ask, therefore, is whether, in the new ball-game that we are seeing in football, with vast amounts of money swirling around the game, the money is going to be used for the good of the game. Currently it is unclear what is going to happen to this money. The choices, though, are relatively simple. Funds can flow out of the game into the profits of owners or investors and the wages of players or, some at least, can be employed to strengthen the game through improved facilities and better opportunities. So far the picture is pretty clear with 'new' investors extracting the value that has taken generations to create or simply squandering assets through conspicuous consumption and inefficiency.

What we are witnessing is a whole series of new challenges, which are going to affect not just the short-term viability of individual clubs but their long-term success. These challenges pose new questions, which take football into new territories. We need to be asking ourselves whether we have the skills or capabilities within the game to face up to these challenges. So what are the issues? Among the most important is the amateur tradition of football in the UK.

THE 'AMATEUR' TRADITION

Football in the UK has a deeply rooted 'amateur' tradition in its governance and management. Even today, despite the fact that we now have an increasing number of specialists, experts and accountants involved in the game, it is important to recognise that the fundamentals of professional football in the United Kingdom are amateur. An examination of the boards of even Premiership clubs will show that they are peopled largely by non-executive, amateur directors. Only a handful of clubs have chief executives who are directors. Some of the largest clubs have entirely non-executive boards.

When the structure of the clubs is examined more deeply, the amateur tradition continues to dominate, with few dedicated or qualified staff in key business areas and little dedicated training and development in leisure or sports management, marketing, customer service, media relations, finance or people management. This amateur tradition is suddenly faced with taking on new roles, which are expected of their enterprises, and of their fans (whom I would distinguish from their supporters), the shareholders, the directors and the employees of the businesses. The line between fans and supporters is important as it distinguishes between fans who have positive attitudes to a team but do not, usually, have any active involvement e.g. through attending games; and supporters who have an active involvement e.g. through attending games. Some analysts are using the terms secondary and primary support to make this distinction with secondary supporters akin to fans and primary supporters being close to the above definition of supporter. The distinction is important commercially but has a potentially greater importance in defining the relationship between the club and 'its support' (incorporating both groups). Some of the most recent changes – greater access to full games through cable TV, wider accessibility of merchandise – are targeted on the large fan-base rather than the much smaller supporter-base. In Manchester United's case, for example, there are around three million fans but fewer than 150,000 supporters. Some planned developments, notably pay TV, seem likely to further discriminate in favour of fans against supporters. Other proposals such as ground moves and expansion of executive facilities at the expense of traditional space seem designed to reduce the opportunities of supporters to the benefit of fans. Reducing this 'active' involvement weakens the link between the club, its roots and its community. It seems likely to produce the type of passive link between 'producer' and 'consumer' that characterises most markets. This, in turn, changes the nature of the game as we know it.

These are complex and challenging issues, which pose dilemmas for those responsible for shaping the future of the game. Effectively and responsibly managed, the challenge of balancing these interests could strengthen the game. Badly managed, the failure to balance these interests could weaken the game for generations. It is fair to ask whether those with the responsibility or those whose task is it to deal with these challenges have the knowledge, skills and understanding to deal effectively with the task in hand. Equally important, do they want to deal with these challenges in ways that meet the long-term interests of the game or their own short-term interests?

MONEY, MONEY, MONEY

So let us explore this amateur tradition a little further. We all have our own experiences of the amateur tradition in football. The following example relates to Everton FC but it could just as easily have occurred at any of the other English clubs in the recent past. As football supporters we have all been to those grim fixtures where your team is playing poorly against uninspiring opposition, such as Wimbledon. You have sat through a dreary nil-nil draw on a cold, wet Monday night. Towards the end of the game there's a Tannoy message which tells you that tickets for the next away match are available after the game. So you trudge along in the rain to the box office to buy your tickets and there you are confronted with the living embodiment of the amateur tradition. Typically, there is no cover while you stand in line. Waiting there in the rain, with only the excitement of that nil-nil draw to keep you warm, facing you at the Goodison Park ticket desk is a sign which reads: 'What is it about the word No you do not understand?' Happily the sign has now gone, but this attitude towards supporters was an intrinsic feature of the amateur tradition. That was the kind of message typically coming out from clubs, and which, in some senses, is still the case.

The typical supporter makes a massive investment in his or her club. Over a lifetime, the direct expenditure of traditional supporters, those behind the goals, exceeds £20,000 excluding money spent on merchandise. Fans will spend £3,000 to 4,000 on merchandise, related products and occasional visits to the ground. For some, this outlay is the largest personal commitment outside of their home and food that they make in their life. This level of investment has, traditionally, been ignored by those running the clubs. In the past this mattered less as the administrators – at least at club level – were largely drawn from the same pool of support as those on the terraces.

Today, that amateur tradition manifests itself not just in the way the businesses are (and were) run, but is expressed by most directors' lack of understanding of the relationships they need to manage between the organisation, the club and the different groups of people who are committed to the club. In this respect it is worth recalling the story about the great 1940s player Len Shackleton, who famously left a blank page in his autobiography under the heading 'What club directors know about football'. Experience tells us that he perhaps should have added a second blank page covering what directors know about business, management and strategy.

EXTRACTING THE VALUE

In truth, the amateur tradition still dominates the boardrooms of most clubs. This explains why people like Alan Sugar, John Hall, Peter Johnson and others, none of whom have any real love for the game, can come along and capitalise on decades of amateurism and poor management to extract enormous capital value growth out of their investments in football clubs. The sharp increases in the value of their investments do not reflect great, outstanding or even competent management of their football interests. Their skills lie in extracting the value accumulated over decades in the clubs they now control. This economic value was vastly underestimated before first BSkyB, then others, discovered ways of exploiting the hidden assets of clubs. The process by which Martin Edwards, Alan Sugar, John Hall and Peter Johnson have, between them, added over £300 million to their personal fortunes for investments of less than £30 million has more in common with the asset-stripping of Slater Walker during the 1960s than any miracles of 1990s strategic management.

Wealth extraction rather than the greater good of the game is the reason most of the new breed of football club owners are in this business. Vast fortunes are being made – and they are not being made by the players for all that Alan Sugar and others whinge about spiralling wages. The people making the really serious money in football are those who have made enormous capital growth from investments in relatively under-utilised assets.

Alan Sugar, Martin Edwards, the Hall family at Newcastle United and others have seen the value of their shareholdings in their respective clubs soar. Even Jack Walker at Blackburn Rovers – who was unusual in acquiring a comparatively poorly supported club with no tradition of recent success and which required an extraordinary high level of investment – managed to make a positive return on his investment up until the time of Blackburn's relegation from the Premier League at the end of the 1998–99 season. In 1997–98, the increase in the asset values of the investments of Peter Johnson at Everton (despite the team's poor performances) exceeded the total player wage bill for the Premiership. The increased value of their shares between 1993–94 and 1998–99 of five of the new generation of owners exceeded the entire player wage bill for the Premiership and all divisions of the Nationwide League over the period.

Enormous capital gains have been made by relatively small numbers of people. They have tended to surround themselves with fellow board directors who are non-executive amateurs and who perceive their real role as 'yes-men' for the chairman or the majority shareholder. Where clubs do recruit credible non-executive directors, such as at Newcastle United, they rarely stay around when the fundamental disrespect for any sense of wider stewardship is revealed by some crisis or scandal. And who can blame them? What serious professional person would want to take on a role as a cipher for a domineering chairman?

So, on the whole, most clubs are still run fundamentally by non-executive boards of directors with limited experience of the types of business issues facing modern soccer. Again, using Everton as an example, the club has faced the prospect of acquisition by an outside interest for most of 1999. There is, however, no one on the board, apart from Peter Johnson, with any direct experience of a friendly or hostile takeover. Johnson, however, is likely to be the primary beneficiary of a takeover, which maximises his short-term earnings – even if this is at the expense of the club's long-term interests.[1] Changes in ownership at Leeds United, Nottingham Forest and others were taken against a similar background.

CONSTRAINED BY THE RULES

There are reasons for this. Clubs which are not plcs are still governed by the FA's Rule 34, which stipulates that the articles of association of clubs include a clause which, among other things, precludes club directors from drawing a salary as a football club director. As a result, you don't see the traditional structure that you see in most organisations (especially commerial enterprises) where you have experts in marketing, finance and even human-resource management on the main board giving the board the benefit of their expertise. Instead, what you have is a collection of amateur, non-executive directors who come in and very often run their clubs the way they run their golf clubs.

PROFESSIONALISING FOOTBALL CLUB MANAGEMENT AND BOARDROOMS

Modernising football club business management and overcoming the legacy of amateurism in the boardroom will require a fundamental change in the culture and ethos of the game. If you are going to have a professional game, frankly you need professional management systems and well-organised strategies to build up the value of the clubs and the businesses that underpin the game. That will require the transformation of the skill base at the top of football. By way of example, it is absurd that not one Premier League club has on its main board a human-resources/personnel director as a full-time executive member of staff, even though football clubs are a quintessential people business. Even Premier League chairmen describe their industry as a people business. It is not surprising that you get the kinds of problems that are the consequence of this amateur tradition in football club boardrooms. There needs to be a clearer view, or set of views from the top, about the levels of professionalisation and the true skills that are required to manage clubs efficiently. You can separate this management challenge, at some levels, from what is happening in relation to team affairs, but it is not completely independent from it.

A simple illustration of the problems lies in the career development of young players. It is generally accepted that the attrition rate among young players is very high. Every year a Premiership club might recruit up to 20 young people in some form of playing apprenticeship. Most clubs would be surprised if one in ten eventually make it to the first team. Even assuming that some end up in other teams, perhaps in lower divisions, most are forced to quit the game at the time when their peers outside football are completing their training or studies and moving on in a career. Few clubs make serious efforts to design policies to address this challenge. The issues are similar for senior professionals leaving the game. And players, actual or potential, probably get better treatment than other club employees.

VISIONS AND VALUES

The challenges facing football clubs have to be addressed at a professional and strategic level. At the core has to be a strong sense in most clubs of the club's purpose. It is true that most clubs have a general statement or club motto. A classic example is Everton's *Nil Satis Nisi Optimum* – roughly translated as 'Nothing But The Best Satisfies' – which appears on almost all the club's published materials. But, having said that, there is no real sense in which this, or similar expressions at other clubs, articulate a meaningful mission statement or sense of purpose for the organisation that is any different from a strapline on the bottom of a box of club-branded choco-lates. These mottoes are vastly important to the fans, supporters and smaller shareholders but seem meaningless to those responsible for deliver-ing their goals.

Achieving this fit between purpose and mission, role and responsibility demands a proper understanding of the relationship between the executive and non-executive directors. This is not to say that if you have a proper set of executive directors who understand and accept their executive respon-sibilities, you can't then balance them out with non-executive directors who represent the other interest groups or stakeholders in clubs. Clubs must develop a more sensible approach to the relationship between chairmen, presidents, chief executives and the great plethora of job titles which are exploding across football. In truth, most clubs have a virtually non-existent skill base but any number of job titles.

STEWARDSHIP

At the same time, if you start then asking serious questions about the stewardship of the business, in corporate governance terms, you are confronted with serious confusion on the part of those with responsibility for such matters at clubs. Again the example of Everton is instructive on this issue.

In early 1999 a group of Everton shareholders was involved in some fairly complicated arrangements to force an extraordinary general meeting (EGM) at the club. This was prompted by the great dissatisfaction of most shareholders and supporters with the way the club was being managed. Over a decade the club had spent around £100 million on players while the team moved from being league champions in 1987 to relegation fodder in 1997. In just four years £25 million of new capital was invested in the club through new share issues, but the club's indebtedness soared from under £5 million to around £20 million. In sum, this meant funds haemorrhaging at the rate of £10 million a year in a business with a turnover that barely averaged £10 million per annum over the decade.

The response to the proposed EGM indicated that key officials, like the club secretary, were seriously confused about their roles and responsibilities. The role of the company secretary seems relatively clear. Formally, he or she is accountable to the shareholders who own the club, who have rights according to corporate law and rights according to the articles of association of the business. In practice, is the company secretary accountable to the people with whom he or she deals with on a day-to-day basis, typically the directors and the chairman? In calling for the EGM, the rights of the shareholders were very clear. The club's articles of association were clear. In the face of their demands, the club first denied their rights then delayed calling the meeting until the normal AGM was called.

There has to be a proper sense of the stewardship role in football. As the Everton example illustrates, that is not there at the moment. Instead, there is a reluctance to implement fundamental tenets of the law on corporate governance. The situation is made worse by the limited resources available to the typical smaller shareholder in soccer. They simply cannot afford to execute their rights in law. Alongside this, the authorities, notably the FA and the Premier League, are reluctant to back fans, supporters or small shareholders against those in control of the game.

Again, the difficulties at Everton illustrate the problem. Some years ago, the football authorities regulated to prevent any one individual taking a controlling interest in more than one club. Five years ago, Peter Johnson, then chairman of Tranmere Rovers, acquired a controlling interest in Everton. At the time, he issued a prospectus clearly stating that he had divested himself of his controlling interest in Tranmere. Four years later, faced with a financial crisis at Tranmere, it emerged that Johnson still controlled the club. In response to protests from supporters and shareholders in both clubs, the football authorities have completely failed to act. This failure has made it impossible for those regulating company law to act. The fans, supporters and small shareholders have lacked the resources to force action through the courts.

That's why, when we are talking about a system of governance, that system of governance has to be articulate, explicit, accessible and actionable. The current system of governance in English football meets none of these conditions. Effective action on the stewardship of the people's game is out of the reach of the people.

STAKEHOLDER VISION

Strategic vision is required at the top of the game in the FA, at individual clubs, and most of all in the Premier League. This means leadership, which is based on recognising the authorities' responsibilities to everybody in football. It does not mean having at the head of the Premier League or the FA someone whose job is basically to be non-threatening to a group of chairman who don't want to be threatened by anything or anyone.

Fundamental to this strategic vision is some concept of football clubs as 'stakeholder' corporations. We need to articulate and internalise the notion of a stakeholder view of our clubs and our sport and that stakeholder vision means recognising who the legitimate stakeholders are.[2]

We need to understand that those stakeholders have a vested interest in understanding who is really building value in professional football in the United Kingdom, and how this value is being created. They need to understand the internal and external portfolios of businesses that exist in soccer. The internal portfolios are those directly involved in delivering the game to its core support. This means the team, its grounds and the immediate activities. The external portfolios are all those activities, which surround the club from the merchandise to the credit cards.

What is happening at the moment is that there are two main business drivers reaching different groups of people and serving different needs. Firstly, there is the primary or core support, the people who actually go to the game. And, secondly, there is the new external, secondary, group who mainly watch the game on television (on BSkyB TV) but who nevertheless still participate in supporting clubs, and who represent an increasingly important source of emotional and financial support. By and large both drivers draw on ordinary working people. It is a misconception, and a ridiculous one at that, to try and argue that simply because there is money in the game, it is simply a rich man's game. Football clubs, if properly managed, do not need rich benefactors to bail them out.

This is vividly illustrated by the scale of investment and expenditure in the Premiership era and BSkyB TV-related changes. Traditional supporters investing by traditional means through tickets remains by far the dominant source not only of total revenues for Premiership clubs but the growth in this income exceeds all other sources in the years since the start of the Premiership. The new investors (i.e. the new owners like John Hall, Alan Sugar and Peter Johnson) have provided the smallest share of both total income and the increase in income. Over this period, revenues from merchandising have exceeded the investment of the newly enriched owners. Less than 10% of the growth in capital values of Premiership clubs has been reinvested.

STAKEHOLDER CORPORATIONS, NOT CARPET-BAGGERS

In truth the search which has occurred in soccer, the preoccupation with seeking out more and more rich men to come and put money into the game, is a nonsense. These so-called 'investors' have made massive sums while giving little back to the development of their clubs. At the same time, the supporters and fans have poured vast sums into the clubs with virtually no return in terms of better facilities, superior quality or greater responsiveness to their needs.

In key aspects of the football business, the track record of the multi-millionaires going in and buying football clubs is appalling. Totalling up what Alan Sugar has invested in Tottenham against its current market value, carrying out a similar calculation for Jack Walker at Blackburn Rovers, the Hall family at Newcastle United, Peter Johnson at Everton, and all the others like them; and comparing their extraordinary financial gains with the paltry number of trophies their clubs have won, it is clear that for the clubs the involvement of these 'entrepreneurs' represents an appalling investment. The track record of the rich entrepreneurs who have bought into football clubs has been poor when compared to the track record of those enterprises and those organisations that have actually been built up by a proper understanding of the dynamics of the business they are in. You need financial strategies at football clubs which are not just based on capital growth but which are looking for returns over the long-term for everybody who has invested in the game, including the supporters; we need a better balancing act in terms of rewarding all stakeholders than has hitherto been the case.

The mediocre capabilities of most club directors is borne out by the poor historical financial performance of most clubs. The old saying 'I think I would probably function much better if someone more qualified than I was in charge of me' probably sums up the inherent problem. Nevertheless, the efficient execution of the director's role is central to the effective management of a football club. We need to understand the nature of the current breed of directors, how they have been recruited from too narrow a base, their shallow knowledge, their lack of dedicated expertise and the pervasive culture of amateurism alluded to earlier, as well as what shape their involvement should really take today.

Critically, in many cases directors appear to have the most rudimentary understanding of the obligations imposed upon them by legislation such as the Companies Act, and sensible attitudes to stewardship. Their relationship to team affairs is often that of Pontius Pilate. They frequently authorise huge investments in player transfer fees and wages and then wash their hands of the problem, leaving the team manager to carry the can when these investments fail to produce a return.[3] Directors have to learn to balance their different roles and face up to these challenges. In my view we need a new generation of directors. That is the kind of challenge which exists in professional football at the moment.

CONCLUSION
What is the solution? First and foremost it is to internalise the challenge. Gerry Boon of Deloitte & Touche has made the valid point that football is still a small industry and most of the businesses that exist in football are small businesses. But the reality is that most small businesses are proprietor-owned and proprietor-managed. The person who founded them is usually running that entrepreneurial concern. Therefore it seems to us not unreasonable for that risk-taker, the Richard Branson at the Virgin Group, or the Anita Roddick at the Body Shop, the people who started the business, to generate an entrepreneurial profit.

What is not acceptable is the situation in football where people are buying up largely undervalued assets and making massive returns because of poor stewardship and poor standards of governance. They are taking value out, without putting value in through bringing to the game the kind of professional and strategic expertise which is essential for any organisation to prosper.

What do we do about it? What is required is to open out the ownership base of football. Clubs need to open their share register to a much wider range of shareholders drawn from the communities they support. In this regard the decision of Fergus McCann in October 1999 to sell the majority of his holding in Celtic to season-ticket-holders and existing small shareholders was progressive and welcome. It was in marked contrast to Martin Edwards' decision, in the same month, to sell £41 million worth of his shares in Manchester United exclusively to institutional investors in the City of London. Shareholder rights have to be reinforced as currently the rights of small shareholders are abused by dominant majority investors. There is an excellent case for government support for football trusts. The reform of company law which is in train at the moment needs to take more account of the unique nature of businesses like soccer.

Football needs an efficient system of corporate governance and regulation. Well-crafted state intervention, as was demonstrated through the work of the Football Trust in facilitating the reconstruction of Britain's stadiums from 1990 onwards, has a role to play. But football's existing governing bodies and the boards of football clubs must also play their part. Pressing requirements are that basic standards of corporate governance best practice be applied within the clubs and some form of stakeholder philosophy should be encouraged to take root. The game needs to professionalise but not at the cost of forgetting its sporting roots and its obligations to the wider communities that have sustained it.

4. The players' perspective
GORDON TAYLOR

The great strength of football is the extraordinary passion it excites in its followers and supporters. It is tremendous that we all feel so passionately about it. Everybody feels they own a part of it and have an opinion on it. And so they should. Football, after all, is the world's greatest spectator sport.

Some observers argue that in purely financial terms football is still a very minor industry. However, it is important to remember that its central role in people's lives lends it an importance in national life over and above the financial value of the clubs themselves. That is why people like Alan Sugar and Sir John Hall are attracted to owning clubs, because the publicity value of such ownership has a value beyond any direct financial profit made. So I believe football is and always has been big business. That is why it is so important that it is governed and regulated in an appropriate way.

PLAYERS' WAGES
Two major interlocking themes in the current debate about football are the huge scale of the infusion of television monies which has recently come into the game and how this has been distributed, and the recent dramatic increase in players' wages. As chief executive of the players' union, the PFA, representing over 4,000 professional footballers in England and Wales, I have some views on these issues. The first point I would like to make is that football is a tough game and has not always been financially rewarding for players. By way of illustration: I remember when I played at Bolton Wanderers in the early 1960s just before the maximum wage was removed. The tough-tackling full-back Roy Hartle used to say, 'Never mind the ball, let's just get on with the game.'

A recurrent theme in the writings of many commentators on recent developments in football is that players are being too well rewarded. I think that it is worth remembering at this point that ultimately the game is about players, and they should get some credit for this. I detect, sometimes, an undercurrent of envy about players earning good money, while at the same time there is no envy of our top film, TV or popular music stars earning a lot. I recall the fears when the maximum wage was removed in 1961 about how this move would damage the game. It had to be removed because it was infringing basic rights and freedoms, represented a restraint of trade, and was beyond the law. Five years later England won the World Cup. It is therefore quite ironic that nearly four decades later we have the Bosman ruling (which ensures freedom of movement of players who are out of contract) which in the essence of the spirit of its judgement only reflects what Judge Wilberforce said back in 1963 when judging the retain-and-transfer system to be illegal. Now clubs and governing bodies are saying that the Bosman ruling has unleashed unsustainable wage inflation to the extent that some form of salary-capping is being seriously discussed as a counter-measure. I would see such a measure as also a restraint of trade and the PFA would oppose it vigorously.

I can recall the regional meetings about removing the maximum wage and one particular delegate stood up and said, 'I don't see what the problem is with a maximum wage of £20. My father works down the pit and earns a lot less than that.' And Tommy Banks, in his broad Lancashire accent, replied: 'Yes, I hear what you say. I admire your father's profession. In fact I've been down the pit, I've done his job. But you try and tell your father to come up out of that pit and mark brother Stanley Matthews next Saturday.' The point I want to make is that being a footballer is a very special skill and it is only right that the players should be rewarded fairly for that.

On the other hand we are trying to introduce a sense of responsibility amongst the profession along with other interested parties in the game such as supporters, the FA and the government, through the PFA in England and the International Players Association (FIFA-PRO). We are trying to develop a recognition that the problems of football cannot be solved by one interested party alone, but only through a coming together of what other authors in this collection might describe as stakeholders. By way of illustration, if you think back to the 1980s when the game reached its nadir and we had the Bradford, Heysel and Hillsborough tragedies, it is important to note that football on its own could not have resolved these problems. It would therefore be naïve of me, as a football administrator, to think that we, or any other interested party, can operate purely on the basis of the pursuit of their particular constituency's self-interest. You need to be aware of both global and local perceptions of your organisation and its members. You need to keep abreast of legal developments: government has to be actively involved in the football industry, for example with respect to such issues as health and safety, particularly at stadiums; or in relation to the granting of work permits to overseas players, a particularly important issue for the PFA.

THE ROLE OF SUPPORTERS' GROUPS

The importance of the involvement of a wider range of interested parties is nowhere better illustrated than by the very positive influence brought to the game when, after Heysel and Hillsborough, football supporters started to get themselves better organised. This had the effect of reasserting the central role of supporters in the theatre of the game. By way of example: as a player you used to think you were responsible to the manager, who you perceived as having the easier job as your situation was very insecure. The manager was responsible to the board and it stopped there; there was no sense of any network of obligations beyond that. But of course it doesn't stop there, because every board of directors is responsible to its supporters if not to its shareholders (and both if its supporters are also shareholders). And I would not like to think that the game could ever be taken away from the influence of its supporters. The game has to be about packed stadiums. The way supporters responded after Heysel and Hillsborough should never be forgotten. The fact that since that time supporters have been involved, together with the Football Trust, local authorities, the police and many other bodies in addressing the issues of ground safety and improving the quality of the experience at football grounds, has been very important in laying the foundations for football's renaissance. It is important to remember that in 1986 Margaret Thatcher would have closed down football quite willingly, and a sizeable minority of the public would have supported her in doing so. But it was the work of the aforementioned fans' groups and other interested parties which has contributed to the game's rebirth and to making it so popular today. This success is the reason why there is so much interest in the game today. As a consequence, everybody feels they have a piece of it and everybody wants to mould it in their own particular way. But they all have to remember that to maintain the current level of success we need to continue to treat the interests of all these interested parties in a balanced way so that no one group's interests dominate. For example, we cannot and should not ignore capital coming into the game, via individuals like Jack Walker at Blackburn Rovers; on the other hand you do not really want any particular club to become too dependent on one individual, which is unhealthy.

THE ROLE OF TV

Similarly, with reference to Rupert Murdoch's BSkyB's attempt to take over Manchester United, you have to acknowledge that while there were problems with this particular case, the influence of satellite TV money on football has largely been beneficial. In the 1980s, when the game needed television money, it was completely dependent on contracts with the terrestrial networks. At one point the FA and the Football League thought there were too many televised games and that this was affecting attendances. For a period of some months, between contracts, there were no televised games and at this point the FA, the Football League and the clubs realised they needed the TV money. They then had to go cap in hand to the BBC and ITV (this was in the era before the introduction of satellite TV) for a £1 million a year deal, a very small sum of money indeed.

While it may be an unpopular thing to say in some circles, I feel you do have to give some credit to the satellite TV companies for the way they entered the televised football marketplace. They took a gamble on football. At the time BSkyB was not trading profitably. Rupert Murdoch saw what a lot of his competitors, as well as nearly all the commentators on the game, did not see at that time, which was the value of sport as a television spectacle because of how much it meant to people, how important it was in our social fabric. And BSkyB's dedicated sports channels have been particularly successful, a success they deserve.

However, while acknowledging the contribution of satellite TV to football's rebirth, I am not in favour of BSkyB achieving an undue, monopolistic dominance over the running of the game, similar to that which they currently enjoy over football broadcasting; particularly through taking over a football club. There were many people who felt it was inevitable that BSkyB would be allowed to take over Manchester United and that such a development was not problematic. But the PFA made clear at the time, through its submission to the MMC enquiry, that it felt that such a move would be unhealthy. Firstly, it would have dramatically increased the competitive power of one club, Manchester United, to the point of an unhealthy unchallenged domination, a point I discuss in more detail in the next section. Secondly, a TV company controlling a very desirable club would have a totally unfair advantage over its rivals, and for all intents and purposes would dominate any future negotiations over TV rights and the division of TV revenues. This would soon result in many small clubs either having to be wound up or being absorbed as nursery clubs into the dominant clubs in their particular areas. At present, football is a social sport enjoyed by large numbers of people every week; the fear was that it might become a TV sport where people wishing to view top-class football had no option but to stay at home and watch the same dominant clubs playing each other each week. We therefore welcomed the recommendation of the MMC, and the decision of the government, to block the bid.

THE RESTRICTIVE PRACTICES COURT CASE AND THE IMPORTANCE OF COMPETITIVE BALANCE

A key reason that the MMC gave for rejecting BSkyB's bid for Manchester United was that it would increase polarisation within the Premier League by opening the door to a handful of clubs with financial links to media companies to become much more powerful than the rest, an analysis with which I would agree. It is therefore doubly ironic that it is another government agency, the Office of Fair Trading (OFT), who, through their decision to challenge the right of the Premier League to negotiate collectively on behalf of its member clubs by taking a case to the Restrictive Practices Court (RPC), came very close to undermining the ability of football to try and maintain the fairest and highest level of competition within the game. The OFT proposed that the Premier League's exclusive rights to negotiate broadcasting rights for all its members was a restraint of trade and that individual clubs should be free to negotiate their own deals. If they had been successful in their case, they would have unleashed a free-for-all which would have created an imbalance in resources among the Premier League's membership and destroyed competitive balance. Thankfully the RPC rejected the case.

If you are serious about regulating football efficiently, your top priority has to be to ensure that competition is as healthy as possible so as to create maximum uncertainty in results. Now that particular job is becoming more difficult. England is unique in the world in that it has 92 full-time professional clubs. We also have the highest aggregate attendances. More people watch football live in the Football League than in the Premier League. You cannot ignore those statistics, which are a credit to our game. The reason supporters go to our games in such large numbers is because both the Football League and the Premier League are so competitive.

We would not be doing our job in sport if we allowed the erosion of uncertainty of results; if we undermine a system that, prior to the formation of the Premier League, in the last 30 years saw 50 different clubs in the top division; if we allow to continue a system where the three clubs that get promoted into the Premier League from the Football League each season are odds-on with the bookmakers to go down after one season in the top flight. In that case I would not be doing my job as a sports administrator and neither would the FA, the Premier League or the Football League. Such a scenario is not in the best interests of the game because it is counter-productive. The only way we are going to maintain an interest in football is by keeping high level of uncertainty of results. That is why it is doubly important that we do not see the Premier League dominated by a handful of clubs and where there is no effective and long-lasting mobility from the Football League to the Premier League. In this respect, the recent blanket dominance of the domestic game by Manchester United does raise the question as to how healthy the competition levels are in the domestic game when United are able to consistently dominate the main domestic competitions.

Proof of the imperative to have aggressive regulatory structures in your league in order to maintain a high level of balance and competitive uncertainty is provided by that arch-capitalist country, the United States of America. I regularly visit US sports associations and see how they genuinely try to give the bottom club the very first choice of the college football draft pick system in order to make them more competitive; the way that the National Football League (NFL), for example, organises commercial income and then distributes it equally to the League's member clubs to ensure that clubs have sufficient resources at their disposal to remain competitive. That is why it is imperative that football's main world governing bodies, UEFA and FIFA, curb the political in-fighting that has bedevilled them and concentrate on the main job in hand maintaining a high level of competitive balance in the game at all levels.

The success of football depends on a strong infrastructure with effective and independent governing bodies. If financial and administrative control of the game were to be concentrated in the hands of a few clubs and TV companies worldwide, the game would suffer.

THE INFLUENCE OF THE EUROPEAN COMMISSION

It is imperative that UEFA concentrate on the problem of creeping imbalance within the game because of the stance that has been adopted by the European Commission in relation to the development of young talent. The European Commission believes that sport and football, in terms of competition legislation, should be treated exactly the same as any other business. But it never has been, and in my opinion, it never will. In order to be successful, sports leagues need to foster a high level of competition; in conventional business sectors the emphasis is on eliminating your competitors.

It was interesting to reflect on the outcome of a recent Belgian court case involving a Finnish basketball player playing in Belgium. The court decided that it was good for the competition to have windows of time when players cannot be bought or sold to avoid, for example, the richest club suddenly buying in a number of expensive, high-performance players in a desperate bid to avoid relegation.

It is also interesting that the Court of Arbitration for Sport (CAS), the leading international court for sports issues, is still considering whether it is appropriate for football that one owner has more than one club in the same competition. This is in response to an appeal by ENIC, an investment vehicle, which combines interests in four clubs – a majority stake in Slavia Prague (the Czech Republic), a minority stake in Rangers (Scotland), and full ownership of Vicenza (Italy) and AEK Athens (Greece) (see also Chapter 8 by Adam Brown). ENIC challenged UEFA's ruling that only one of its clubs could compete in the same competition. Now, I find this episode extraordinary. Look at what happens in Formula One motor racing, where it is not unusual to see a number-two driver on the point of winning a race take his foot off the pedal to let the number-one driver pass to win. Similarly, in horse-racing, you see what happens when an owner has two horses in a race and the outsider usually wins, to the extent that in France they quote the prices of the two horses together. The FA's own rule prohibiting multi-club ownership came about because of the way in which Robert Maxwell took control of Derby, Oxford and Reading, and the consequent fears of the implications of this move. You would not think you would have a difficult job convincing politicians of the undesirability of having one owner with more than one club in the same competition. But because of politicians' central role in determining competition policy, it is critical they are involved in this debate, as there are a number of siren voices out there who are arguing that multi-club ownership is not a problem, which it very definitely is. Politicians need to understand the imperative of maintaining competitive balance.

Similarly, administrators need to take on board the views of everybody – supporters' organisations, business and television which, after all, has been the driving force of all this new income. Fortunately, because of the Taylor Report, that money has not been totally wasted. But I would say that any administrator needs to convince his club that a certain large percentage of any future income needs to go into capital projects for the future; in youth development programmes; in positive community work such as drug-awareness programmes where my players do their best to act as role models; in anti-racism programmes. And particularly that they concentrate their efforts on ensuring that the next generation of supporters will be able to afford to enter the grounds. We need full stadiums and we cannot afford to let football become an armchair spectator game. We need to address the issue of low-income fans, families with young children, the disabled, the unemployed being excluded or priced out of the grounds, because this is where a large section of the next generation of supporters is going to come from. We ignore this fact at our peril. We need live spectators in the grounds for a healthy game. A purely television spectacle will not work.

CONCLUSION

Finally, I would make this point: public companies say their first priority is to their shareholders. I don't agree with this proposition in the context of football clubs. If a football club is a public company in a professional league then the FA must say to them that their first priority is to their football supporters and not to the shareholders. Ultimately the successful clubs are the ones which are centred in their local communities, and that is as it should be. That is why the football authorities should not allow schemes such as Wimbledon's proposal to move to Dublin.

This link between football and community is what I think of when I remember living in Manchester at the time of the Munich disaster and all the sadness surrounding it. Yet that club, just a few days later, provided a team that still stayed in the FA Cup and still stayed in the European Championship. Contrast that with the 1999–2000 season when the same club was offered an exit for commercial and political reasons and withdrew from the FA Cup. If that illustrates the way the game is going, it is certainly not going down a path which I would want to travel.

5. Why football needs a regulator

ROGAN TAYLOR

What are the prospects for a new regulator either inside or independent from the game of football? This is a question which has been increasingly raised as the deliberations of the government-appointed Football Task Force progress. The implication of the question is that there is a problem with the way in which the game is being regulated at the moment. This is a proposition which I, for one, would agree with, particularly following my experiences as a member of the Football Task Force.

REGULATORY PATERNALISM – THE FA'S FIRST HUNDRED YEARS

I think the problem at the beginning of any discussion about whether there should or shouldn't be a regulator is that you have to decide both what the game is at the moment and what you want it to be in the future. We certainly know something about what the game was for the last hundred years or so. Though professional football has been almost entirely privately owned through limited companies throughout most of this century, that fact has made little difference to the kind of social, and perhaps even religious, hold that football has had on the hearts of a huge number of ordinary British people.

The problem for us in 2000 lies in the fact that the game is changing so fast. It is not what it once was and it has certainly not yet completed its current transformation into what it will become. After a decade of seemingly incessant restructuring, football has still not stabilised into the shape it is likely to hold even for the early part of the new century. It is difficult to make predictions, or policy, in such a fluid environment. Nevertheless, this should not mean that we, or more pertinently the football authorities, should shirk the responsibility of looking for policy solutions where obvious problems have manifested themselves.

In order to decide whether we need a regulator and what that regulator might do, I think we have to decide what we want from the game, what we think it is and what we think it should be. What place should football occupy in our national life in the next millennium? Football has been regulated for 'the good of the game' as a primarily sporting organisation, almost from its inception by the FA. Much has been wrong with the way the game was regulated by the FA, perhaps especially regarding the level of professionalism and competence employed. But I think there is one thing that we can say for the much-criticised 'blazers' of Lancaster Gate. The 'old buffers' were also *real* buffers; they did protect and defend this game. In the history of the development of professional football, under the regulation of the FA, you can see how the leftover 'Corinthian' vision of what the game ought to be about protected football from the outright predations of commercial business forces.

For example, right from the very beginnings of professionalisation and private ownership, strictures such as the FA Rule 34 (which deterred commercial asset-strippers) and restrictions on directors of football clubs drawing salaries or paying out dividends over a token amount were made in an attempt to ward off a kind of Americanisation of English football. The 'franchise' concept of sports clubs where there is very little relationship between clubs and the places they play was actively discouraged. The effect of the FA restrictions meant that football clubs were not seen *in themselves* as potentially profitable institutions. This in turn had the effect of immobilising them where they were born, giving them the chance to send down undisturbed and deep roots into their local communities. You could move the Brooklyn Dodgers from New York to California but who could contemplate moving Newcastle United to a more convenient location down south? I suspect that not enough people really recognise that it was this aristocratic, Corinthian vision of the game that (unintentionally) enabled it to play so significant a part in the lives of ordinary people. And this Corinthian vision did not fade within the FA for over a century after those ex-public schoolboys wrote the Rules of Association Football in 1863. You should remember that Sir Frederick Wall was playing for the Royal Engineers in the FA Cup in the 1880s, and he was still secretary of the FA in 1933. Almost a caricature of an upper-class English gent, Wall and his like ran the FA for its first 70 years. Even after Wall was succeeded by Stanley Rous, a very similar approach was adopted, if not quite so heavily moustachioed. These administrators might have been conservative and staid, but they did offer stability, and a commitment to prioritising sporting over commercial imperatives and the redistribution of income throughout the game.

Many people feel that the FA finally abandoned any last vestiges of this custodial role at the beginning of the 1990s, just one year after the Hillsborough disaster. The birth of the breakaway Premier League, encouraged secretly at first by the FA as part of its squabble over power with the Football League, was the first and most critical manifestation of this opting out. In an increasingly desperate attempt to 'modernise' (under a constant welter of criticism from the media for their poor management of the game), the FA, as a regulatory 'buffer', simply abandoned ship. At this point those traditional duties of care for the game seemed to drop down the agenda in terms of priorities. The real priorities were to secure the supremacy of the FA by, paradoxically (possibly fatally), promoting the powerful – the big clubs – into the pilot's seat, via the Premier League. The failure of the FA to negotiate and manage their relationship with the Premier League – when they were in an all-powerful position as midwife at the birth of this new creature – was a crucial mistake. The FA Premier League (as it was first called) was allowed the full respectability of life under FA approval without any 'caring' responsibilities being required from what soon became the richest league in the world. Only recently – and under considerable pressure from other sources, including first the Football Task Force and now the government itself – has the Premier League agreed to send money back down the football pyramid to its roots.

Though the FA operated in a protective role for so long, I do not believe that this rather peculiar organisation demonstrated any great concern to involve supporters in the way they managed the game from 1863 onwards. The regulatory process was private. Even 'respectable', conservative fan associations were excluded. For example, the National Federation of Football Supporters Clubs (NatFed), formed in the late 1920s, was an extremely respectable organisation representing many of the supporters' clubs who contributed so much to the game through running lotteries and other fundraising initiatives at football clubs, generating the cash to build and roof the popular ends of grounds all over the country. The members of these fan groups and their dedication are the major reason why we still have 92 professional clubs in this country. Many of the 92 have only survived through private and public benevolence: of organised supporters and of local individuals. (The same can still be the case today as we have seen at Northampton Town where a supporters' trust was instrumental in saving the club from bankruptcy in 1992.)[1] Yet, extraordinarily, the FA's regulatory process did not even allow an organisation as respectable as NatFed inside the doors of its Lancaster Gate headquarters until well into the 1970s when the game had become mired in the hooligan crisis. There were a few informal meetings, inevitably off-the-record, but the FA did not officially meet these eminently respectable, be-suited, representatives of the supporters' groups (despite their often looking more like the directors of small football clubs than real football fans) until nearly 50 years after the organisation was formed. So there was never any question that the vast mass of football fans (in the 1948–49 season there were 42 million attendances at League games alone) were ever properly represented at any level in the game's administration.

THE FA'S REGULATION OPT-OUT

Now, with the FA's opt-out, there is a double vacuum at the heart of football's administration. There is the vacuum that was always there: the absence of representatives of fans with any serious input into policy-making in the game. And there is a second vacuum where once the regulatory body, the FA, did some regulating in the interests of the game as a whole, however paternalistically this operated in practice. Suddenly, a decade ago, this role was substantially abandoned. To many, the FA does not appear to be entirely neutral any more in the way it uses its power. This is, of course, anathema to the principles of regulation of which the cardinal rule is neutrality in the application of power and influence. Clearly there are now some favoured parties – one in particular. The current restructuring ('modernising') of the FA will represent an even greater capitulation to the Premier League who (it is rumoured) want a complete veto over any regulations the FA enacts which might affect the way they run their affairs.

To these prospects must be added the fact that there has been a kind of stage-two privatisation in the game in the 1990s; the result of a number of processes which gathered speed during the previous decade. One of these was a change in the *type* of owner of football clubs. During the 1980s, men like Irving Scholar at Spurs, modern 'entrepreneurs' in a changing economy under Mrs Thatcher's government, began to view football clubs in a different light from more traditional owners (who had often made their fortunes locally in more traditional industries). The move onto the stockmarket by many clubs in the 1990s confirms this shift in vision towards a profit-orientated ownership. There is an additional danger now which threatens the traditional relationships between fans and their clubs. Local supporters (and for a club like Manchester United that means within the UK) are becoming even more marginalised from the core agenda of England's leading clubs. For the balance of power of the established interests in the game is shifting from administrative organisations to the big clubs, and the focus of the latter is shifting from the local to the global. This is exemplified by Manchester United's decision to opt out of the FA Cup to go to the World Club championship in Brazil. I believe the extent to which this was a straightforward commercial decision by United has been obscured by the FA's self-destructive decision to support it. Consequently, the decision has been cloaked and disguised – wrapped up in the Union Jack – by the FA's insistence that it was part of the wider campaign to have the 2006 World Cup held in England. I think that United's decision would have been the same regardless of any World Cup bid. Critically, Manchester United's duty to their institutional shareholders requires them to prioritise global markets over local ones.

When one remembers that a football club is an odd kind of monopoly supplier of a product which some people just have to buy – almost like an essential service – the ownership of clubs is an important public affair. Despite decades of television exposure of the big, glamorous clubs, most fans' choice of club is still largely based on family or local affinity – blood and soil – and once chosen you stick with it for life. These factors alone produce quite a strong argument for some form of independent regulation if the traditional, 'neutral' regulator has abandoned that role.

My experience as a member of the Football Task Force has only added strength to this belief. The actions and words of some of those who represent the Premier League, and to a lesser extent the FA, have given the impression that they do not think there are any problems in the game at all, bar a few minor matters which they can take care of. Their complacency is almost tangible. It is as if they cannot work out quite why the Minister for Culture, Media and Sport has bothered to set up a group like the Football Task Force. Until July 1999, at no point in our lengthy deliberations had any positive suggestions been made about how the Task Force might address the most difficult problems that the Minister had raised as serious concerns.

For example, every suggestion various members have made about tackling the problem of exclusion has been met with the insistence that the FA and the Premier League have done all they possibly can on this issue and there really is nothing else they can do about it. It is as if the fact that supporters are being priced out of grounds because of the rapid increase in match-day ticket prices – priced out of a game that they may have spent 40 or 50 years supporting – is an unassailable process. If they believe this, they should say so explicitly. Up until July 1999, they had made no serious attempts to solve these kinds of problems – or even at least to alleviate some of their worst effects – despite their presence on the Task Force agenda. The subtext of their contributions read: 'Football's fine and dandy. There are rising gates, massive media exposure, the financial turnover of clubs is exploding. If it ain't broke don't fix it!' They think the game is so healthy it does not matter if some of the old 'core' support misses out.

Finally, in late July 1999, the Premier League and FA did make a submission to the Task Force which did involve some promising proposals including the setting up of an independent scrutiny panel to examine vexed issues in the game whose appointees would be selected in consultation with the Secretary of State for Culture, Media and Sport. While this proposal has some promise, until the final report of the Task

Force appears there is no way of telling how committed either the Premier League or the FA is to such potentially radical reforms of the game's administration.

The problem I have with this attitude of begrudgery to the need for reform – apart from its obvious injustice – is that I think football is a much more delicate plant than some representatives of the FA and the Premier League appear to believe. True, the game has survived some extraordinary crises despite being poorly managed in many respects from its inception by the FA and the Football League. (It might be said to have survived despite their stewardship rather than because of it.) For example, it has treated its paying customers, on average, abominably. It has presided over a game that has regularly killed its supporters, in significant numbers, in virtually every decade of this century except the 1990s. Yet, until very recently, the FA and the Football League never consulted those customers about any important decisions that they have taken throughout the twentieth century. And largely they have expected them to pay for the privilege of standing in death traps.

Nevertheless, the ability of football and its fans to survive that kind of battering points us toward the game's current weakness in a rather odd, ironic way. Where did that strength to survive come from for most of this century? Even, in 1985, after 20 years of chronic hooliganism and disasters which took the lives of hundreds of football fans, there were *still* 16.5 million attendances in the season after Heysel. That figure is an amazing tribute to the power and depth of fans' relations with the game.

But did that fantastic hardness and fastness of supporters' connections to football and their clubs – that cultural diamond at the heart of the game – did it have anything to do with the *kind of people* who attended games? 'The Labour Party at prayer' was one eloquent description of traditional football crowds. (The Old Labour Party at prayer as opposed to New Labour!) Did it have anything to do with the sense of place and ownership that those people and their communities had, and felt, for their football clubs? I think that it did. But now it seems that the newer type of football fans that the game seems so keen to attract will not demonstrate the same kind of diehard commitment that the old ones did.[2] What worries me is not the arrival at grounds of the kind of people who did not attend football matches before, and who might not attend in the future, but the systematic exclusion of many who represent the communities that have sustained the game for so many years. Not only is this not fair, but it is not good business either. It looks like a very short-sighted pursuit of short-term advantage to target higher-spending fans whose loyalty may be fickle, over more traditional lower-income fans who will stick with you forever if you maintain strong links with them. If we want a game that remains in touch with a broad swathe of the British public, it seems like some form of independent regulation may be the only way to persuade football to do itself a favour.

WHAT ROLE FOR A REGULATOR?

That said, I think the running of some kind of independent regulatory régime is not unproblematic. A host of questions regarding how such a body would be funded, what would be its remit, its relationship with other football bodies; all these questions remain to be answered. But one thing is clear from a scrutiny of the game's history. The players and the mass of fans were traditionally always the last in line when football's governing bodies were drawing up their list of priorities for action. At least for the players, in recent years, matters appear to have improved significantly on this score. It is well past the time when the game should be properly involving its fans.

In Liverpool the cry for 'justice' for supporters in football is most often associated with the cause of the families of the victims of the Hillsborough disaster. While a discussion of the consequences of Hillsborough is outside the scope of this chapter, I must say I do believe that these families deserve a justice they have yet to receive. But I would also like to remind you of the other half a million fans who were out at matches that fateful Saturday afternoon, 15 April 1989, stuffed into other football grounds throughout the country which we now know could easily have hosted similar horrors. What about *justice* for them? Those fans also deserve some justice, at the very least to have someone to look out for their interests in this period of traumatic change. There is a case for the establishment of some independent ombudsman – the 'ombudsfan' – to whom they can take their grievances. It was Hillsborough and the consequent Taylor Report which persuaded the government that public money must be drafted in alongside private money to reconstruct the game. This government intervention was a core building block on which football's recovery in the 1990s was based. It was imposed by *external* regulation and it paved the way for football's renaissance.

PART II

IMPLICATIONS OF THE BSKYB/MANCHESTER UNITED CASE

6. The attempted takeover of Manchester United by BSkyB

PETER CROWTHER*

INTRODUCTION

The Monopolies and Mergers Commission's decision[1] to recommend an outright prohibition of the acquisition of Manchester United by BSkyB surprised many commentators. Speculation had been rife that the transaction would be allowed to proceed, but that BSkyB would have to give certain undertakings, in particular in relation to its future dealings with the Premier League. Among competition lawyers, the decision was also greeted largely with surprise. There too it seemed that many had thought the transaction would go ahead.

Shareholders United Against Murdoch, a group of Manchester United fans and shareholders mounted a large campaign to block the transaction, and Rosenblatt Solicitors agreed to assist them at the stage of the MMC inquiry. The initial advice given to SUAM was that, to block the transaction, SUAM should see the transaction primarily as a 'broadcasting' merger rather than a 'football' merger. As a result, SUAM's submissions were focused principally on the implications of the transaction for competition in broadcasting.

This chapter discusses the arguments submitted by SUAM,[2] when the transaction was referred to the MMC as well as the MMC's findings; in less detail, the chapter also considers the lessons which may be learned. Many submissions were made by other third parties in relation to the impact upon football generally, but these are not considered here. In any event, the MMC report itself placed by far the most weight on the competition aspects.[3]

Section 1 discusses the approach taken towards defining the relevant markets. Section 2 examines the arguments which were submitted as to how the transaction would hinder competition. Section 3 considers the points made in relation to undertakings which BSkyB might have offered,

---

*Peter Crowther advised Shareholders United Against Murdoch (SUAM), who mounted a large campaign to block the transaction. Opinions expressed in this chapter are entirely personal and should not be taken to reflect those of SUAM or Rosenblatt Solicitors. SUAM has subsequently reformed itself as Shareholders United (SU), an organisation to represent the interests of shareholders in Manchester United plc who are also supporters of Manchester United Football Club.

to remedy any potential anti-competitive effects. Finally, section 4 sum-marises the implications of the MMC's decision for the future relationship between broadcasters and football clubs.

1. MARKET DEFINITION

Defining the market is the starting point for any competition investiga-tion. The task is – in a nutshell – to identify a framework for investigating the competition implications of a particular transaction. The market in which the two parties are active is defined, and then the assessment moves on to how the competitive position would be affected by the merger. Not surprisingly, competition authorities are usually concerned where two parties are active in the same product or service market (for example, the broadcasting market), since such a transaction would increase the market share of the competitors, possibly to the point where they can act indepen-dently of customers and competitors.

Having said that, even where the parties are active in separate (but usually related) markets, competition concerns can arise. However, such concerns do not arise unless at least one party is dominant in a particular market. Consequently, it was important to establish that at least one of the parties had a sufficiently high share of a particular market to give a preliminary indication that it was dominant.

BSkyB   The MMC identified four markets in the broadcasting value chain:
   (a) the supply of rights for broadcasting purposes
   (b) supply of programmes
   (c) supply of channels at wholesale levels
   (d) distribution and retailing of channels to subscribers

BSkyB is active in all of these markets in the UK. SUAM argued that there was significant evidence that BSkyB should be treated as dominant for the purposes of the merger, in particular in the light of the European Com-mission's findings in its investigation into British Interactive Broadcasting, as well as the 1996 Review of BSkyB's position in the wholesale pay TV market. In particular, SUAM submitted that BSkyB was dominant in:
   • the retail pay TV market;
   • the wholesale pay TV market generally; and
   • the wholesale supply of sports channels for retail pay TV.

The MMC considered whether free-to-air broadcasting and pay TV should be treated as part of the same market. This was significant since if the free-to-air 'market' was included, BSkyB's position in the market would be considerably diluted. SUAM submitted that the MMC should follow the approach taken by the OFT in its 1996 Review of BSkyB's position in wholesale pay TV. The MMC agreed with the conclusion arrived at by the

OFT, but disagreed as to the reasons. The MMC decided that free-to-air broadcasting had to be purchased before pay TV could be considered by a potential subscriber. Hence the subscriber would regard pay TV as a complement to rather than substitute for free-to-air content.

In the event, the MMC concluded that it was more appropriate to treat pay TV as a separate market, and, further, that 'based on conditions of substitutability, we concluded that the relevant market for our purposes was for sports premium TV channels'. The ability to enter and compete with BSkyB depends upon ownership of live rights, which are themselves a limited resource. The MMC decided that there were not enough such rights to sustain many sports premium channels. This, together with the fact that BSkyB currently provides three sports premium channels, led the MMC to conclude that BSkyB is dominant in this market.

United   The MMC found that United enjoyed strength in three particular respects: its financial performance, the size of its supporter base and its sporting success. SUAM argued that, at the very least, Manchester United was part of the market for the supply of Premier League football (as opposed to football generally). SUAM also submitted in the oral hearing that it may be appropriate to identify a narrower market, including:

(a) a market for the supply of top-quality Premier League games; and/or

(b) a market for watching Manchester United games.

In relation to the former, SUAM argued that the consistent quality associated with the top four or five Premier League teams meant that viewers would choose – when not watching their own team – to watch matches involving these teams. On the basis of Manchester United's recent performances, it was clear that Manchester United was an important player in that market. One possible way to gauge the accuracy of this would be to examine the gate receipts at clubs placed low down in the Premier League, when visited by those clubs at the top part of the league.

SUAM also submitted that it was possible to identify an even narrower market, that for watching Manchester United games. There were two dimensions to this: the market for watching the games at the stadium, and the market for watching the games live on TV. Clearly, to the extent that these were actual or potential substitutes, competition would be completely eliminated. The MMC did not have to decide on the matter, but did state 'there is at least an arguable case for treating the live matches of Manchester United, whether watched at the ground or on TV, as a separate market.'

SUAM did not seek to argue that the appropriate market should be that for Manchester United live football games, but stressed that this was a possibility. SUAM provided evidence from independent surveys which appeared to support this conclusion – in particular evidence demonstrating the massive amount of support for Manchester United from younger members of society.

The MMC concluded that: 'The market in which Manchester United operates is no wider than the matches of Premier League clubs.'

Comment   It is submitted that the MMC took the correct approach since the circumstances did not require the MMC to define a narrower market than the market for Premier League football.

An important question for the future is where this 'narrowing' process should naturally terminate. There is an intuitive argument that each football club is supported by a certain number of individuals for whom watching another club is no substitute (so-called 'infra-marginal customers'). While this may be strictly true, in practice a line must be drawn, beyond which a market cannot be considered sufficiently important *for the purposes of competition policy*; it is of course a different question whether, from a perspective other than that of competition policy, there should be restrictions on which entities should be permitted to control football clubs.

While this is, at the time of writing, a theoretical issue, it may in the future assume practical importance. As the law currently appears to stand, broadcasters may acquire up to 25% of Premier League clubs, as long as the gross worldwide assets of each club is below £70 million, before a significant risk arises that a further acquisition would qualify for investigation by the OFT. This is because an acquisition would have to result in at least 25% of 'services of a particular description' coming under common control (or a lesser degree of control), before the OFT would have jurisdiction to investigate. On current views, the services of a particular description would probably be 'Premier League games', but the OFT could in theory take a narrower view, e.g. 'top-class Premier League football clubs' or even football clubs in a particular area.

More immediately worrying from the point of view of consistency in the application of competition law and economics principles is the fact that the Restrictive Practices Court came to a very different conclusion on the appropriate way to define the market. This is dealt with separately in this book by Professor Martin Cave (Chapter 22).

2. IMPACT ON COMPETITION

In common with many other third-party submissions, SUAM argued that if BSkyB acquired United, BSkyB, irrespective of any undertakings given, would acquire a competitive advantage in negotiations on the future sale of football rights. In particular, SUAM developed what it referred to as the 'Marks & Spencers' analogy – in which other 'shops' (football clubs) want to locate closely to Marks & Spencer on the high street. Extending this analogy, the link-up of United with BSkyB would encourage other football clubs to sell their rights in future to BSkyB, since it is the dominant broadcaster in pay TV and thus would have access to the largest sources of revenue. (Of course, SUAM submitted this argument before Marks & Spencers' most recent trading figures had been released!)

Moreover, BSkyB would simply have to acquire the rights to a further two or three top clubs (whose assets would be below the £70 million threshold), and it would have an almost unassailable position in relation to subscribers (see Chapter 8). Even just acquiring the rights to broadcast the matches of the next two or three football clubs placed after Manchester United would be made easier due to the fact that Manchester United commands the largest amount of support from the football-watching population. This process would affect the following possible relevant markets:

- the market for watching Manchester United football;
- the market for watching top-quality Premier League football;
- the market for watching Premier League football.

Although SUAM did not have the resources to have a full survey carried out, SUAM submitted that owning the rights to just three top clubs which attracted a large amount of subscribers would result in those middle- and lower-ranking clubs being attracted to BSkyB due to the possibility of increased revenue through a broader retail football-following subscriber base. This is logical in the sense that unless the pay-per-view or subscription channel was excessively priced (unlikely since BSkyB would have an incentive to increase the number of subscribers and could not price discriminate between those supporters of a particular football club who, all things being equal, may pay a higher price than the marginal football viewer), a process of 'tipping' would occur after critical mass had been achieved.

SUAM also argued that competition between Premier League clubs themselves would also be affected, due to the increased buying power of the club, backed by immense financial resources. However, the main detriment identified by SUAM would be the development of pay TV in the UK, in particular in relation to premium sports channels.

Undertakings   When assessing a merger, the MMC is obliged to consider whether the parties can give any appropriate undertakings to remedy anti-competitive effects that have been identified. The outright prohibition of a merger must be a proportionate response to the seriousness of the anti-competitive concerns identified, and the MMC generally tends to let mergers through wherever possible. SUAM's line on this was clear. No undertakings would be appropriate, for a number of reasons:

- the nature of the industry was changing and therefore undertakings would become at best irrelevant and at worst inappropriate;

- price regulation may be necessary, the consequence of which would be the permanent introduction of regulation into an industry which was hitherto unregulated; and
- even if the MMC could identify undertakings which could in principle be suitable, Rupert Murdoch's own history suggested that there was a significant risk that any undertakings may be breached.

With regard to the last argument, SUAM submitted a paper containing all instances in which Rupert Murdoch had previously given assurances which had not been honoured. These included assurances given to the Department of Trade and Industry.

The MMC considered an undertaking that Manchester United should be prohibited from taking part in future discussions about the sale of live Premier League football rights. BSkyB had objected to this on the grounds that this would unnecessarily adversely affect BSkyB's share price, and would unfairly discriminate against Manchester United. In the event, the MMC found that such an undertaking would not be appropriate:

- it would not prevent informal information flows between United and BSkyB;
- United could influence other clubs in the run-up to the allocation of future rights, without necessarily taking direct part in the final decision-making process;
- the undertaking would not be credible to other broadcasters when preparing bids for the broadcasting rights;
- this would be unfair to United since Premier League rights represented a significant element of United's income, and it should therefore play a part in the Premier League's decisions;
- if collective selling were to break down, this undertaking would no longer be appropriate.

The Report reveals that the parties increasingly offered more stringent undertakings. From the contents of the Report, it appears that the parties initially denied that the merger would give the parties any advantage in bidding for future rights. After the MMC objected, BSkyB offered two assurances, which were weaker than the hypothetical remedy considered by the MMC above:

- United would bar itself from receiving any information in advance of final bids being prepared;
- United would abstain from voting on the future collective sale of rights, where BSkyB had submitted a bid.

In the circumstances, it was not difficult for the MMC to conclude that these assurances would not be satisfactory: the MMC had already rejected a stricter undertaking as insufficient.

3. BROADER IMPLICATIONS

As adviser to SUAM during the MMC process, this author may not be particularly well placed to comment independently on whether the decision was the right one. However, my own view is that this was not just another 'vertical' merger, in contrast to the views expressed by many commentators both before and after the decision. There are instances where a vertical merger can generate horizontal effects (in this case an impact on competition in the broadcasting market), and it is submitted that the merger fell into this slightly uncommon category.

The decision has been severely criticised by some competition lawyers. However, the Report is carefully reasoned, and the MMC was simply not convinced by what the parties offered by way of undertakings. With the obvious benefit of hindsight, it is interesting to speculate whether the MMC might have allowed the transaction through if a different approach on the issue of undertakings had been taken by the parties. It is, however, immensely difficult to 'second guess' how the MMC will react in any given case, and to devise a strategy on hypothetical remedies accordingly. In the final analysis, of course, if the parties were not prepared to offer undertakings at least as strict as those which it might be foreseen would be required by the MMC, the transaction should not have been allowed to proceed (assuming that the MMC's reasoning itself stands up, which I submit it does).

In my view, the Report is not a 'setback' for the even-handed application of competition policy. Moreover, it was not a 'political' decision as has been reported. The Secretary of State had no choice but to accept the MMC's carefully reasoned recommendations. On the contrary, it would have been a political decision to reject the recommendations.

4. CONCLUSION

From a purely personal point of view, this was a very exciting merger to be involved in, especially because many did not take SUAM seriously, and those who did thought we were pushing a very large boulder up a very steep hill. The outcome of this particular MMC inquiry, it is submitted, turned on the inadequacy of undertakings offered by the parties. Of course, it may be that the commercial cost of undertakings which might have been suitable was too high, hence the parties' apparent cautious approach on this issue. Moreover, even though SUAM's focus was on the broadcasting market – to create the reasons to block the merger – sitting time after time in a room full of ardent Manchester United fans did not allow one easily to lose sight of the real aim: to keep Manchester United!

7. The MMC's inquiry into BSkyB's merger with Manchester United plc

NICHOLAS FINNEY

INTRODUCTION

When the merger between BSkyB and Manchester United plc was referred to the Monopolies and Mergers Commission (now the Competition Commission) for consideration, the panel assembled to undertake this task needed to be highly experienced, something which was demonstrated by the decision for the case to be chaired by the chairman of the Commission itself, Dr Derek Morris. From the outset it was clear that this was going to be a difficult case to examine, since the merger not only brought together two substantial enterprises with different operational and trading objectives, but also involved a very substantial degree of third-party representatives (over 300 individuals and 57 organisations). Closer examination of the third-party evidence, as handed over to the panel by the Office of Fair Trading (OFT), revealed them to be universally hostile to the merger apart from six Premier League clubs who had submitted letters in which they raised no objections.

In determining how the panel should conduct the inquiry, care was taken to ensure that both parties were given adequate facilities for oral representations, and that in addition, third parties were also afforded an opportunity to give oral evidence. As a consequence, the panel held an above-average number of hearings including three hearings in Manchester. In total, five hearings were held with the main parties: three with BSkyB (including a remedies hearing) and two with Manchester United. Despite objections from the main parties: the panel decided that it would be helpful if the issues letter, which laid down the main issues it wished to raise with both parties, should be formally published in the form of a press notice. This was the first merger inquiry to apply this procedure and one which, in the event, did not have the effects feared by the main parties. Indeed, the stock exchange reported that it had no discernible effect on the share prices of either BSkyB or Manchester United. Ironically, subsequent alleged leaks and comments by third parties actually led to an *increase* in share prices.

THE REFERENCE ITSELF

On 29 October 1998, the Secretary of State for Trade and Industry, Peter Mandelson MP, referred to the MMC the proposed acquisition by British Sky Broadcasting Group plc (BSkyB) of Manchester United plc (Manchester United). The references were made under the powers granted the Secretary of State under sections 64, 69(2) or 75(1) of the Fair Trading Act 1973. The MMC was required to investigate and report on certain matters regarding the merger, including whether the situation may be expected to operate against the public interest.

THE PANEL'S ANALYSIS OF THE EVIDENCE DURING THE INQUIRY

The panel decided that it was going to be crucial for it to establish an agreed market definition. Given the outstandingly successful profiles of the two merger parties, although in different fields, it was going to be important to distinguish 'broadcasting markets' from 'football markets'.

One additional complication that faced the MMC was the earlier referral by the OFT of the collective selling of broadcasting rights used by the Premier League to the Restrictive Practices Court (RPC). This case was running concurrently with the MMC's own inquiry. (It is interesting to note that this issue is now being looked at by the Competition Secretariat in DGIV of the European Commission.)

MARKED DEFINITION ISSUES

The panel looked for what could be considered as a formal link between the activities of the two merger parties. It found that it was, in fact, the sale of TV rights by sporting organisations to broadcasters which provided the main connection between the market for football and the broadcasting markets (para 2.9). The panel also noted that for the first time in the UK, the proposed merger would involve the vertical integration of a major supplier of sports rights and a broadcaster. Obviously, the panel then had to go on to consider the potential impact of the merger on the sale of Premier League TV rights (itself a subject being considered by the RPC).

BSkyB BSkyB operates in all four markets of the broadcasting supply chain: it buys TV rights, makes some of its own programmes, packages programmes into various channels, and retails these channels to both 'direct-to-home' subscribers and as a wholesaler to other platforms. The panel took note of the previous definitions of broadcasting markets (1996 Directorate General IV – EC Competition Policy Newsletter 1998) and compared them to those proposed by the parties to the inquiry. It focused on the market for channels at the wholesale level because this was a key determinant in ascertaining the competitive framework both upstream for rights and programme-making, and downstream for channel distribution and retailing.

In the end, it came down to the panel taking a view on whether 'free-to-air' TV was in the same market as all forms of pay TV. BSkyB argued strongly that they were all part of the same market, but the panel disagreed. It found that sports programmes on free-to-air TV were not ready substitutes for those on pay TV. The latter involved the purchase of attractive and *exclusive* live rights for which free-to-air could not compete, partly on revenue restriction grounds, but also because of programme scheduling difficulties particularly in relation to fitting in 60 live Premier League matches. Important evidence to support this conclusion came from the fact that in the 1996 sale of Premier League rights, all three bidders were planning to broadcast on a pay TV channel (or pay-per-view). No free-to-air channel was a contender.

Manchester United   The club's outstanding financial performance, strong international support base and on-field achievements make it the most successful English football club. Manchester United's activities clearly had to be studied carefully in order to determine the relevant market. The panel noted Manchester United's revenue sources included advertising and sponsorship, the retailing of merchandise and services such as catering and hospitality associated with Old Trafford. It focused particularly on the supply of football matches and looked at whether a wider market might be appropriate, such as leisure services, or a narrower market, such as Premier League football or Manchester United's own matches.

One of the tests used to assess monopoly supply influences on a given market is whether or not the supplier can charge prices 5% to 10% above competitive levels. The panel applied this test to Manchester United's products and doubted that BSkyB's proposed 'leisure activities' market was realistic, particularly since a 5% or 10% price rise would not cause Manchester United supporters to switch to other leisure activities. After careful consideration of the various potential football markets, it decided that the evidence of consumer performance suggested the Premier League might be the relevant football market for the purposes of considering the effects of the merger.

Broadcasting Markets   DGIV had earlier concluded that free-to-air TV was unlikely to provide sustained and effective competition to pay TV in relation to sports programming for the following reasons:

(a) free-to-air TV was capacity constrained so it was unable to provide adequate line viewing opportunities;

(b) the ability to charge subscription charges (and ultimately 'pay-as-you-view' charges) meant that many sports events could be purchased for more than could be reasonably afforded by free-to-air broadcasters.

BSkyB put forward various arguments to refute DGIV's conclusions, none of which managed to persuade the panel otherwise. In need of examination were the relative values paid for executive rights for live sporting events, particularly football. Clearly Premier League football was a primary product attracting high values, and this situation was likely to be exacerbated in 2000–01 when those collective rights, if permitted, were to be auctioned again.

The panel, however, did not find the DGIV's conclusions convincing and instead looked carefully at demand side considerations to assess substitutability. The conclusion reached was that there was a separate market for pay TV whilst recognising that the existence of free-to-air broadcasters would place some upper limit on the prices of pay TV broadcasters (para 2.39).

The panel then considered carefully whether a narrower market was appropriate. Again, substitutability was a key consideration. It agreed that sports programmes (particularly those offering exclusive live coverage of an event) could not readily be substituted for non-sports programmes. The availability of this particular product was largely confined to sports channels. Market evidence tended to suggest that because of demand side considerations there was a 'sports premium channel market' (para 2.44).

It also approached the question of new market entry and concluded that creating a new premium sports channel is a step that cannot be easily and rapidly taken. Given BSkyB's virtual monopoly of sports channels, the panel looked at the case for defining the market even more narrowly in terms of football, or some sub-set of football on pay TV (paras 2.45/2/46). There was evidence suggesting that football, and Premier League football in particular, played an important part in persuading consumers to purchase sports channels, and to an extent a recent NOP survey lent weight to this conclusion (para 2.46). The possibility that the development of the pay-per-view market could start to blur the distinction between different types of sports channels was accepted by the panel. However, it found that this market for football was, as yet, undeveloped and that, on balance, the relevant broadcasting market was the market for pay TV sports premium channels (para 2.51).

MARKET ACCESS TO PREMIUM SPORTS CHANNELS
The potential for new competitive sports premium channels was analysed by the panel, who concluded that there were unlikely to be enough rights

to sustain many sports premium channels. In addition, BSkyB's very high market share, together with entry difficulties, gave BSkyB market power in the sports premium channel market (para 1.5).

BENEFITS OF THE MERGER TO THE MAIN PARTIES

Before going on to examine public-interest issues, the panel took evidence from the main parties on the merger itself, in particular to ascertain the benefits to each of the parties.

At oral hearings, BSkyB had emphasised the importance of 'owning content' as a means of securing their future role as 'programme-makers'. The panel was shown the internal documents that had been prepared to support the offer for Manchester United. The BSkyB executive confirmed that:

- sport was an accepted part of BSkyB's brand-building strategies;
- football was the leading sport in European TV market;
- sport could be used to build the value of TV networks and/or distribution;
- Manchester United would provide a solid UK football product base;
- acquisition of Manchester United would buy a 'seat at the table';
- through Manchester United, BSkyB might be in a better position to deal with developments such as a European super league.

It became evident that BSkyB's case detailed only positive consequences which the merger would bring about, but these were ones which would, ultimately, extend their already dominant market influence. The panel did not feel that without the merger BSkyB would be commercially threatened in any way (para 2.75/76).

Manchester United, on the other hand, felt the merger would offer the club an opportunity to be part of a *new* group, one with greater financial means and additional resources. Thus, merging with a media business that could offer both of these would merely be a logical venture for Manchester United's business interests.

PUBLIC-INTEREST ISSUES

Public interest raised by the merger fell into two broad groups:

- competition amongst broadcasters; and
- possible effects on consumers and football generally.

COMPETITION FOR TV RIGHTS

The panel took care to examine whether the proposed merger would give BSkyB further significant advantages in the competition for rights. The problems that it encountered in the course of this examination concerned, first, the uncertainty over future selling arrangements for Premier League rights and, second, the extent to which the merger might precipitate other mergers between broadcasters and Premier League clubs. These uncertainties led the panel to scrutinise the merger using four main scenarios:

(1) Existing collective selling arrangements/single merger

Third-party submissions focused on the importance and influence of Manchester United within the Premier League – indeed, many parties felt that it would be objectionable if BSkyB, or any other broadcaster, bought any Premier League club, since it would give them a 'seat on both sides of the table' when rights sales were negotiated. It was seen as particularly detrimental for BSkyB, the incumbent broadcaster of Premier League football, to acquire the most influential club. Both BSkyB and Manchester United argued against this conclusion, claiming that Manchester United, with one vote in 20, was no more influential than the bottom club. Manchester United argued strongly that the way in which the collective rights were negotiated and sold made it impossible for Manchester United or any other club to exercise any influence. Finally, BSkyB said that it did not need to own Manchester United to ensure support for its bid for collective rights.

On balance, the panel was not convinced that these arguments held water. It believed that the 'seat at the table' arguments had value and that this might give an organisation the facility for inside influence by legitimate means (para 2.87). The ultimate threat of withdrawal from the Premier League by Manchester United seemed unlikely, but not inconceivable in certain circumstances. The difference if the club were to be owned by BSkyB would be that broadcast considerations, rather than football club considerations, might dominate.

The panel considered all the information advantages, toehold effects and BSkyB fall-back options (paras 2.99 to 2.135) with the parties, but in the light of third-party submissions it concluded that, despite arguments to the contrary from the parties, certain information advantages would be likely to accrue to the merged entity. In relation to toehold effects, the panel was inclined to agree that the effects which would arise as a result of the merger would not give BSkyB the major advantage over its competitors that some third parties claimed it would. However, it did think that some benefit would accrue from the overall rights-selling process, in the form of its financial stake in the revenues received by Premier League clubs.

BSkyB's assertions that it was not its intention, or desire, to end the Premier League's collective selling arrangements or to damage the League in any way was accepted. However, the panel felt that BSkyB's fall-back options, which included splintering the collective selling arrangements, whilst unattractive, could be used as a spoiling tactic, and other potential bidders could be expected to see such options as credible. Consequentially, the panel felt it likely that the bidding behaviour of BSkyB's competitors would be inhibited to some extent (para 2.135).

The panel also looked to the ownership of football clubs by broadcasters in other countries as a useful comparison, but found that their experiences did not really provide a helpful basis for reaching conclusions about what was likely to happen in the UK were the merger to proceed (para 2.139).

Whilst the matters analysed by the panel would not individually give BSkyB a decisive advantage over competing broadcasters, taken together they could be expected to improve significantly BSkyB's chances of securing the Premier League's rights. This advantage was felt to be a real one, indeed one which might be expected to improve BSkyB's chances of winning – whatever the response of its competitors (para 2.140).

It was because of the OFT's challenge to the collective selling of rights by the Premier League (which was referred to the Restrictive Practices Court prior to the BSkyB/Manchester United reference to the Commission) that the panel felt it necessary also to examine the remaining three of the original four scenarios which it thought might arise should the OFT win the case.

These were *(2) new selling arrangements/single merger, (3) existing selling arrangements/multiple mergers and (4) new selling arrangements/multiple mergers.*

Whilst accepting that conclusions were bound to be speculative, the panel nevertheless felt it appropriate to see what the effect of these developments might be on competition for Premier League rights.

The removal of collective selling rights from the Premier League would not prevent individual clubs from putting together agreed collective packages. BSkyB's ownership of Manchester United, however, was felt to give it a strong hand in any such negotiations. The panel felt that no other broadcaster could put together such a package (because no one else owned Manchester United's rights), so BSkyB would be able to outbid their competitors (para 2.150). The panel looked at the likelihood of exclusive rights being abandoned, and sales of rights being distributed widely amongst different broadcasters. It concluded that this was highly unlikely in the short to medium term because the economic value of exclusivity would be of significant financial advantage to most clubs.

The panel then looked at the likely consequences if BSkyB's bid for Manchester United precipitated a range of bids for other clubs by broadcasters. In reality, broadcasters that owned clubs might then seek to share the rights of Premier League clubs. Such an agreement to not compete with each other would have at least as damaging an impact on competition for these rights, and in any event might all be investigated under the Competition Act 1998 (para 2.165). In circumstances where only individual selling rights were permitted and the BSkyB/Manchester United merger had precipitated other mergers between broadcasters and Premier League clubs, the panel decided that this might be expected to reduce competition, compared with the possibility of no such mergers (para 2.170).

In conclusion, the panel found that in any of the four scenarios they looked at, a reduction of competition, less innovation and reduced choice would be the result.

EFFECTS ON FOOTBALL

A strong concern of the panel was to ensure that its inquiry adequately covered the many concerns expressed by third parties about the consequences of the merger on football. Although the concerns expressed often went further than the competition and consumer concerns that normally arose in a merger inquiry, the panel felt obliged to ensure that such concerns were examined, if relevant in terms of the public interest. It decided to look at three issues: effects on consumers; effects on competition between football clubs; and the effects on the organisation of football.

Consumers   The panel categorised consumers in two ways: those who were committed fans of a particular club, and those who regularly attended matches. Clearly, there was a considerable degree of overlap between the two groups. Third-party submissions claimed that the merger would have an adverse effect on ticket prices because local community pressures would no longer be effective once BSkyB owned Manchester United. The panel disagreed, believing that Manchester United already had sufficient commercial incentives to exploit local monopoly opportunities. It then examined the implications of the introduction of pay-per-view, but concluded that since no widespread application of pay-per-view was imminent it could not reasonably form an expectation of an adverse effect (para 2.192).

The panel went on to examine another widely expressed concern of Manchester United fans, namely that following the merger, starting times of matches would be fixed to suit broadcast considerations. The evidence was not, however, felt to substantiate these allegations and whilst there was little doubt that broadcast considerations now played a part in determining starting times, this was occasionally occurring already at the request of some clubs with specific security concerns. The panel felt that some trade-off was inevitable given the very large sums of money paid by broadcasters to football clubs for the rights, and that if clashes between fans' interests and broadcasters occurred, the football authorities were the right people to intervene.

Competition amongst football clubs Fans, and organisations represen-ting them, were deeply concerned about the effect of the merger on competition between football clubs. However, the panel found that there were two opposing views:

- Manchester United could be held back or artificially weakened;
- the merger would make Manchester United so strong that it might be virtually unbeatable.

At the heart of these concerns was the feeling that once a broadcaster owned a club, commercial broadcast considerations could require strategies to be adopted which distort the purity of competition.

The panel thought it unlikely that it was in BSkyB's interest to weaken the club, thereby reducing its attraction. However, it did believe that under certain circumstances, the strengthening of the club could cause adverse public-interest effects. In particular, the panel stated the concern of many parties that if the merger led to Manchester United becoming too strong, this would worsen an already marked trend towards greater inequality of wealth between football clubs (para 2.205). The panel had taken quite a lot of evidence on the distribution of the very considerable sums of TV money that had flowed into the industry over recent years. Even within the Premier League, there were wide disparities between the most successful and least successful clubs. But outside the Premier League, great worries had been exposed about the impact of increasing inequalities of wealth on the whole structure and quality of British football.

Somewhat surprisingly, the panel accepted that major structural changes to British football were matters within its terms of reference, but only in so far as they were affected by the merger. It concluded that the merger would tend to increase the inequality of wealth between clubs and that, as a consequence, the ability of many clubs to compete would be hampered and the demise of some smaller clubs could well follow (para 2.206).

The organisation of football It was put to the panel that the merger would strengthen the hand of BSkyB in its dealings with football authori-ties, and that the interests of broadcasters would lead to changes in the game and its presentation that might be against the public interest.

BSkyB continued to make a heartfelt plea which focused on how the importance of football to its viewing profile would mean that it would never do anything which might be regarded as detrimental to the game.

However, once again, the panel concluded that by increasing BSkyB's influence over the Premier League's decisions, the merger could lead to a situation whereby some decisions taken would not be in the long-term interests of football, giving rise to the adverse effect that the quality of British football would be damaged.

These public-interest findings on the adverse effect of the merger on certain aspects or football were somewhat controversial. In practice, whether or not the panel had so found, the merger would have been recommended for prohibition on broadcasting competition issues alone.

RECOMMENDATIONS

At the same time as the issues letter was publicly distributed, the panel had also sent a letter solely to the main parties, setting out hypothetical remedies. The panel had indicated some areas where undertakings might be explored, but the parties were unable to develop these and the panel 'went cold' on the potential effectiveness of any undertakings. This was for two primary reasons. Firstly, the only undertaking that might get close to alleviating the principal public-interest offences would be one that effectively removed Manchester United from the entire rights-selling process. This proposal was clearly flawed since it was both demonstrably unfair to Manchester United and it would not prevent other bidders from recognising the informal influence still available to the new group.

The second reason was a belief on the panel's part that developments in broadcast technology (such as digital television) and, consequently new product availability (such as pay-per-view), were so rapid that any undertakings might quickly be overrun and rendered obsolete.

During the later stages of the inquiry, both BSkyB and Manchester United did offer a number of concessionary assurances, but none that the panel felt could combat these two important realities.

In the end, the panel felt that 'the only remedy which would deal with the full range of the adverse effects it had identified would be prohibition of the merger'.

8. Sneaking in through the back door? Media company interests and dual ownership of clubs

ADAM BROWN

This chapter outlines the main developments in the media ownership of English football clubs in the aftermath of BSkyB's failed attempt to take over Manchester United, and highlights the dangers these pose for football. It focuses on two main concerns: firstly, media penetration of football clubs' ownership; and secondly, the dual ownership of clubs.

The chapter argues that key decisions made by the Monopolies and Mergers Commission (MMC) and the Restrictive Practices Court (RPC) are in jeopardy because of moves made by broadcasting companies in the wake of these decisions to own stakes in clubs. Briefly, the judgement of the MMC was designed to protect competition within the pay TV sports market, and the RPC decision was that it is in the public interest to maintain the collective negotiation of TV rights and its concomitant redistribution of monies. Furthermore, I argue, those developments since the MMC ruling and the RPC outcome have also raised concerns over the dual ownership of clubs. These problems are exacerbated because it is media companies that are involved, but dual ownership *per se* is something that has been outlawed by football authorities here and across Europe.

The chapter concludes that only quick and robust action by competition authorities and the football authorities will protect football and the pay TV market from undue influence and unfair competition by certain companies. The government has shown itself to be prepared to call in competition authorities to protect competition in the pay TV field and it now needs to secure the progress already made. The football authorities have an obligation to uphold their own rules regarding the dual ownership of clubs by outlawing the integration of media companies into the ownership of more than one club. At a time when there is unprecedented interest in the regulation and governance of football, these developments pose a serious challenge to existing regulatory structures and, crucially, will test the efficacy of those structures.

1. MEDIA OWNERSHIP

The two key decisions made in relation to the ownership of clubs and the negotiation of television rights this year were made by the Monopolies and

Mergers Commission in April 1999 and the Restrictive Practices Court in July 1999. It is worth remembering what they said.

The MMC was asked by the Office of Fair Trading to investigate the merger of BSkyB and Manchester United. Their report was unequivocal in its opposition to the merger, a report that was subsequently accepted in full by the Secretary of State for Trade and Industry, Stephen Byers, on 9 April 1999. The MMC's main areas of concern were fivefold. Firstly, that the merger would be anti-competitive in the pay TV market because it would give BSkyB an unfair advantage in the negotiation of Premier League and other TV rights. Secondly, the already dominant position of BSkyB and the market power of Manchester United would exacerbate such an advantage. Thirdly, any advantage that BSkyB might gain could not be overcome by the imposition of 'Chinese walls' (barriers to the flow of information such as between subsidiary and parent boards), non-exclusive deals or even exclusion from the rights negotiations. Fourthly, the merger would also damage the quality of British football by increasing the 'wealth gap' between richer and poorer clubs through a greater retention of TV revenue by the most popular clubs. And finally that the merger would give BSkyB additional influence over Premier League decisions which would be against the long-term interests of the game.[1]

Following complaints from cable TV operators, the Office of Fair Trading took the Premier League, BBC and BSkyB to the Restrictive Practices Court. This was on the grounds that the sale of live Premier League TV rights to BSkyB and the BBC was both collective and exclusive. The OFT believed that the Premier League was acting as a cartel in its sale of rights and as such was being anti-competitive; and that the 'exclusive' nature of the deal was restrictive in that it prevented other TV companies screening games which BSkyB chose not to.

After a nine-month court case, the judge, Mr Justice Ferris, ruled in favour of the Premier League. In this second landmark case, he again raised the 'public interest' concerns he had with the way football is financed through television. In particular he supported the notion that the collective sale of rights allowed for the redistribution of income in the game:

> Indeed we see no need to differ from the view of the Football Task Force that, from the public point of view, it is desirable that resources generated by professional football should be invested to a greater extent than at present in the lower levels of the game. The removal of restrictions now under consideration would therefore deny to the public a benefit or advantage.

However, despite these unequivocal rulings, a number of matters remain unclear in relation to both cases. In his statement to the stock exchange on 9 April 1999, Stephen Byers acknowledged the MMC's concern 'about the scope for the competition authorities to examine mergers involving football clubs'. Primarily, most clubs fall below the £70 million threshold to be considered 'qualifying mergers', and existing regulations seem unclear about the partial purchase of clubs by media companies. Mr Byers announced that he would seek views on whether changes were needed in the guidelines so that other club mergers could be examined, with particular reference to public-interest concerns. No such changes were announced by the DTI during the time the developments outlined below happened.

In fact, no takeovers occurred in the wake of the MMC decision on BSkyB/Manchester United. Indeed, financial analysts believe that:

> predictions that broadcasting companies would rush to snap up clubs to gain ownership of valuable media content have proved unfounded, not least because of regulatory hostility to such potentially anti-competitive deals. A few media groups have bought small stakes in some clubs but, beyond these, takeover interest has all but died.[2]

Of primary concern, therefore, is the question of whether the spate of media companies buying minority stakes in clubs in the wake of the MMC and RPC decisions do, in fact, raise many of the same problems which the MMC highlighted. The adequacy of the regulatory functions of both football and competition authorities to protect the long-term interests of the game is now being tested.

In the months after the MMC and RPC decisions a number of developments occurred in relation to the media ownership of football clubs. NTL, who hold a 6% stake in Newcastle United, withdrew their takeover offer in the light of the MMC's ruling in April 1999. However, they maintain their stake in the club. NTL are quite open about why they continue to hold their stake in Newcastle United. In an e-mail letter dated 27 October 1999, Bruce Randall, NTL's public relations manager, outlined the reasons for their continued investment thus:

> NTL is interested in gaining a seat at the negotiating table when it comes to television rights . . . We believe that entering into a partnership with Newcastle United is an excellent opportunity for us to enter the UK sports pay TV market . . . Clearly, media

companies like ours taking stakes in football clubs puts them in a better position to be involved in screening top-level football in the UK.

The motives are crystal clear here: NTL see their investment in Newcastle as strategic in that it buys them something more than a return on their stock – it buys them a seat at the negotiating table for TV rights. This should set alarm bells ringing with those authorities that blocked BSkyB's takeover of Manchester United on these grounds.

Granada Television bought a 10% stake in Liverpool – still a limited company – on 13 July 1999 for £22 million. 'The deal,' said *The Guardian*, 'effectively earns the television company a seat in football rights negotiations,' and a 'senior Granada executive' would be appointed to the board. The role in relation to TV rights negotiations, said chief executive Rick Parry, would be to 'advise, guide and represent us'.[3] Again, it is clear that this investment is not straightforward in that it has additional benefits and roles for Granada, primary of which is increasing their chances of accessing live football.

Having lost their bid to take over Manchester United, BSkyB maintained their 11.1% stake in the club. Due to the sale of shares by chief executive Martin Edwards in October, BSkyB are now by far the club's biggest shareholder and they also maintain their one-third ownership of MUTV.

In August 1999 BSkyB announced that it was to take a stake in Leeds Sporting, the listed parent company of Leeds United. Following the approval of shareholders, 9.2% of Leeds was sold to BSkyB for £13.8 million on 11 October 1999. Central to the deal was the agreement that BSkyB would act as 'media advisors' for Leeds United and that they would take a huge 30% commission on any increase in revenue from television contracts over the next five years. Again the nature of the deal leaves no doubt as to BSkyB's expectations to be centrally involved in the negotiations for TV rights.

In November 1999, BSkyB secured a similar deal with First Division leaders Manchester City who, like Liverpool, are not a listed company. Here BSkyB bought 9.9% for £7.5 million and they have a deal very similar to the Leeds one to act as media agents for the club, with similar remuneration. BSkyB's role is not to invest in Manchester City merely for the possible long-term return that might give, but to place the company in a strategic position with regard to the negotiation of TV rights.

It is likely that further penetration of football club ownership by these and other media companies will occur – it is reported privately that a number of deals are already in progress. The current collective Premier

League TV deal is due for renegotiation in 2001, with speculation already mounting about possible bids. Questions still remain over the nature of these negotiations – although the Premier League remains committed to collective negotiation; whether this happens and whether it allows non-exclusive deals to be made is uncertain. Thus, the developments outlined above suggest that media companies are positioning themselves to influence those negotiations. This threatens the free and open competition in the pay TV market as well as football's ability to determine its own future and structures of finance. Furthermore, it is clear that BSkyB's roles at Manchester City and Leeds United will be to negotiate media deals on behalf of each club. This places BSkyB at a clear and blatant advantage to other broadcasters in relation to the sale of those clubs' TV rights. As the dominant shareholders in Manchester United and as partners in MUTV, BSkyB have a similarly powerful position in relation to that club's negotiations, which, as the MMC have already highlighted, have an unusually powerful position in the market of pay TV Premier League football. Granada's position as media agents at Liverpool and NTL's openly stated reasons for investing in Newcastle United illustrate clearly that their aim is to secure access to screening live football of their respective clubs.

These factors mean that the ownership changes outlined pose a significant and serious threat to football and to competition within the UK pay TV market for a number of reasons. There are a number of scenarios. Were Manchester City to get promoted, BSkyB could have tie-ins with three clubs in the Premier League. This will significantly increase their ability to win future rights for Premier League matches, when, as the MMC concluded, they already enjoy great market power and any extension of this would be damaging to competition. It is perfectly possible that through purchasing stakes in yet more clubs, BSkyB could effectively 'buy' enough votes at the Premier League to block any other broadcaster getting the collective Premier League contract. Ironically, this would be achieved for considerably less than their attempted takeover of Manchester United. Even if no more stakes in clubs are taken, the broadcaster will have, through its stakes in Manchester United and Leeds, access to privileged information in relation to the sale of Premier League broadcasting rights. The same applies to NTL and Granada. As the MMC concluded, 'no undertakings . . . could ever prevent the informal flows of information, nor would they prevent [the clubs] influencing the rights negotiations in advance of the formal negoti-ations'. The broadcast company could therefore gain competitive advantage over their rivals, whether 'their' clubs were part of the negotiations or not. That BSkyB and Granada have agreements to act as their clubs' media agents, merely exacerbates this concern.

However, such agreements also raise a conflict of interest in that, in BSkyB's case, the leading broadcaster of live football will effectively be negotiating with itself, and, extraordinarily, be paying itself commission. In this there will be a clear conflict of interest for the broadcaster: their chief concern will be to get TV rights for as little as possible while their role as clubs' agents will be to get as much as possible for these rights (for which they will then be paying *themselves* commission). In such a scenario, the clubs (fans, players, managers and shareholders) will be put at a disadvantage. Whether rights are sold collectively or individually, the adverse effect on competition of having leading broadcasters acting on behalf of clubs will be detrimental to the clubs. There is also the danger that there may soon be enough broadcast companies with stakes in football clubs who see their best interests served through the individual sale of TV rights to use their voting power at the Premier League to prevent a collective deal, against the long-term interests of the game and its customers as highlighted by the RPC judgement.

There is a secondary concern, to do with the ownership of stakes by media companies in more than one club. If Manchester City win promotion, BSkyB would own stakes in three clubs in the Premier League in the 2000–2001 season; they will certainly hold stakes in three clubs competing in the FA Cup and League Cup. Such a situation appears to be against the rules of the football authorities (see Section 2, below) and as such should be dealt with by their regulatory structures, as would be the case whatever kind of company it involved.

However, dual ownership of clubs by media companies (as opposed to other companies) raises additional concerns about competition within the football market, which should be of interest to the competition authorities. Problems of dual ownership are exacerbated when it comes to media companies because of television's strategic importance in terms of football's finance and the horizontal and vertical integration of the two. If one media company has an undue interest in more than one club a number of problems may occur, including favouritism for clubs they own in terms of numbers of matches screened, arrangement of fixtures, reporting of games and disciplinary factors. There may also be restrictions on access to players and other staff for other media companies and platforms. There could be a gradual erosion of the collective and redistributive function of the Premier League, exacerbating the 'wealth gap' problems of which the MMC made special mention in their report. Media companies would have guaranteed access to matches at clubs in which they have an interest, which are not covered by existing, or future, collective agreements (e.g. Champions League and UEFA Cup). The more clubs, the bigger the section of the market they could secure through ownership, rather than through fair competition in the sale of rights. Suspicion may also arise over the validity of results involving clubs owned in part by the same media company.

Media Ownership – Summary   The MMC ruled that BSkyB's purchase of Manchester United would give BSkyB an unfair advantage over their competitors in terms of access to Premier League TV rights, which would be detrimental to competition in the pay TV market as a whole and which would adversely affect the health of British football. BSkyB's 'Plan B', therefore, has been to gain strategic roles within clubs without leaving themselves open to the scrutiny of the competition authorities: coming in quietly through the back door, rather than the front.

The role of other media companies pursuing similar strategies does not lessen the effect of this. It increases the threat to the collective negotiation of Premier League TV rights. This collective and redistributive function was upheld *in the public interest* after a lengthy court case but now needs further safeguarding.

It is clear that the strategic nature of the stock purchases at both floated and private companies raises many of the same concerns as the BSkyB/Manchester United merger. They are *deliberately and explicitly* designed to increase the ability of those companies to secure TV rights. The warnings in the MMC's report, it appears, still need to be heeded. Nicholas Finney, a retired member of the MMC panel which ruled against the BSkyB takeover of Manchester United, and who also writes in this book, has said that further action is needed by the authorities in order to adequately confront the threat to competition which these purchases represent.

Furthermore, following the RPC decision, it was widely recognised by commentators that the judge's support for collective and exclusive selling of Premier League TV rights was by no means a guarantee that the new TV deal, in 2001, would be based on these lines. It was recognised that pressure from television companies and the desire of a minority of top clubs to increase their share of the money from TV deals could lead to a breakdown of the collective arrangements. This threat to the public interest exists anyway, but it is increased hugely with the trend in the part-ownership of clubs that we have highlighted here.

In almost every scenario, the public interest, competition within the pay TV market and the good of football – which Justice Ferris, the MMC and the Trade Secretary all upheld earlier this year – will be jeopardised. The Office of Fair Trading and the Department of Trade and Industry should act quickly to prevent any further part-purchases of football clubs by media companies. Media companies who currently have stakes in football clubs should be forced to divest themselves of those shares.

2. DUAL OWNERSHIP

Dual ownership by media companies is an issue dominated by BSkyB in English football. BSkyB now own 9.9% of Manchester United plc, who wholly own Manchester United Football Club. They are by far the company's largest shareholders. BSkyB also own 9.2% of Leeds Sporting, who wholly own Leeds United. BSkyB also own 9.9% of Manchester City. Furthermore, they have agreements with both Manchester City and Leeds United to act as 'media agents', with seats on each board, in which they will have a role in TV rights negotiations and benefit from any increase in TV revenue. Clearly, BSkyB enjoy a powerful position in making key decisions in three clubs.

All three football authorities in this country – the Premier League, the FA, and the Football League – have clear rules to prevent clubs being owned by the same person or company. Traditionally, the basis for these rules is to maintain fair competition in football and avoid suspicions of clubs coming to agreements with each other over results, finance and transfers. Within the context of the developments outlined above, a new and additional threat is that dual ownership by media companies will be used to help them gain access and preferential deals for TV rights. The current competition rules of the football authorities are outlined below.

The competition rules of the FA Cup, run by the Football Association, the English game's governing body, are explicit. Rule 30 states:

'a) Save with the prior written permission of the Council no club may compete in the competition at any stage where that club is interested in another club which is participating in the competition or wishing to participate in the competition ('the Second Club'). The Second Club shall similarly not be permitted to participate in the competition at any stage.

b) Save with the prior written permission of the Council no club may compete in the competition at any stage where a person or any associate of that person is interested in such club and a Second Club . . .'

The FA define a club, person, or associate as one who:

i) holds or deals in . . . the securities or shares of that club; or

ii) is a member of that club; or

iii) is involved in any capacity whatsoever in the management or administration of that club; or

iv) has any power whatsoever to influence the financial, commercial or business affairs or the administration of that club . . .

The FA can disregard the holding of less than 10% of the share capital, but *only* if 'those shares are, in the opinion of the Council, held purely for investment purposes only'. The additional factors in BSkyB's ownership of Manchester City and Leeds – their seat on the board and agreement to act as media agents – seem to override this condition.

The FA Premier League have similarly comprehensive rules regulating the involvement of persons or companies in more than one club:

Except with the prior written consent of the board, no club may either directly or indirectly:

2.1 hold or deal in the securities or shares of another club;

2.2 be a member of another club;

2.3 be involved in any capacity whatsoever in the management or administration of another club;

2.4 have any power whatsoever to influence the management or administration of another club.

Further, Rule 3 of the Premier League rule book states that:

'no person, by himself or with one or more associates, may at one time, either directly or indirectly be involved in any capacity whatsoever in the management or administration of more than one club.'

Rule 4 makes a similar distinction to the FA rules with regard to a 10% shareholding by saying that:

'no person, by himself or with one or more associates, may directly or indirectly hold or acquire any interest in more than 10% of the issued share capital of a club while he or any associate is a director of, or directly or indirectly holds any interest in the share capital of any other club.'

The Premier League also follow a similar definition of 'associate' to the FA and their conditions outlined in 2.1–2.4 suggest, again, that the intention of the 10% rule would be effectively bypassed in relation to BSkyB's investment in Manchester City and Leeds.

The Football League have almost identical rules to the FA, but state that they are in place to prevent associations and dual interests which might 'undermine the integrity of league competitions and the reputation, credibility and image of professional football clubs'. The League can force any club in breach of these regulations to 'take such action as is necessary to rectify the breach' with the ultimate sanction of expulsion from the League.

The European governing body, UEFA, have similarly strict guidelines on associations between clubs. Their rules were invoked in relation to media company ENIC's majority stake in Slavia Prague, part-ownership of Rangers and full ownership of Vicenza and AEK Athens. Although UEFA's ruling that two teams in which ENIC had interests could not compete in the same UEFA competition was challenged within the European Commission by ENIC, UEFA's rules were found to be legal under European law.

It should be restated that for all football authorities, regulations on dual ownership are quite explicit in a number of areas. Firstly, that a shareholding of 10% or less is not considered to be an interest. Secondly, a shareholding of 10% or more precludes a company having any interest in another club. Thirdly, any shareholding which is not solely for investment purposes – whether under 10% or not – shall be considered an interest; and finally, that any power or agreement to influence the business decisions of one club shall preclude that person's (or company's) interest in any other club.

BSkyB's holding in Manchester United, their recent acquisitions at Leeds and Manchester City, and their strategic roles at the latter two clubs, are a *prima facie* transgression of competition rules in English football.[4] It should be remembered that all three clubs compete in the Worthington League Cup; that all three compete in the FA Cup (except for the 1999–2000 season); and that Manchester United and Leeds compete in the Premier League. Manchester City will also compete in the Premier League in the 2000–2001 season should they gain promotion. There are a number of areas where rules on dual ownership appear to have been broken: BSkyB's holding of 11.1% of Manchester United should have precluded them from owning *any* shares in *any* other football club with whom Manchester United might be competing. This was acknowledged by the Premier League, who obliged BSkyB to reduce their holding to below 10% at the end of November 1999. Even with their current holding of 9.9%, however, they are still by far the largest shareholder in Manchester United and as such they could certainly be deemed to have 'any power whatsoever to influence the financial, commercial or business affairs or the administration of that club'.[5] In any case, BSkyB must have the *'prior* written permission' of the football authorities (the board of the Premier League, the FA Council or the board of the Football League) for holding stakes in more than one club. This had not been given.

BSkyB's agreements with Leeds to act as their media agents and to sit on their board should preclude them from holding any interest in any other club as this constitutes 'any power whatsoever to influence the financial, commercial or business affairs or the administration of that club'. Likewise, BSkyB's agreement with Manchester City should preclude any other interest or agreement with any other club. Even if all these agreements were terminated, it is clear that BSkyB's holdings in these clubs are not 'held purely for investment purposes' but to be able to influence the sale of television rights. They are 'buying a seat at the negotiating table' in NTL's words.

Recommendations   BSkyB's ownership stake in Manchester United and its recent purchase of stakes in Manchester City and Leeds, as well as its agreements with those clubs, represent a multiple transgression of the football authorities' rules. These rules were designed to protect the integrity of football. It is absolutely essential to the credibility of the football authorities' regulatory functions that they uphold their own rules regarding the dual ownership of clubs. It is particularly important in this case, as indicated above, because of the nature of the company concerned – already the dominant market force in sports pay TV and seeking to further enhance this position. The importance of TV revenues to football make this a matter of central concern for the whole game.

The following action by the FA is therefore appropriate with regard to the FA Cup: if BSkyB wish to maintain their shares in Manchester United, they should divest of their interests in Leeds and Manchester City. Alternatively, BSkyB should divest of its shares in Manchester United and one of the other two clubs. BSkyB's additional agreements with Manchester City and Leeds should, if they are not ruled anti-competitive by the competition authorities, be nullified. Under existing rules BSkyB could maintain their agreement with one of these clubs, provided that they divest of their interests in all other clubs. *To ensure that these measures are implemented, the FA should make it clear that the only alternative is expulsion of the clubs concerned from the FA Cup.*

The Football League should also apply the same action to the Worthington League Cup. *To ensure that these measures are implemented, the Football League should make it clear that the only alternative is expulsion from the Worthington League Cup.* Similarly, the FA Premier League should take the following steps with regard to the Premier League: BSkyB should end their ownership either of 9.2% of Leeds or of 9.9% of Manchester United. If BSkyB were to maintain their ownership of 9.9% of Manchester United, they should end their agreement with Leeds United to act as 'media agents'. Should Manchester City gain promotion to the Premier League, BSkyB should be made either to divest of their holdings in Manchester City and terminate their agreement with that club or divest of their interests in other Premier League clubs. The Premier League should prevent BSkyB buying further stakes in any other Premier League club and prevent the company from making similar agreements with other Premier League clubs. *To ensure that these measures are implemented, the Premier League should make it clear that the only alternative is expulsion from the League.*

Dual Ownership – Summary   The football authorities in the UK and Europe have robust rules to prevent the dual ownership of clubs and to prevent associations between clubs. It seems clear that Manchester United,

Leeds and Manchester City are in contravention of these rules relating to three English competitions – the FA Cup, the Premier League and the League Cup. Should both Leeds and Manchester United qualify for the Champions League in the 2000–2001 season, they may also be in contravention of UEFA rules. The fact that these dual associations involve the biggest broadcaster of sport in the UK, BSkyB, and that BSkyB has board membership and additional agreements with Manchester City and Leeds to act as their 'media agents', makes the case compelling. It raises additional concerns about the integration of media companies into the ownership of football to those outlined in the first part of this chapter, and places a question mark over the future finance, organisation and governance of football.

ENIC – A Test Case   The football authorities should be confident of their position in relation to these matters of dual ownership. The right of membership associations in football to enforce their rules on dual ownership was upheld in the ENIC test case at the European Commission. This followed a complaint by ENIC when UEFA challenged their ownership of a number of clubs in different countries which were competing in UEFA competitions. In a third landmark ruling relating to media companies in 1999, UEFA were allowed to enforce their own rules preventing dual ownership of clubs. Their example now needs to be followed in England.

CONCLUSION

There has been considerable debate and discussion in the UK in relation to the governance of professional football. The government's Football Task Force was established to make proposals for the better governance of the game and in the course of this has deliberated about what form of regulatory mechanisms are needed in English football. The developments which this chapter outlines, and the contravention of FA, Premier League and Football League rules which they appear to represent, are a test for the authorities and their regulatory function. Quick, unequivocal and firm action is needed to safeguard both the integrity of professional football in England and its long-term financial health. Although other matters concerning media companies owning strategic stakes in football clubs ought to be dealt with by the competition authorities, the concerns of dual ownership and common associations are in themselves matters for regulation by the football authorities.

A failure to police adequately its own rules in this case will not only damage the health of English football but also strengthen the calls for an independent regulatory structure for football.

PART III

THE NEW COMMERCIALISM AND PLCS

9. The changing face of football: a case for national regulation?

JOHN WILLIAMS

THAT WAS THEN . . .

The onset of the close season. When I was growing up in the 1960s on Merseyside, for the seasonal footballing last rites we used to end up, late at night, on BBC TV (always the Beeb) with flush-faced young men in the FA Cup-winners' post-banquet booze-up courtesy of, if I'm not mistaken, Jimmy Hill. During the day, and as the years wore on, we had come to 'know' uncomfortably more and more about these football players in the Wembley pre-match build-up: who roomed with whom; the pranksters and the introverts; the breakfast and luncheon rituals; superstitions – usually, shorts on first, and who was the last one out, etc. Most of this TV fare was excruciating, embarrassing even. We got more out of the managers, too, some of them perceptibly freezing in the media headlights as the years wore on. In 1974, Liverpool's Bill Shankly and the visibly shaking Newcastle United manager, Joe Harvey, were interviewed on a split screen on the morning of the tie between the keen northern rivals. At the end of the exchange and thinking himself off camera (perhaps!) Shanks made the telling aside that Cup-final rookie Harvey was, clearly, 'a bag o' nerves'. On the field, Liverpool crushed the jittery Geordies. The power of the media?

On national TV, after the annual big match and the feast which followed, these impossibly young football heroes were usually now quite spent, nerves and trauma far behind them – and they were also gently, but transgressively, pissed. Strangely, on these occasions drink and glory seemed to make otherwise monosyllabic young men, with brains in their feet, more, rather than less, articulate. Certainly more interesting. Nothing, it should be noted, seemed to have this effect on Jimmy Hill. All this was, above all, the signal for footy obsessives, that it had all ended, the beautiful game, for another year.

The FA Cup final was still pretty much the only live football anybody saw on TV in the 1960s; certainly the only club football of this type. So, there were important things to look out for here – the players' once-a-year presentational tracksuit tops, for example, stylish but hated by some of the older pros as unnecessary and 'too continental'. In the early 1970s Leeds

United, breathtakingly, even had the players' names on their Wembley tops. There was also the special edition FA Cup final shirts to admire, complete, for the only time in the season, with embroidered club badge, and even with the match date. Usually, certainly until substitutes were allowed in the early 1970s, only ten of these shirts were made, plus the goalie's green (always green) top. They were produced then just for the combatants, not for fans, as the hundreds of thousands of replica shirts sold today are. Not to wear the 'traditional' club home colours at the final – to have to change on the coin toss to accommodate opponents – was regarded as rank bad luck.

Then there was the famous Wembley turf itself, proudly unblemished, and depthlessly green compared to the mud heaps or the dust bowls of the semi-finals only weeks before. But the turf was also notoriously cruel, lying in wait to cramp up those for whom the nervous tension proved simply too much. And, of course, there was the inevitable sunshine, the north London summer heat, which was surely made for foreigners, for the languid but explosive Brazilians, rather than the doughty, honest, British journeymen of the English game, now fully exposed in this last crucial act of an over-long season.

Very occasionally, even back then, FA Cup finals brought no clear way of connecting strongly to the match itself other than to the event as a national rite of passage which marked the gathering of the sporting clans and another season almost gone. Usually, the quality or glamour of at least one of the sides involved (the Tottenham side of '61 and '62; the emerging Man United of '63), or the underdog status of others (Second Division Preston North End in '64; Leicester City in '69) or the sheer drama of the match (Everton against Sheffield Wednesday in '66) was enough to get you gripped.

Howard Kendall, the youngest Cup finalist at 17 years of age, played for 'brave' Preston, who lost to West Ham in 1964, probably only partly because the hicksville hooped socks the Lancastrians wore for the day could never have been allowed to lift the Cup. David Nish, still the youngest FA Cup final captain, led Leicester City, a boyish Peter Shilton in goal, to a fourth Cup final appearance – and a fourth defeat for the East Midlands club – against Man City in 1969. These were proper Wembley stories.

For northerners, at least, the 1967 final was much harder work. A new (but not improved) Tottenham overcame flashy Chelsea; no one in our Bootle street got overexcited about this one. Down in 'the smoke' they probably said the same thing (in spades) about the 1968 bore when West Brom wore down an inspirationless Everton. Howard Kendall, four years older than in his Preston days but apparently no wiser, picked up more losers' tat here. Half of Liverpool – my half – both enjoyed this torture and 'felt' for family members and friends who had, inexplicably, taken up the blue sash. Not too deep down we probably felt they also got what they deserved.

On Merseyside, as elsewhere in those days, local finalists brought a new intensity to Cup final day. Special souvenir editions of the local newspapers emerged. The Road to Wembley, plus pullout team photos for display in the front window. People 'dressed' their houses then to advertise Cup final footballing allegiance, though my mother would never allow my brother's Evertonian blue to go up in case neighbours or passersby mistook us for Catholics. Some people in Liverpool still do this now, put up their football pictures, though the gusto and some of the collective spirit has inevitably gone out of Cup final fever. In triumphs in 1965 (Liverpool, for the first time) and in '66 (Everton, the 'bluenoses') the city of Liverpool boasted back-to-back FA Cup winners. We had no real sense then, I think, that people from outside the city – unless they were actually from Merseyside, doing missionary work elsewhere – might also be closely following our cause.

In those days, each side in the FA Cup final received around 12,000 tickets each, 24,000 in total, for a ground which then held the magical 100,000 fans. As far as I can remember, we never knew anyone who actually got a ticket for the match – for the FA Cup final. These people, it seems, were privileged season-ticket-holders, or liggers, or club secretaries or local football officials living down in the home counties and elsewhere who fancied a big football day-out in Brent. We knew none of these. Going to home games was affordable, but for the Cup final we drew the curtains and watched the drama unfold on telly. This, to my young eyes, was England; the FA Cup final and all that went with it defined what it meant in sporting terms to be English.

In the 1960s, after all the FA Cup hype and the TV drama was over, there was – well, nothing. Unless, of course, as in 1966, the World Cup finals came to town. Or, your club had actually won the Cup, in which case it was a few days more, hanging onto lampposts, and draping bunting on the town hall for the obligatory double-decker parade with the trophy in the city centre. Even following a Cup final triumph, and Shankly's mad and inspired speeches about how we, the fans of the 'Pool, were stronger and more passionate even than Mao's Red Army (which division were they in?), fans, players and football staff, well, they soon just melted away, they disappeared into pubs and local neighbourhoods. Goodbye to all that: then it was cricket, Ken Barrington, Cowdrey and John Edrich, at least until late August. (One or two footballers even played professional cricket in those days.)

Few top footballers left in the close season unless, of course, the club wanted rid of them. No one could leave. Few new players, if any, arrived. Managers were generally secure and resolutely in charge. Largely anonymous chairmen wrote gnomic match-programme notes and made sure the pies were hot. We expected the same guys to return, reassuringly, to do battle again in the following campaign. This was football.

. . . AND THIS IS NOW

Recalling all this 1960s material is not simply an exercise in pleasurable nostalgia – though I have enjoyed it, and it is nostalgia. And there is, clearly, a burgeoning market for this sort of fans' exploration of the game's allegedly 'warmer' past.[1] My recalling the 1960s is more a marker for talking about what is different about 1990s football – and about England, itself – and to warn against the kind of 'back to the future' theorising which idealises and reifies the past (when, exactly, was the game more 'democratic' and transparent?) and which often accompanies 'serious' debate about what is wrong with the game today and how we should try to solve its various 'problems'.

I have also, purposely, used the 1960s here because those who enjoy remembering the so-called 'pre-commercial' variant of the sport, and who seem to yearn for its return, tend conveniently to bypass aspects of the game's real difficulties of the 1970s and 1980s and retreat to an earlier, happier, period. Or else, as Ian Taylor has pointed out, they tend to idealise terrace culture of that time, draining it of its often racist and violent excess.[2] The message here seems to be about a preferred return to the more innocent pre-teens of the sport rather than to its troubled adolescence. Here, though, some of the real problems begin. Little of this kind of thinking has any useful purchase, I would argue, on producing realistic policies for football in the 1990s.

So, what is different about football today? Too many things to cover in a short chapter. Let us mention just a few here. For one thing, increasingly, the sun seldom sets on the sport in the national consciousness these days. Rather than disappear, and give way, reasonably, to other seasonal sporting interests after the Cup final, top football players now seem to move into even sharper media focus at the season's end. TV coverage of post-season competitions (new tournaments, exhibition games, friendlies) and media excitement about, and appetite for, football and 'news' about football proliferates – especially as the fortunes of satellite operators, such as BSkyB, have become increasingly indistinguishable from the success of its football coverage, and as other marginalised TV outlets scramble for any available 'live' football opportunities. FIFA and UEFA summer events have multiplied. Football has become a 12-month sport, both in terms of extended playing periods, and in terms of its non-stop media promotion.

This 12-month football cycle is partly due, too, however, to the new commercial imperatives and the increasingly 'global' reach of top English clubs (Manchester United play matches for sponsors in Australia, China and Hong Kong; they open up new merchandise outlets in South-East Asia, etc). But it is also connected to the inexorable movement of top players into the sort of media-orchestrated realms of the culture of celebrity, unmatched even by George Best in the 1960s: the summer 'royal' wedding of Victoria Adams and David Beckham; Michael Owen's Boyzone-like international fanclubs; Ian Wright's dreadful TV shows, etc. Football 'personalities' exert an extraordinary sporting and cultural hegemony these days, colouring front and back pages, and offering hours of speculation and ad-hoc coverage on TV and radio, both in and out of season.

And this all-year-round cycle is connected, too, to struggles over the effective commercial control and the intellectual property rights of the sport and its players – the so-called new global 'economies of signs and space'.[3] Today, these intense struggles, over the ownership of sporting images and brands, involve agents, clubs, national associations, international confederations, transnational corporations, sponsors and, increasingly, international media moguls. Players and their advisors are also increasingly aware of the growing value of their own commodification. The latest expression of this has come in the so-called 'player power' transfer cases in England in 1999, involving Nicolas Anelka, Jimmy Hasselbaink and even, briefly, 18-year-old Francis Jeffers of Everton, as clubs attune to the full impact of the Bosman ruling and to a world in which players and their advisors are much more self-reflexive about shaping their careers, about the expanding global marketplace for footballers, and about their alarmingly escalating earning potential. In this sort of 'winner-takes-all'[4] jungle of the international free market for scarce sporting talent, clubs are culpable too, paying, as they do, wildly inflated contracts, and also busily destabilising contracted players elsewhere while wailing as their own local stars try to rubbish their contractual commitments. Top players now come and go pretty much as they like.

This model has all the markings of the 'hyperreal', a world in which many quite moderate players grow rich as the dubious 'democratisation' offered by wall-to-wall radio and TV supporter phone-ins, and the desperate media appetite for 'football copy', accelerates managers and coaches into job-threatening 'crises' following even a couple of early defeats. Media talk of possible titles and trophies follows, correspondingly, at the first small signs of any real cohesion and success.[5] Far from expecting the same players to return next season for the sake of continuity and team building, new (increasingly from abroad) signings must be procured by top clubs in the close season, it is argued, in order to boost season-ticket sales and to stimulate jaded fan palates and to puff up expectations. Match-ticket prices, accordingly, escalate. For all the talk about fans' reflexive awareness of the real nature of this media circus or of their anxieties about the 'business' of football, nothing succeeds, it seems, in quelling spectator discontent quite like a multi-million-pound spending spree. If club chairmen were largely anonymous patricians in the 1960s, they and their colleagues have an increasingly high profile and are measured by fans by the depth of their pockets in the much more cut-throat, media-hyped and ambitious 1990s.

As well as these important developments, certainly, the central role of the FA Cup final and of the BBC itself in uniting and defining the national audience for sport – and, indeed, the nation – has diminished markedly since the 1960s.[6] In the new competitive markets for TV sports coverage, the BBC can apparently no longer even afford to purchase live coverage of the FA Cup final, which has now gone to ITV and to satellite TV, the latter being the new power brokers of top sport. There are few fans now who, truth be told, would probably actually prefer BBC football coverage to that offered by Sky Sports today, which, notwithstanding the 'flattening' hype about all its televised sporting contests,[7] has both the necessary cash and the almost endless air-time to lavish on its prize possessions. Ironically, Sky also offers young male fans, at least, the prospects of collective and participatory pub TV coverage, the 'new terraces', in an age of what are for them 'sanitised' and allegedly atmosphere-free all-seater grounds.[8] The age of interactive sports coverage on digital systems, which now allows viewers to control and switch camera angles on live events and to 'shop' for additional information about clubs and players, will further individualise the experience of the TV watching of sport as well as add to claims about the 'empowering' and 'skilling' of the armchair viewer in important ways even relative to the 'live' attender.

The future of the BBC and of its public-service remit are also under deep scrutiny today as TV and radio channels, lifestyles and choices proliferate in response to pick-and-mix post-national entertainment and sporting cultural preferences. Recent polls suggest there is little support, especially among the young, for a non-commercial public-service channel in the traditional sense.[9] This public opposition to the role of the BBC threatens the extent to which the existence of national public broadcasting contributed to a sense of a society 'under control': of national public institutions being accountable to a larger public and being influenced by it.[10] Top football clubs also depend, increasingly, of course, on their own TV markets for finance as the age of independent TV deals and the 'electronic turnstile', or pay-per-view match coverage, looms into view. New partnerships and new ways of exploiting the football/television relationship seem likely to emerge directly at clubs as the larger 'European' clubs seek competitive advantage and as 'domestic' clubs simply try to hold on.

Also, far from being unique these days as it was in the 1960s, live coverage of the FA Cup final now takes place alongside literally hundreds of 'live' football matches covered each season by terrestrial, cable, satellite and now digital TV outlets. Live football on TV is now available – for those who can pay – pretty much round-the-clock and from all parts of the world. This part-inversion of the mantra from the 1960s – that the world was watching our Cup final, and who cares how they play the game – also reflects how Britain has slowly been opened up to the new sporting global flows and to foreign influences on how the sport should be staged and played. In the 1960s, the exotic exceptionality of foreign players in the FA Cup final – South Africa's Albert Johanneson, for Leeds United in 1965, for example – was enough to trigger media profiles and 'special' (often racist) news features. These days, following a dramatic influx of foreign talent to these shores, it is not too fanciful to say that English players in FA Cup final teams can excite media activity for some of the same reasons. Some committed football viewers in England, newly versed in the nuances of foreign leagues and in the international trade in top players, can also now get almost as excited by live TV coverage of, say, Barcelona v. Real Madrid as they do by any big club clash in England. Some also travel abroad to watch these international club confrontations, as global football tourists.

Finally, this more 'globalised' meshing of previously diverse interests in football, and the complexities of the struggles for control and influence in the international game, also challenge the very integrity of historic national football competitions. Back in the 1960s this idea – the abuse of a treasured national sporting ritual – would have seemed incredible. But, in 1999–2000, the FA Cup, the world's oldest and most revered knock-out football competition – now in an era when the knock-out format is not only unloved abroad but is also regarded as 'bad business' – is taking place without the FA Cup-holders, Manchester United. Extraordinarily, United have apparently been urged by the competition's own originators, the

Football Association, to play instead in a FIFA-organised international club tournament in Brazil.

The FA Cup has already been changing slowly in the new football world. Such recent developments mark not just the increasing power of top clubs in Europe – a fact already signalled by the threatened 'privatisation', and the subsequent forced reorganisation, of UEFA club competitions for 1999–2000 – but also the changing role and priorities of FIFA and of the FA itself. The FA's sights here are set squarely – in blinkers, some might say – on attracting the World Cup finals to England in 2006, hence the 'sacrifice' of the Cup-holders in the 2000 FA Cup. FIFA, strategic and increasingly compromised 'guardians' of national team football,[11] but itself alarmed by the growing influence of the 'G14' top clubs in Europe, harnesses, by way of an England 'sweetener', the richest and most popular club in the world for a prominent FIFA event in Brazil. And United? Well, they can claim the altruistic defence of the wider public good, while their sponsors and shareholders rub their hands at the promised TV exposure in the important new markets in South America, Australasia and the Asian regions. Fans, being fans, want United to be World Club champions, sure; but, hey, why can't we do it all, they also ask.

REGULATION AND OTHER MATTERS

This sort of jockeying and horse trading – the bargaining of local priorities against international ambitions; the tensions between club and national team interests; and the new, highly commercial, global interests of the Football Association – makes it hard, it seems to me, to argue, as some now do, that Lancaster Gate itself should be promoted as a serious candidate for some sort of independent football regulator for football in England in the 1990s. (I will return to the general question of regulation in football in a moment.) Remember, also, that it is the FA which can apparently guarantee lowest ticket prices at the World Cup finals in England in 2006 of £15 for adults and £9 for children, while in 1999 some clubs in the FA's own Premier League insist, unhindered, on a minimum ticket price of £25 or more. Early FA Premier League gate returns in 1999, and the dramatic fall-off in season-ticket-holder renewals at 'middle-range' clubs such as Leicester City, Derby County and Aston Villa, suggest that consumer limits might already have been reached – and passed – on price, at least at some clubs at the top level. This does seem to be a matter largely of price rather than of the 'unpredictability of outcome' arguments which have warned against the dangers of allowing a small number of rich clubs to dominate domestic competition. The latter is something which pretty much happens in football around the world, certainly in Europe. In team sports, its control seems even only partially effective in countries, such as the USA, which have 'closed' sporting competition, mobile franchises, no competing international markets for players, and with ceilings to any sort of progressive, 'European' system of promotion and relegation.[12]

Arguments, generally, for stringent financial regulation in English football of a kind which is independent of European markets for sport are, in any case, rather difficult to sustain, not least because of the various market 'seepages' which are likely to occur – players, income, and so on – but also because of the real and complex ambivalences which many supporters at top clubs, understandably, hold towards their own club's and the game's future both here and abroad. These are difficult matters, often expressed in the nature of the divergences between public issues and private interests. There are not too many accounts of the 'new era' for football which deal with them at all adequately. Let me say a little more on this.

Arguably, much of the critical and often sophisticated writing on the 'new business' of football proceeds, for example, with apparently little reference to, or understanding of, the social, political, economic and global shifts which have underpinned and helped to sustain such developments.[13] Such accounts are often impressive and heartfelt, but they tend to isolate the sport from wider changes, to be strongly national-based, to begin with unexplained assumptions or assertions about the 'rights' of football fans, and also to have a powerful masculinist emphasis. They also tend to be quite static and sometimes fixed in their ideas about late-modern sports fandom. They often threaten simply to set up, as binary oppositions, for example, 'fans' against 'consumers', 'live' attenders against TV fans, and 'traditional' supporters (good) against 'new' fans (obviously, bad). They sometimes seem to conflate judgements on claims for fan 'authenticity' largely with assessments of their sex and social class background – and this in a period when actually analysing and 'reading' class is, itself, no simple task. They seem premised, finally, on what I would contend are rather overly simplistic and economistic arguments about a new, largely domestic 'business class' which has, allegedly, strategically ransacked the sport for profit in the face of concerted and apparently homogeneous opposition from 'the fans' who, themselves, have fully worked through and agreed upon social democratic (or better) solutions to the sport's now rather entrenched inequalities.

Despite the important and impressively critical edge of much of this work and, not least, its conclusions on the real corrosive effects of the 'free market' on football (high ticket prices, crisis clubs, and so on), I would like to argue we also need other, much more broadly based, analyses of 'new' football in order to tease out the real significance of recent changes in game. Fortunately, other responses to recent developments are available. Richard Giulianotti's complex, sociological and anthropological, account of football's international transformation from a 'traditional' sport to its 'modern' and, now, 'postmodern' forms, for example, has much more to recommend it.[14] But it is also restricted in its usefulness, in my view, by its own 'masculinist' frame and, ironically, by the fact that it actually lacks a really convincing political economy of the changes which have occurred, admittedly in a global context, at different rates and in different ways at particular moments in a range of footballing cultures and economies.

John Sugden and Alan Tomlinson's work on FIFA has no such problem.[15] Instead, it is a sophisticated, invaluable and properly sociological analysis of transnational political and economic change in the history, structure and dynamics of one of sport's, and the world's, most powerful and influential non-governmental organisations. As we have seen, FIFA is now a key actor in the new socio-economic international relations of football, including club football. Theorising FIFA's role in the new future for football will, surely, have to be a key part of any real understanding of the reshaping of domestic and international football markets.

Ian Taylor's extremely perceptive and subtly critical analysis of the emergence of the FA Premier League, and of what he calls 'market football',[16] is singled out in its importance by his unusual determination to move beyond conventional conceptions of 'fandom' and to look at how supporters connect with the sport at what he calls 'the level of the imagination'. This is especially persuasive in this context because, as Taylor argues:

> If, with the editors of fanzines and the organisers of the Football Supporters Association, we spend too much time bemoaning the loss of the 'true' terrace football follower we may be missing the significance of the emergence, rather closer to home, of new ways of being a fan, for example, and new ways of proclaiming, in an increasingly globalised world, one's local origin and identity.[17]

Accounts of this kind are premised, at least in part, on associated psycho-social shifts in late-modern identity formation, including what the sociologist Ulrich Beck has called the rise of 'individualisation'.[18] One does not have to accept the dubious premise of the 'inevitability' of 'free markets',[19] or the quite ridiculous claims about 'classlessness' in Britain, or even cling to the impossibilism of a return to a reworking of the post-war Keynesian settlement to see, as Will Hutton argued recently,[20] that we are, indeed, living in an age when some of the old parameters of identity construction, through gender relations and the family, work, social class and local community networks are, certainly, eroding or changing. As these old sources change, we are pressed more to become the creators of our own identities, primarily through diversifying patterns of leisure and consumption. Hutton and Martin Jacques[21] argue that these shifts can be used to account for the recent huge rise in the popularity of sport and of personal fitness and even for the recent growth of individual (over team) sports.

The uncertainty and 'risk' involved in the construction of late-modern identities may also account, of course, for some of the important new ways that fans now connect with their favoured football clubs. This is especially the case in relation to the ways emerging club/fan links might now contradict more normative gender and class identities, and also the changes in the specifically modernist ties of family and place which have traditionally connected especially male football fans with their local clubs. It will not deal, however, with the very real cleavages which have clearly opened up between less affluent, local male followers and football clubs at the highest levels of the sport in England in recent years, and at a time when inequality in Britain has generally been rising.[22]

The extent to which such barriers, of price and ticket access, act alone against live football match attendance, and can now be said to constitute a key form of 'social exclusion' in the 1990s is a moot point.[23] This is especially so in the light of the wide range of other, mediated, relations with football clubs which are available and which are increasingly mobilised today, and the arguably much more pressing and more fundamental sources of social exclusion which have become more solidified in the last 20 years, for example: the relative lack for the urban poor of reliable forms of employment and decent pay; of good social housing and health care; of reasonable educational and training opportunities; of public safety at home and on the street, and so on.[24] Certainly, however, it is undeniable that previously well-established ways of passing on important traditions of 'live' working-class male football support, specifically from father to son, have indeed been seriously disrupted in many major English footballing cities in the recent period and have probably added to the very real sense of social and psychic isolation of white urban working-class males in Britain in the 1990s.[25]

Anthony King's recent work on 'masculinist' Manchester United fans takes up some of these important themes,[26] but it is also significant for the ways it tries to locate the 'new consumption' of football within this wider discourse on the post-Fordist transformation of social and economic relations in Britain, and also of the new importance of cities and regions – rather than nations – in emerging new global cultural and economic networks. Again, aspects of King's approach are, arguably, overly economistic and, like almost all accounts of contemporary fan culture, he focuses too much on a relatively small part of the football audience: young, working-class, white males who follow a very large club. But he is successful in identifying both forms of resistance and compliance, for example, among 'the lads' in Manchester to new forms of football consumption. Young United fans such as these are strongly opposed to aspects of the new consumption of football – for example, the so-called new 'consumer' fans, the excessive merchandising, the seats – but they are also very proud of the business acumen and success of the club's administrators, and even of its stadium and products. They see the club in a very new cultural and market position *vis-à-vis* other large European clubs. In this sense, even 'masculinist' fandom in the 1990s both resists and, paradoxically, contributes to the new consumer trends in the sport and, indeed, to its 'globalisation'.

King also highlights, importantly, the new preferred guise, for these fans, of United as a post-national, regional but fully European club, a club which now increasingly strains at its identification by the British media as a signifier for England, or a 'representative', for example in European club competitions, of the FA Premier League itself. Instead, the club signifies for these supporters, specifically, new and important aspects of the search for ways of expressing a properly European cultural identity which both has strong regional resonances with United's north-west Manchester location but which also profoundly bypasses the national. Talk here, therefore, in any simple terms at least about the regulation of football in a national context is to lose sight not only of the new global economics of top football but also of the extent to which the new traditions of articulating and expressing attachments to major football clubs – and also what such clubs now mean to their followers – already extend some way beyond the domain of nation states and of their own signifiers.

CONCLUSION

In this chapter I have tried to look at recent changes in global, 'market' football by comparing it with the national, 'Keynesian' model of football in England in the 1960s. I have used a case study of the FA Cup because of recent indications that the new conditions of 'market' football require that the current holders of the cup, Manchester United, will play elsewhere during the 1999–2000 competition. The role of the FA itself in United's absence from its own prized national competition reveals, I have argued, both the complexities of new post-national football tensions, and reasons why the FA may not be the most appropriate choice for a new and effective regulatory role in English football.

I have also argued that journalistic and some academic accounts of recent changes in the game, impressive as they often are, are much too narrowly focused and too economistic, and that they miss, for example, important aspects of the effects in sport of 'de-traditionalisation', as a social and economic process which creates the conditions, not only for increasing personal insecurity, but also for the 'reflexive' renegotiation of personal identity – perhaps through sport and sports spectatorship.[27] The obvious need for some form of regulation in football, of a kind which limits some of the recent damaging effects of the free market – and of increasing general inequality in Britain in the 1990s – must be assessed against this wider canvas of recent social and economic changes. It must, if it is to be effective and relevant, I have argued, take into account, above all, the changing nature and context of football 'fandom' in the 1990s and the new post-national interpenetrations of football cultures.

At lower levels of the league structure in England, where finances are especially tight, there is a good reason to argue that the old 'commercial' models for smaller football clubs are now simply outmoded, and that imaginative new forms of club control and financing – which centrally involve supporters and other local stakeholders – are likely to be much more desirable and more successful in the longer term than any simple reintroduction of traditional forms of economic cross-subsidisation between professional clubs.[28] Any economic support system linking larger clubs with smaller clubs must deal, it seems clear, with issues of club structure and control as well as with simple finance. Fans, it should also be noted, can be strikingly conservative, too, even when potentially 'progressive' changes to club structures are in the offing.

Finally, it should be clear that – even if Merseysiders and others who have suffered in the 1990s might want it – there can be no return to the English footballing 'island state' of the 1960s. This is not to accede, limply, to the view that 'nothing can be done'. Far from it. It is simply to recognise that the new millennium holds the sorts of new challenges for the game at national and 'global' levels which will have to be very differently addressed from those faced when Hunt, St John, Yeats and their colleagues at Shankly's inspirational Liverpool were in their pomp.

Author's note: I would like to thank Stephen Hopkins for his comments on an earlier draft of this chapter.

10. Tomorrow's football club: an inclusive approach to governance

MARK GOYDER

So, football has become big business. Is that the end of civilisation as we know it? No. From Manchester United through to Mansfield, football clubs have to learn about the way businesses behave if they are to build lasting success. In this contribution to the debate I want to draw on the research and the experience of 'Tomorrow's Company', a business-led organisation which champions an *inclusive approach* to business. I do so as a business observer of the football scene, but also as a football fan who has loved the game for over thirty years. Like many participants I am occasionally saddened by the short-sightedness of boards, the excessive rewards of those at the top, at the inadequate support for investment in the future, by the folly of investors who see the whole thing as a bundle of tradable assets rather than as a delicate organism fed by loyalty and human values . . . and I am talking about business here, not just football.

The parallels between sporting and corporate success are endlessly fascinating. Supporters of the top teams at the moment worry about the loss of identity when foreign stars – or foreign managers – jet in, pick up a season's wages, and jet out again.[1] There is interesting evidence from the research literature about the qualities of the businesses that added the most shareholder value over five decades in the USA. The most successful companies were described as having 'cult-like cultures'. You either fitted in or you got out. (Look at Wimbledon – if you don't want to have your new shoes and suit set on fire after the first training session, don't go there.) And among the most successful companies, top executives were rarely hired from outside: there seemed to be something irreplaceable about 'growing your own'. That was over the five decades ending in the 1990s; interestingly, Hewlett Packard, one of the role model companies, has just broken with this tradition to hire a woman as its new CEO. The key test of her success, as with Arsène Wenger or Gérard Houllier, will be in her ability to work with the grain of the organisation's tradition and values, to change what has to be changed while knowing what you must never change.

Perhaps the clearest message from business to football is the one about uncertainty and change. Today, for the top clubs it seems easy, with West

Ham turning people away while charging people £29 a head for tickets, whilst fans of Schalke 04 in Germany pay top prices of around £4 a ticket.[2] Do we really believe that the admission-prices curve can continue indefinitely on its steep upward rise? The history of business failure is full of people who took for granted the continuing demand for their products. What about pay-per-view? What if we elected a government that fell out with the EU and foreign players were prevented from coming here? What if there was a nasty recession or civil disturbance? What if interest rates doubled just as football clubs were busy expanding their stadiums, and they were left half-finished and half-empty for two seasons? What if there is a new wave of amazing interactive cybersport, which leaves football looking boring and staid to a new generation of punters? We do not know what will change, but *something* will change, and when the change comes, the lesson from business is that the survivors will be those that were:

- sensitive to the changing climate around them;
- quick to learn and adapt;
- insistent on preserving their unique character and values;
- prudent with their cash;
- good at growing their own talent;
- well regarded by their local authorities;
- earning the loyalty of the next generation of their fans.

Why do these things matter to successful businesses? It's common sense. Relationships with customers, suppliers, communities and employees are to a business what ears, nose, eyes and touch are to an animal or person. They enable you to sense danger and seize opportunity. Businesses which only think about pleasing today's shareholders destroy their ability to create wealth tomorrow. Relationships depend on human qualities like loyalty and trust: when you are in trouble you want to have a strong deposit account of goodwill to call upon, not a group of people who have felt exploited for years. You can't trust people who have no values.

Prudence with cash gives you freedom of action: if you have gambled away all your reserves you are at the mercy of whatever rich freak may choose to buy you out. It was home-grown talent that rescued Manchester United after Munich. What we sow, we reap: we just don't know if it will take twenty minutes or twenty years.

An inclusive approach to the running of a football club would start with understanding what makes it different. It doesn't need a PhD to realise the central importance of supporters. If you map out the relationships that matter to, say, Tesco, you would go through the employees, the customers, the suppliers, and the community whose permission Tesco needs to operate. Only if Tesco get all that right can they hope to create a return for their shareholders. But what about football clubs?

A few years ago, my family was on a half-term break near Scarborough. My son I and decided to go and watch Scarborough play a home game in the old Fourth Division against Swansea. It was a wet night, and after ten minutes the home team scored. A few feet away from us was a band of Welsh supporters who had just travelled 300 miles, and who had another 300 to travel home, and who had just seen their side concede an awful goal. Yet they were singing, 'We're so great, we're ****ing incredible.' That's what I call loyalty.

Football fans aren't just customers. They are, especially in the case of the smaller clubs who lack a Shanghai branch of the supporters club, the local community. They are suppliers of goodwill, energy and atmosphere. Without the atmosphere of the Premier League, many foreign players say they would not be so keen to come to the UK. And the fans have power: if they withdraw their goodwill and support, few boards can hope to survive. The money that comes from television rights and merchandising may be a welcome extra, but it only grows out of the soil of goodwill that fans provide and over generations may withdraw.

If clubs get it wrong with their fans, they have in one blow messed up three of their key relationships. So my agenda for an inclusively run football club would include the appointment by the board of a director responsible for supporter relations. This would lead to all kinds of innovation. This would include consultation over the fairest way to allocate tickets; how to have a public-address system that actually addressed the public; co-operation with the local community over parking; internet dialogues with the manager; quarterly face-to-face public meetings where the board explains to the fans what it is doing on youth development; a joint approach to difficult issues like fans standing up in seated areas; improvements to the quality of music, entertainment and food at the stadium. Again and again in Tomorrow's Company we talk to businesses who find that if they cultivate the habit of listening, *really* listening, and encouraging the flow of new ideas, they make savings. Recently a construction company had massive problems bringing in skips to remove waste from the shopping centre where its operators were working. One day a manager from the building company was talking to the labourer who swept up round a neighbouring supermarket. 'We have our own waste collected every day. Why do you do a separate collection?' asked the labourer. It seems obvious to them now to collaborate on waste collections: yet nobody had ever thought of it before.

But dialogue with the supporters would not just be about the housekeeping issues. A tomorrow's football club would get into dialogue on the big issues too. Ask the directors to state, in the programme, and in the club's annual report, what they are there for. Few clubs, whether publicly quoted companies or mutuals, would dare to say, 'We're here to rip you lot off and make lots of money for us.' Most would find it much easier to say, 'We are here to win the championship, entertain the fans, and build a better club for the future.' Great. Once you've got that in black and white – or claret and blue – you can start holding them to it. Any time there's a decision you don't like, challenge the club to justify it against their own statement of purpose.

In the same way, challenge the club to state what its values are, what it cares about, what it will and won't tolerate. Get it to make a commitment to dialogue. Few clubs would dare to say, in writing, 'No we won't talk to our fans.' So even the reluctant will be shamed into making some kind of commitment to dialogue. Build on it. Conversation changes lives! Figure 1 below illustrates this model.

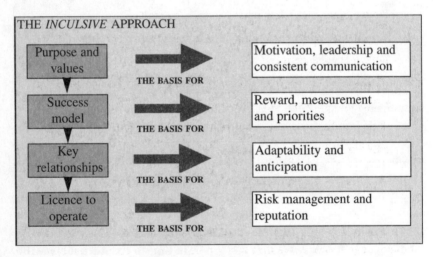

Figure 1: The inclusive approach

One of the benefits, for me, in attending the July 1999 conference at Birkbeck College on the regulation and governance of football was to hear from speakers like Brian Lomax, who had stepped in at a time of crisis for Northampton Town, and started to build an inclusive football club. Mutual patterns of ownership may be part of the answer. I am in favour of experimentation. But there are, sadly, some mutual organisations which have lost touch with their roots. Mutual behaviour, inclusive behaviour is more important than mutual structure. Maybe non-mutuals should start to promote supporter-shareholding schemes through Save As You Earn. It may well be that the defection of the FA from the role of regulator does leave a vacuum, which will need to be filled from above. Be warned, however: regulators do not always achieve the desired result. Compliance cultures are not always the natural breeding ground of innovation and flexibility.

Figures 2 below illustrates what I believe the future agenda for action should be for all companies, football clubs included.

- **Purpose**: do we state this clearly and consistently?
- **Values**: are we clear and consistent about values?
  Do we practice what we preach?
- **Personality**: what gives our company its unique personality?
- **Communication**: are we consistent in what we say to all audiences?
  Do we listen and adapt what we do as a result?
- **Challenge**: do we encourage a culture of challenge?
  Do we engage critics?
- **Measurement, reward and recognition**: do we reinforce the behaviour we want, or do we only pay for results? How do we check up on the health of our relationships? Does the board review these measures?

Figure 2: The agenda for action

Personally, I believe that the next decade can and should be the decade of dialogue in football. We may all then be in time to ensure that come the next downturn in support there is a robust group of inclusive football clubs which are truly built to last.

11. Football, fans and fat cats: whose football club is it anyway?

KEVIN JAQUISS

INTRODUCTION

If you were picking a theme tune for the debate which is going on about the future of football, you might do worse than 'Que sera, sera'. There is a lot of fatalistic talk about the problems in football. People can see that things are wrong but do not believe they can really do anything about it. In the end, people say, money talks and the law will always protect the men with the big bank balances.

To a significant extent that is true – under company law as it now stands the big shareholders in football clubs hold all the cards. There is a difficulty with this approach, though. Football does not operate like other businesses; there are all sorts of dynamics operating outside the simple legal structure. Unless those dynamics are understood and addressed, football will face a mounting tide of criticism and abuse from its customer base. That cannot be healthy in the long term, even for the big shareholders.

This chapter looks from a lawyer's viewpoint at the tension between the legal structures and the nature of football and goes on to suggest how things might be changed.

WHAT'S SPECIAL ABOUT FOOTBALL CLUBS?

If you want to know someone's tastes in food you might ask, 'What's your favourite restaurant?' If you want to know their taste in drink you might ask, 'Which is your local?' If you want to know their tastes in football, though, you say, 'What team do you *support*?' That word tells us a lot about what makes a football club special.

Although we use restaurants and pubs – and sometimes talk as if we own them ('it's my local') – we don't really expect to have any say in the way they're run. Football is different. For a start, a lot of us put up with a very poor-quality product on the field when we would never tolerate rancid beer in a pub. But we also feel that the club owes us things in return for our support, that we are entitled to have a say in the way it is run, and even that we have something to offer. This goes beyond bellowing advice and abuse from the stands. We expect the club to come and listen to us in supporters' club meetings or to answer our letters criticising moves in the transfer market. This sense of ownership underpins the whole of the debate about football which has been going on in recent years.

STAKEHOLDERS

Most football clubs in the UK are limited companies with shareholders and directors. Although they may be the same people, there are two distinct roles. The shareholders own the business. In the 'good old days', very few of them hoped for a financial return – their return came from what happened on the pitch and perhaps also out of feeling that they were keeping an important local institution going. In recent years, some shareholders have made vast and incongruous fortunes out of their ownership and this has changed the football environment. There are now influential shareholders in football clubs who want to see either a return on their investment or some protection so that their investment is not wasted.

The directors run the club and have serious financial responsibilities to the club's creditors. They also have responsibilities to the shareholders to run things in line with their wishes. In most businesses, provided they stay within the law, the directors and shareholders can do what they want. Financial journalists may comment on the running of a plc which is listed on the stock exchange but no one comments on what happens in private companies. If the directors mess things up on a massive scale, it is a matter for them and the shareholders to sort out.

Football is not like that. There have been all sorts of campaigns by fans whose interest in their club would not be recognised in law. It is not unusual to see fans calling on the main shareholder in a club to put more money in – though company law is based on the fundamental position that a shareholder only has to pay for his shares. Fans regularly call for the resignation of directors – 'Sack the Board' – though company law gives that right to the shareholders because it is their money the directors are playing with. Fans see themselves as stakeholders. If they can, they may buy small shareholdings. This gives them some sense of belonging and the right to attend the AGM but they are outgunned when decisions are made by the votes of the big shareholders.

CONFLICT

Football's recent history is one of guerrilla warfare between the fans and the legal owners. In some cases, the fans have been formidable and have outgunned the board in business experience or PR skills. In other cases, the fans have pursued crazy campaigns with no understanding of the real issues. In all instances, the dispute has been damaging to the club because it is a key part of being a football club to be a local (or sometimes national) institution. Although football clubs do now have to be run in some ways as if they are part of the leisure industry, they are not *just* part of the leisure industry.

The essential components of professional football clubs are that they need a ground to play on, training facilities and a squad of players with a skilled (or lucky) manager. They have income from television, sponsorship and gate receipts but they do need working capital in the form of equity or loans or both. They *must* be professionally managed in their commercial activities if they are to exploit opportunities and succeed in the Premier League or keep their heads above water in the lower leagues. And they also need true *supporters,* not just people who turn up regularly or occasionally to watch a game.

The trick is to find a structure which balances these various needs and the interests of those concerned. The problem with any structure based on a traditional limited company is that the supporters never progress beyond a nominal shareholding or a token presence on the board. Some advances might be made if some form of regulation were introduced, but this does nothing directly to improve the relationship between a club and its fans.

USING MUTUAL STRUCTURES

A possible answer to all this lies in the 'mutual' structure – in legal terms an industrial and provident society rather than a limited company – and that is the model I discuss here. Some very interesting work has been done on the use of trusts as vehicles for supporter involvement in clubs and there are some supporter trusts in existence. This chapter does not attempt a comparison between the two approaches. My aim is to suggest the role which mutuals might play in the football clubs of the future.

Mutuals began in the nineteenth century; people began to club together to help each other when there was limited access to finance and no welfare state. This was the origin of building societies, friendly societies and co-ops. Until recently, co-ops or public benefit societies like housing associations have continued to operate in a closed world under nineteenth-century rules. People have now begun to realise that the mutual structure has great potential where the primary aim of an activity is not to make money or where a community need is being met. New forms of mutual will probably emerge over the next few years in situations where a community has an interest in the way services are delivered to it but does not want shareholders in the City or anyone else to profit from the activity.

Some of the thinking which has been developed is relevant to football, particularly the thinking about the nature of a community's interest in a mutual. The point in football is that, although fans like to think they 'own' their club, they are not looking for a financial return. Indeed, many of them feel there is something wrong in people making money out of football.

The first advantage of the mutual structure is that the members of a mutual society are its owners but have only nominal shareholdings – the rules say that they cannot sell their shares at a profit and cannot realise the value of their shareholding on a sale or winding up. Membership of a mutual can accurately reflect the real relationship between a fan and a football club and the pressure of the need to make a return to shareholders can be removed.

The second advantage is that the structure can accommodate the need for professional management. This has been a problem with mutuals in the past but it is now possible to register rules which reflect clearly the balance in power between a representative board which takes a broad view of the well-being of the society and an executive board which has to deliver results on a day-to-day basis.

The third and most important advantage is that the structure can be flexible. I have been involved in drafting entirely new sets of rules which alter the old balance between the interests of members, providers of capital and executives and define clearly where the rights of members begin and end, what issues they are entitled to decide and how significant their representation on the board should be.

There are also advantages beyond the interests of each individual club. Clubs run as mutuals would have reasons to work together – where clubs with the traditional structure do not – in strengthening the links of football as a whole with the community and distributing sensibly the revenue within the game. This makes self-regulation a realistic long-term aim.

THE TOTAL FOOTBALL MUTUAL

A 'total football mutual' would have the following as features of its constitution to build a healthy relationship with its supporters and its community:

- a clear statement in the rules of the nature of the relationship and its importance as a guiding principle;
- a representative board charged with responsibility for setting standards and monitoring the club's success in meeting its community aims;

- a separate executive board chosen on merit with responsibility for running the club efficiently and in line with its constitution and the wishes of the representative board;
- a membership without any right to share in the capital of the club on a sale or winding up so that the board and executive would not be under pressure to secure a return or capital growth for shareholders;
- a modern democratic structure for the election of the representative board and testing community opinion.

Other less radical models might involve a blend of mutual and traditional shareholdings, especially where some part of the club's activities needs risk capital to make it work. In many cases, there will be a nervousness at first about letting people elected by supporters take ultimate responsibility for the running of the club, so that the rights of supporters and their representatives will be strictly limited. The important point is that, in every case, the structure is giving the supporter a form of ownership which matches his or her sense of the relationship with the club.

PIE IN THE SKY?

At present a substantial part of the working capital in most clubs is provided by shareholder equity. In the largest plcs, the paper value of that equity might appear to rule out conversion to a mutual structure. This brings us back to our fatalistic theme tune: except in the most desperate cases, supporters do not think they can raise or borrow the sums involved. In many cases, this may be right. There are, however, some features of football clubs which make me wonder whether it is right to discount the prospects of success in substituting mutual and loan capital for equity:

- the clubs we are talking about have the benefit of two unusually stable and easily collected income streams – gate receipts (which tend to be reliable at a 'core' level) and television revenue;
- many clubs also own a ground with a capital value;
- the disciplines required by a lender are less likely to be unacceptable to members who have no financial stake in the club than to conventional shareholders;
- a club operated in this way would have little difficulty in bettering the financial performance of the vast majority of clubs under their present management;
- the outsourcing of commercial activities, exchanging certainty of return and reduced overheads for the prospect of large profits at higher risk, is a realistic option where there are no shareholders seeking a return.

I think there are clubs where a fully mutual model might be established in the short term. Certainly, the model should be in the thinking of any group of supporters looking at a rescue of a club in financial difficulties. The model may also be useful, however, where there is no prospect of a 'mutual takeover' in the short or medium term. It is possible to imagine a group of supporters starting as a pressure group, progressing to a collective shareholding and a formal relationship with a club, then monitoring and/or managing the club's community activities on its behalf and finally taking control on a fully mutual basis. If the members of the group agreed that they were not in it to make a return on their investment, they might adopt the aims and constitution of the 'total football mutual' between themselves and use it as the vehicle to hold shares in the club. The model would work effectively at all the stages from pressure group to takeover.

CONCLUSION

There will be changes in football over the next few years. The changes will be at best damaging and at worst catastrophic if they do not reflect the concerns of the supporters who make the game what it is. The mutual model makes it possible for this to happen in a structured way, giving the supporters a stake not as investors but as custodians together of the future of 'their' club.

PART IV

INTERNATIONAL DEVELOPMENTS

12. International developments and European clubs

ANDY WALSH

The pace of change within the game of football never slows. Over the last few years the pressure for change has been on the increase. The Bosman ruling along with the influence of media companies and the overwhelming commercialisation of the game have changed the face of professional football and, while many would agree that some change was necessary, the change we have seen has not always been for the better. The administrators of football are its temporary custodians, charged with protecting the game's integrity against both internal and external pressures and overseeing the development of football as a sport with a common regulatory code. It is their role to shepherd the game through difficult times and to ensure that it remains intact as a sport, understanding how important a role the game plays in the lives of many people who trust them to carry out their duty.

The FA in England is responsible for every level of the game from top professional sides to park and schools football. The professional clubs have long expressed their disquiet with what they see as a restrictive and antiquated structure which they believe limits their abilities to operate in a commercial environment. In an attempt to force changes the clubs at the top of the game have often threatened breakaways and some clubs have reconstituted themselves as public limited companies (plcs) in an attempt as much to circumvent the rules as to raise extra investment. The establishment of the Premier League in England was meant to bring stability, giving the 'bigger' clubs a greater share of revenues and more autonomy. The same clubs that pressed for the formation of the Premier League have now set their sights on a European league with the establishment of the secretive and self-selected G14 group of clubs. The directors of these so-called bigger clubs have been involved in discussions that could lead to the establishment of a European league with TV money again being the main driver.

Neither supporters, players nor managers are asked for their views on such developments; they are merely presented with the outcomes as a *fait accompli*. In England we are warned that the proposed changes are an inevitable consequence of the game's global appeal. The directors of football clubs make their pleas for understanding with: 'If we don't join a European super league we will be left behind.' At Manchester United the club's plc board warned fans that unless the BSkyB takeover was successful, 'we will be left behind because rival European clubs are owned by media companies'. At clubs in Germany, France, Spain and Italy the directors of football clubs warn their fans 'unless we float on the stock exchange we will be left behind, as English clubs can attract outside investment'.

It is therefore refreshing that the following chapters in this section report different ideas and experiences from other European countries. The experience of individual supporters will vary but the sense of belonging to 'a club' that a supporter feels for his or her team is shared, a sensation that transcends tribal and national boundaries. The ownership of Manchester United FC, and how that club related to its supporters, was central to the campaign waged by Manchester United fans against BSkyB's attempted takeover of their club.[1] In a similar spirit, the role of President Núñez at Barcelona has seen Barça fans come together to form L'Elefant Blau, an independent fans' organisation established to protect the interests of supporters and Barcelona's true 'owners', the club members or *socios*. In Chapter 15, written by L'Elefant Blau's president, Joan Laporta, the intention of their supporters' group is explained as being to promote reform of Barcelona and to democratise its structure.[2] Barcelona is often cited as an example of how a football club should be run, owned by its members with an elected president and board. L'Elefant Blau fear that the current club president, Núñez, is trying to move the club away from these traditions and this structure by engineering a flotation on the stockmarket.

Núñez recently exceeded his permitted powers and signed a TV deal for the years 2003 to 2008 – going against the terms governing his tenure as club president by binding any future holder of presidential office to a commercial contract and decision that he had made. The famous Barcelona shirts have never carried the name of a sponsor yet it is believed that even this may change. The fear of Joan Laporta and his group is that the very nature of FC Barcelona is coming under threat from commercial interests. At the 1999 Birkbeck College conference from which this book emerged, Laporta summed up these feelings: 'Football is not a business, it is our sport, our emotions, an expression of our feelings on life.'

It is undoubtedly the case that football generally is under tremendous pressure from outside commercial interests who wish to use the sport as a vehicle to promote their own goods and services. At the 1999 Birkbeck College conference, Patrick Mignon, the legal advisor on European affairs to UEFA, explained how in France commerce saw the prospect of the European super league as an ideal way of exploiting the marketing possibilities that football creates. Because of the success of the French national team, football enjoys a high profile in France yet most of the top French stars play abroad where the financial rewards are greater.

Picking up on the same theme, Gordon Taylor, chief executive of the English Professional Footballers Association, draws a comparison with the current 'post-Bosman' era and the period immediately after the abolition of the maximum wage.[3] In his chapter, Taylor describes how, during the time of the maximum wage, top players would stay at one club for almost the whole of their playing career. Once the maximum wage was abolished there was a drift from the small-town clubs to the big-city clubs. Those clubs based in larger conurbations could draw increased audiences and pay bigger wages. Gordon Taylor's argument is that today we see a similar drift – but this time from nations with a relatively small TV audience for football to those with a much larger audience.

The single European market is held responsible for the Bosman ruling and Alasdair Bell explains in Chapter 13 the difficulties that UEFA face in trying to apply and police football's rules and regulations within a framework designed for business and commerce. At the time of the July 1999 Birkbeck College conference at which Bell spoke on these issues, UEFA were preparing for a hearing at the European Sports Tribunal in Lausanne where they were defending their own regulation that prevents one individual or company owning more than one club. One company, ENIC, held multiple stakes in various clubs across a number of different countries and UEFA feared that such ownership could create a conflict of interest should two of those teams meet in a competitive fixture.[4] In the end, a combination of forces including players' representatives and supporters' groups eventually saw that UEFA's rules were upheld. The point is that sport should not be subject to the same rules and regulations that govern commercial activities. Thus, the speculation that Wimbledon FC might move to Dublin may be undesirable for the fans and the sport yet European law would not allow UEFA to block it as it would be viewed in the same way as a bank deciding to move its operations from London to Dublin. In a further example Alasdair Bell reports in his chapter that in 1999, Media Partners, the sponsors of the proposed European super league, had accused UEFA of abusing its power in opposing the establishment of that particular venture. Clearly there is a legal vacuum – the law is currently silent on so many issues that directly affect sport – and commercial interests may well use this uncertainty to gain an advantage for themselves unless football becomes better organised. With so many conflicting interests in the game, this will prove difficult. But as a minimum the European Union should be persuaded to amend its legislation so that supporters have a legal say in the running of their clubs and the wider game itself.

In Chapter 14 Stuart Dykes reports that at Schalke 04 in Germany the club structure has many similarities with the traditions established at FC

Barcelona. The club constitution, drawn up in conjunction with the German FA and redrafted in 1994, was to act as a template for all German clubs and is based on a membership model. Anyone can join and participate in electing the club leadership on a one-member-one-vote basis. Clubs in Germany tend to be sporting clubs rather than commercial companies and pressure to follow the English commercial model is being applied from the directors of a number of the top clubs. The arguments used by these directors echo those of the directors of Manchester United during the BSkyB bid when fans were told that unless the takeover was successful then the club would be unable to keep pace with continental rivals. Ironically, in Germany the cry is 'unless we float then we will not be able to keep up with our English rivals'.

Until recently the Bundesliga regulations did not allow companies to become members – only sporting clubs could compete in the league; however, this was changed at the end of 1998. Earlier attempts to float by Hamburg in 1991 and Werder Bremen in 1992 were blocked by the Bundesliga. Since 1998, instead of ruling out flotation altogether, conditions are being applied such as:

- 50% of shares in a floated company plus one share must be retained by the sporting club members;
- a percentage of the floated company shares should be held in a benevolent fund for smaller clubs.

It is widely believed that Borussia Dortmund could be the first German club to float on the stockmarket but others would then soon follow. Due to an adverse reaction from fans, Bayern Munich have declared that they would not be going public but this could change should Borussia Dortmund or another club do so. The conditions laid down by the Bundesliga have resulted in commerce cooling its interest in football as an investment. The threat of a Murdoch/BSkyB-style takeover has also stiffened the resolve of the Bundesliga to treat flotation with great caution.

There is clearly an urgent need for football fans to join together and create a pan-European fans' grouping which could act as a lobbying force, with branches in every European country to protect supporters' interests and the integrity of the game of football. This need was raised by many at the 1999 Birkbeck College conference, including by Joan Laporta of L'Elefant Blau. The chapters in this section include a number of constructive proposals, many of which are now being actively taken forward, such as the creation of supporter-shareholder groups. An urgent next step is to pursue this work at a European level, both through the European Commission and UEFA, and by linking together supporter organisations across Europe.

13. Sport and the law: the influence of European Union competition policy on the traditional league structures of European football

ALASDAIR BELL

In recent years football in Europe has been enjoying a period of unparalleled public profile and financial prosperity largely as the result of the expansion in the number of broadcasting outlets for the game, and the associated influx of TV monies into the game. Football has always played a central role in the cultural life of most European countries, and from the advent of European club championships in the 1950s the international dimension of such competition has proved a very important and popular complement to the activities of domestic leagues. This rude good health has been achieved under the auspices of the game's traditional national governing bodies under the overall umbrella of football's federal European governing body, UEFA.

Since the beginning of the 1990s, however, the dramatic increase in the financial turnover of the major clubs as a result of the advent of pay TV channels, and the latter's determination to buy the broadcasting rights for European football at ever-increasing prices, has unleashed commercial forces which are actively challenging the legitimacy of the traditional regulatory structures of the game in Europe. UEFA has carried off the difficult task of preserving the primacy of domestic leagues, so that they continue to safeguard the central role of football as a social and cultural activity in their respective countries; administered a highly successful series of European club competitions; and at the same time provided a secure regulatory régime through which to channel the increased revenues coming into the game in a way which safeguards the interests of the widest possible number of clubs and national associations. This is now under threat. The primary reason may be that, since the Bosman case, certain parties see European law as a tool they can use to attack sports rules and structures that they do not like. Furthermore, the European Commission has found it difficult to come to terms with the specific structure of sport, and to accept that it has certain unique characteristics that set it apart from ordinary business or commerce.

Historically it has not been possible for businesspeople to make large sums of money from the ownership of football clubs in Europe. Most local associations had in place rules confirming the primary purpose of clubs as sporting associations. Since the beginning of the 1990s this has changed and increasingly many clubs have been transformed into limited companies run for profit. As a result, UEFA and its constituent national member associations have been subjected to a growing number of legal challenges as to their rights to govern the game in the traditional fashion. The Bosman ruling has encouraged these legal challenges and the atmosphere of legal uncertainty that has prevailed since the European Court of Justice made that ruling at the end of 1995.

In fact many of the sports structures that have been challenged in Europe have already been considered and held legal in the United States. For example, in the US there is a national statute recognising the legality of central marketing of television rights by professional sports leagues. There is no such legislation in Europe, although in the United Kingdom the central marketing of television rights by the English Premier League was held to be lawful under UK competition law by the Restrictive Practices Court. To date, however, the European Commission has taken no view on the issue. Let us look at a number of other examples.

MULTI-CLUB OWNERSHIP

One would have thought that it would be self-evident that allowing the same owner to control two contestants in the same competitive event presents the potential for a conflict of interest. In the UK there has long been a rule forbidding one person from owning more than one club. The need for such a rule is clear from the example of the late Robert Maxwell, who achieved control of Derby County, Reading and Oxford United.[1] The necessity for having such a rule was underlined when, after his death, it was revealed that he was a fraudster on a grand scale who had embezzled huge sums of money from the Mirror Group pension fund whilst chairman of the company. In 1998 UEFA had to invoke its own guidelines on this matter after three teams controlled by ENIC reached the latter stages of the European Cup-Winners' Cup. ENIC challenged UEFA's ruling in the Court of Arbitration for Sport (CAS) and lost. In a lengthy and detailed ruling, the CAS held that the UEFA rule was a legitimate means to deal with conflicts of interest and that it was not contrary to European law. In written statements to the European Parliament, the European Union had also endorsed the UEFA rule.

PRESERVING THE INTEGRITY OF NATIONAL COMPETITIONS

Another area where the integrity of UEFA's regulatory approach is being challenged is on the question of teams from one country playing in another. UEFA still allows national football associations to decide who can compete in their leagues, and largely this consists of clubs located within their national jurisdictions. This structure poses a potential problem for the EU, as the single European market, as it was originally conceived, was about eliminating national barriers to business; in football, national barriers are vitally important in preserving the integrity of individual leagues. This presents the Commission with a difficult legal conundrum when faced with challenges like Wimbledon FC's proposal that they were legally entitled to relocate their home matches in the English Premier League from south London to Dublin on the basis of European law. At its core the logic of Wimbledon's argument was that if, under European law, a Dutch bank can do business in England, why can an English football club not conduct business in Ireland? This position could be supported by the purest interpretation of European law. Yet the danger of allowing this logic to dictate the application of competition policy in the football context is that it will lead to the break-up of existing national league structures which have been so successful and which are deeply appreciated by supporters across Europe.

There is a danger that if the EU does not recognise that sport is a special case then existing structures may be dismembered by the back door through legal cases founded on competition law as it applies to conventional markets and which offers an inappropriate regulatory framework in the sports league context.

THE DANGER POSED BY THE 'SUPER LEAGUE' CONCEPT

The attempt to establish a European 'super league' – a breakaway league from UEFA structures – by a number of leading European clubs in the 1998–99 season led to another legal complaint against UEFA. A complaint was lodged against UEFA that it had abused its 'monopoly' power by allegedly preventing the creation of a European super league.

Of course, it is not so difficult to accuse UEFA of being a 'monopolist' since every sports governing body has some element of monopoly power. The core of the complaint against UEFA was that it had 'abused' its monopoly power by somehow preventing the emergence of a super league. There was no substance whatsoever to this complaint. The reality is that the clubs exercised their own commercial choice to stay within UEFA structures. Nevertheless, in view of the atmosphere of legal uncertainty, it was perhaps not surprising that the whole matter was dragged before the EU.

THE ROLE OF THE EUROPEAN UNION

Under current competition laws it is not difficult to make a complaint against a sports governing body as, by definition, they do have a kind of natural monopoly position; however, if you are organising a league it is essential that there is one central body to organise the league and adjudicate on disputes. This leads to a situation where any time UEFA does something that any other party is unhappy with then they lodge a complaint to the European Commission and accuse UEFA of an abuse of monopoly power and they have at least some kind of *prima facie* case. Such complaints are often devoid of any substantive basis. In any event, European law needs to recognise that sports governing bodies, providing they are democratically elected and that they reflect all the varied interests of the sport, have some area of discretion and manoeuvre and cannot be subject to legal challenge for everything they do.

The absence of such recognition has led to what can only be described as quite bizarre cases in Europe in the late 1990s. Probably the best example was where an athlete sued the Belgian Judo Federation for failing to select her for the national team. Her argument was that the failure to select her deprived her of the opportunity to 'provide services' under Article 59 of the EU Treaty. While the case clearly has a surreal quality to it, the matter was still referred to the European Court of Justice. It has not yet been adjudicated on, but one assumes that the court will say it is for a national federation to select its own national team. Nevertheless, the case does illustrate how, in the absence of clear leadership on this and related sports administration issues by the European Commission, as conventional business organisations play an increasingly influential role in sports marketplaces virtually every last sports association rule and regulation is subject to legal challenge. I think that UEFA and other European sports governing bodies are operating to a large extent in a legal vacuum, and there is a need to convince the European authorities to take account of the specific and special characteristics of sport when it applies new laws to them.

THE ROLE OF POLITICAL PRESSURE IN REFORMING EU COMPETITION LAW

I also think there is a role for the football supporters' organisations in that process. The European Commission as it currently functions is a rather undemocratic institution. It responds primarily to pressure exerted on it by national governments. It is really through influencing the Sports Minister, or the Prime Minister if possible, of the individual national governments, that we can influence the European Union countries to persuade the Commission to reform competition law regarding sports leagues. In this respect the effective manner in which supporters of Manchester United were able to organise was an important reason influencing the UK in deciding to block BSkyB's bid for the club. That decision was based not only on narrow competition law considerations but also took account of the wider interests of football, and the influence of the supporters was particularly significant in this latter respect.

At the moment we are certainly witnessing a growing influence by the European Commission on sports matters, but in UEFA's view this influence could be negative unless the Commission is able to understand the specific nature of sport. Sport is not a conventional commercial commodity, a mere business. Furthermore there is no reason to suppose that the European Union would regulate sport any more efficiently than the governing bodies do at present. The European Union and sports governing bodies have differing objectives. The EU is not actually about protecting the traditional structure of sport and national structures; it is about the abolition of national frontiers and national barriers to business. The primary mandate of the European Union is to create a single European market, not to respond to the characteristics of a special case industry like football. The EU has, thus far, demonstrated little ability to recognise the validity of these special characteristics. As Gordon Taylor, chief executive of the PFA, has noted, the structures of sport in the United States actually allow and respect balance in the league, and allow collective selling of TV rights.[2] We are still trying to convince the European courts that these are the correct things to do. It is proving to be a tough job.

CONCLUSION

In conclusion, I would reiterate the central point, namely that until and unless the EU actually show some more sympathy and understanding regarding the special characteristics of sports leagues, in my view any continued involvement by the Commission in the regulation of the sector is unlikely to be helpful.

14. Commercialisation and fan participation in Germany

STUART DYKES

I am a supporter of Schalke 04, the Bundesliga club from the city of Gelsenkirschen in the industrial area of Germany between Dortmund and Essen. I am also a member of the Schalker Fan-Initiative, an organisation of fans that is probably unique in Germany in that it is organised along much the same lines as an independent supporters' association as exists in England. In Germany most of the fans have organised themselves around fanzines, so we publish a fanzine as well, but we also have an organisation that we use to campaign for fan-related issues. In this chapter I intend to discuss the commercialisation of football in Germany, particularly the situation regarding the transformation of German clubs into plcs.

It is important to remember when looking at Germany that the vast majority of clubs, all but one or two, are *not* limited companies; they are sporting clubs, sporting societies, similar to FC Barcelona. Our supporters' club in Krefeld where I live had until recently the same type of structure and constitution as Schalke 04, based on the same law and registered with the local court. To all intents and purposes the situation had not changed for 130 years. So it is rather an anachronistic structure, and it is ironic that people are looking in some cases towards Germany for a way ahead when the system has been in existence, almost unchanged, for 130 years. The president of Borussia Dortmund says that this structure, this way of organising football, of having sporting clubs rather than a limited company, either private or public, 'has all the charm of a dinosaur'. But I think even now clubs are still rediscovering the charm of this 'dinosaur' and I will touch upon that later. Firstly, though, as regards our club's structure, there is an executive committee, made up in a lot of cases by amateurs, not necessarily people from football. There are some ex-players moving into management positions, such as Rudi Assauer, the Schalke 04 general manager, but this is not generally the case. These people are elected by the membership of the general meeting and the general meeting is the body that has all the power within the club. This is how it works in theory. How it works in practice is another thing. But there is pressure now in Germany to move away from this old structure into a more modern era, and German clubs look towards Britain for the way ahead. To use Borussia

Dortmund as an example, the money that they take through their membership fees is about DM700,000 and yet their turnover the year before last was DM150 million. There is absolutely no relationship between the two figures. There is a call for a change towards a more professional management structure and the introduction or the formation of companies to run the clubs. Even as recently as ten years ago, the chairman of Borussia Dortmund said they ran the football club like they would run a chip shop, it was so amateurish. Eight years later they went on to win the Champions League and now they are widely tipped to be the first German club to go public. So there was recognition of a need in Germany for the game to be run in a more professional manner. Three or four years ago the German Football Association argued that the constitution of a sporting club should be changed so that the club reflects more the corporate structure of a limited company. Schalke 04 was the guinea pig where they introduced a new constitution that is roughly based on this structure of a plc, a German plc. This is not exactly the same thing as a British plc in that it has an executive committee, or managing board, that is elected at the moment by the members and in future by the shareholders. They are professional people who actually run the club full-time, and are paid for doing so. This committee, or managing board, is supervised or controlled by the supervisory board, which is a compulsory feature of all German plcs. The managing board must go to the supervisory board every six months or so and the supervisory board will approve or disapprove their work and recommendations. This is the constitution that has been introduced at Schalke 04.

Therefore even though the clubs are organised as sporting clubs, they are *de facto* fully functioning companies, even if they do not yet have the structures of those companies. So taking a lead from Britain in the early 1990s, from a club's point of view it seemed obvious and logical to want to go public, to launch public companies. The main sources of income would be gate receipts, selling TV and advertising rights and merchandising, but as yet clubs have not branched out into any of the other areas British clubs have entered such as buying hotels and property, but there is perceived to be a need for the clubs to do so. The Bosman ruling has also caused clubs to look elsewhere for other sources of finance, with the potential loss of income from transfer fees. Another important factor is that hardly any of the clubs own their own grounds – most of the stadiums in Germany are council-owned. A lot of them were built with public money for the 1974 World Cup. Kaiserslautern is the only major club in the country that currently owns its own stadium (although Schalke is in the process of building a new ultra-modern arena) and obviously this is a factor in any consideration if they want to go public. Gerhard Niebaum, the Borussia Dortmund president, has said that 'if we want to keep up with Madrid, Milan and Manchester in footballing terms, we must go public' and this was the general feeling, at least two or three years ago. I detect a trend away from that, which I return to below. But while Borussia Dortmund was likely to be the first, Bayern Munich was also widely tipped to go public, perhaps obviously so, for a club of their size and success. Other clubs have also been mentioned, such as SV Werder Bremen, Schalke 04 and Kaiserslautern, although none of these clubs at the moment is seriously considering going public.

The major obstacle to clubs going public was only removed on 24 October 1998. Before then clubs could not have gone public or floated on the stock exchange even if they had wanted to because the statutes of the German FA did not permit it. These statutes said that only teams who have a licence granted by the German FA can play in the Bundesliga, and the only clubs that will be granted a licence are those that remain sporting clubs. In other words there was no way that a private company could have a team playing in the Bundesliga, as it was not allowed under the statutes. This was the case until 1998. Bayer Leverkusen was one club funded by a company but the company was forbidden from directly running the sporting club. The German Football Association was always very suspicious of attempts by any Bundesliga club to go public. The first attempt was in 1991 by Hamburg and then again by SV Werder Bremen in 1992. Both were disallowed under the German FA rules. However, with the lifting of this restriction in 1998 the authorities are now saying that limited companies, private or public, will be allowed to run Bundesliga clubs and compete in the Bundesliga. A number of conditions have been attached to this, which may seem a bit strange in the British context. At the beginning of the 1990s Britain was seen as leading the way forward, but now some of the more negative effects of flotation in Britain have inspired the authorities to seek to introduce some sort of control on shareholders and companies. The German football authorities have introduced a clause approving conversion into a limited company, but have stipulated that 50% of the shares plus one must be retained in the hands of the actual sporting club. The sporting club must retain the majority of the shares so that no shareholder can come in and, for example, demand that all the best players be sold to finance the payment of dividends to shareholders. Under this ruling such action would not be allowed because the club would always have the last say, in theory at least.

What the German FA dreads more than anything is a situation where, for example, Adidas gains control of Bayern Munich. The German FA is very wary of such a scenario and is looking to introduce controls and checks to prevent it from happening. Whereas Manchester United have been a kind of role model for leading clubs such as Borussia Dortmund and Bayern Munich Germans can perhaps be grateful to Rupert Murdoch. The whole business of BSkyB's attempted takeover of Manchester United set alarm bells ringing throughout the country, where leading figures reacted by saying that rules and regulations should be introduced to prevent anything similar happening in Germany should any club decide to go on to the stock exchange.

In Germany there is real concern about the gap between rich and poor clubs getting even bigger, which is seen as being inevitable if clubs go public. So what has been mooted is a kind of solidarity fund where all the clubs that go public, clubs such as Borussia Dortmund and Bayern Munich (who could sell 49.999% of their shares and raise up to £200 million in the process), would be forced by some mechanism to place a proportion of that money in a fund which would then be redistributed to the smaller clubs. How the German football authorities want to go about doing this is another matter. Of course the consequence of football officials in the Bundesliga trying to impose all these conditions and restrictions on any club that wants to go public is to make football clubs a less attractive investment. Obviously people who are looking to invest or companies that are planning to invest in clubs are less likely to do so if regulatory restrictions are imposed. Investors will have no voting rights, and so there seems to be a less sympathetic mood towards going public. This has prompted the head of the Bundesliga (who was also the president of Stuttgart) to say that he did not think that going public at the moment was the right thing for football clubs to do. I cannot imagine the head of the Football League or the Premier League in England or Scotland making a statement like that but it shows you the level of concern in Germany. Bayern Munich have now stated in public that they do not intend to go public at the moment because their thinking is 'if it ain't broke, don't fix it'. The club is doing well. Their reasoning is that if they went public and accepted all the reforms, in a way they would be out of a job because they will then be little more than minders for the company and would lose the power that they have now. Uli Hoeness is the general manager at Bayern Munich but would not be able to make the decisions he does now if he was answerable to the shareholders. At the moment he is only answerable to the members and in most cases the incumbent management can get through what they want to do. At the moment, therefore, there is little incentive to change.

In the summer of 1999 Hertha Berlin announced that they intended to go public subject to the approval of the members. But the way they are going about managing the process is not to launch a public limited company in the normal German sense or in the British sense, but to use a type of company only occasionally used in Germany (in fact there are only 22 such organisations), which is basically a combination of a partnership and a public company (*Kommanditgesellschaft auf Aktien* – KGaA). In this partnership, one of the partners can be a company that can sell shares to raise money for the club, but all the power and all the decision-making rights are held by the owner of the club, i.e. the sporting association. This is one model to get round the situation in which shareholders will be able to exercise too much influence, and it leaves Hertha Berlin with 100% control of the football club. The German FA recommend the club controls 75.7% of the shares; 75% is regarded as the key shareholding needed to push through any changes in the constitution of your club, as 50% plus one does not really leave clubs with enough protection. Also if a club needs to raise capital at any time, they need to sell shares and if a club only has 50% plus one it loses its majority straightaway and the power to get through any changes in the constitution. So whereas the original trend was to go to the stock exchange and go public by forming a plc (*Aktiengesell-schaft*), now the trend is not to go public or to form a private limited company (*Gesellschaft mit beschränkter Haftung*) but to form this 'third way' kind of company. There is a trend to look for alternatives to prevent undue shareholder influence over football clubs in Germany.

In terms of fan representation, I referred above to clubs taking on new structures so that they resemble plcs. This means they have a supervisory board alongside the managing board which exercises a control function on what the management board does. At German Second Division club St Pauli, the supervisory board has seven members and three of them are fan representatives elected by the membership. These officers are elected by the members of St Pauli at the general meeting, and are ordinary fan represen-tatives, not experienced politicians or anything like that. They are not in office to control the actions of the club management, but they do have a supervisory function. This basically means that the president of St Pauli is subject to the regulation of the supporters via the fan representatives on the supervisory board. At that particular club there is a fourth member on the supervisory board who supports most of the positions of the fans, which gives supporters' interests a majority on this supervisory board. This gives the supporters the power to block anything that the president wants to do if they believe it is against the interests of the club. If the president has to re-submit proposals to the supervisory board more than twice, the constitution requires there to be elections at the club. The supporters use it tactically in St Pauli. This is a unique situation in Germany where the fans have a high level of representation. The club has a very active fan organisation and they have been able to exert a strong influence at club general meetings. The meetings are only attended by about 250 people and so if they go along with 40 or 50 members, they do not have to win over a lot of members to gain a majority of that meeting.

It is a different situation at Schalke 04. We have a supervisory board with 11 members and only one fan representative on it, who is the person who runs all the supporters' clubs at national level. For us to go along to a general meeting and try and win over the majority, we have to win 800 votes to get a fan representative elected. Even so, this is a possibility. I believe this does show, in Germany at least, the powers that fans can have and can exercise. St Pauli has attracted some criticism because the supporters' representatives on the board have gone beyond their remit by taking over functions that the managing board and the president have neglected. They have involved themselves in the operating side of the business, for example, by starting membership drives, which, strictly speaking, they are not allowed to. This has caused some in Germany to claim a fan takeover has taken place.

The fans feel the need to become more involved because they believe the club has been mismanaged. In the 1998–99 season the club spent almost the entire season just above the relegation spots of Division Two. The president hired a new manager with a good reputation to save the club from relegation, especially important because Germany only has two professional leagues – if a club gets relegated out of the Second Division it is in big trouble because all the lower leagues are run on an amateur basis. So they hired a well-known trainer to come and save them from relegation. Although many thought they were never really seriously in danger of relegation, the threat was there, so the new coach had a clause included in his contract promising him something in the region of £20,000 to £30,000 as a bonus if the club finished higher than tenth place at the end of the season. All season the club were never higher than tenth, apart from the last game of the season which they won 6–2, taking them up to ninth place! So the club were forced to spend another £30,000 on this bonus when they were really strapped for cash. It was amateurish decisions like this that the supporters at St Pauli felt were damaging the club's interests and so they are now using their place on the supervisory board to try and exert some form of control.

Postscript   As expected, Borussia Dortmund has announced its intention to go public. Contrary to all the previous expert opinion, the executive committee recommended the formation of a KGaA for the professional football department of the club. Only the merchandising side of the business has been earmarked for integration in a plc. The decision was taken by the members at a general meeting held on 28 November 1999. Owing to the lack of any organised supporter opposition, the proposal was accepted with just a handful of votes against. Bayern Munich continues to state that it has no intention of going public.

This chapter is derived from edited transcripts of a speech given to a conference on 'The Governace and Regulation of Professional Football' at Birkbeck College, University of London, 8 July 1999.

15. The struggle for democracy at FC Barcelona and the case for a European independent regulator of professional football

L'ELEFANT BLAU*

Throughout Europe football is changing. The expanded Champions League has had a marked effect on national leagues and competitions and has provoked serious concerns among many supporters. Many fans across Europe feel that the destiny of their clubs is guided more and more by the financial rewards available to them via participation in lucrative competitions. Massive increases in revenue from television coverage has reduced the reliance of many football clubs on their supporters for the major part of their income, and as a consequence many supporters feel alienated from their clubs. L'Elefant Blau is a non-profit association of members and supporters of FC Barcelona working to ensure that the historical democracy of the club is maintained along with the club's traditions of ownership by the local community and strong identification with that community.[1]

FC Barcelona is a prime example of a club in transition caused by the changes mentioned above. The club's traditions of ownership by its members are increasingly under threat from those seeking to exploit global economic forces. Television revenue is increasingly important to the club's finances. Players' wages have increased at an incredible rate throughout the 1990s and the subscriptions of club members have become significantly less important to the club during that time. Sponsorship of the club shirt was even considered for the first time in the club's 100-year history in 1999. L'Elefant Blau recognises the benefits brought by the increased money in the game but campaigns to ensure that, at the same time, the members' democratic rights are upheld. Through such campaigns, our organisation has become a centre of control and opposition to the management of FC Barcelona under the presidency of Josep Lluis Núñez.

Núñez has held on to the presidency of FC Barcelona for 21 years and during this time has tried to radically alter the constitution of the club. At the time of writing, the club is still a non-profit association, but this traditional constitution is in danger. We remain a non-profit association because

---

* The contributors to this chapter were Armand Carabén, Alfons Godall and Joan Laporta.

of the loyalty of our members and the citizens of Catalonia. Núñez has tried to manipulate and diminish the role of the members in the management of the club. His application to convert the club to a plc was done in a manipulative way and without the consent of a majority of the members. But he has managed to hold on to his position for so long because he has sought support from powerful interests. L'Elefant Blau campaigns for the open, democratic management of the club on behalf of those members that Núñez tries to ignore and manipulate. The members do not elect delegates at the club's general meeting. This is another aspect of the constitution that we would like to reform. L'Elefant Blau believes FC Barcelona needs more democratic rights otherwise the club will be ruled by people and directors who will only ever regard the club as a profit-making business.

The club has 100,000 members. On 27 July 1997 there were elections for the presidency. Núñez won by 25,000 votes against 5,000 votes for the other candidate. Yet when he tried to convert the club to a plc L'Elefant Blau organised a vote of censure; only seven months after the presidential election he gained the same level of support, 25,000 members voting for him, but this time 15,000 members voted for the L'Elefant Blau censure. We believe this demonstrates significant opposition to the president when the active participation of the members of the club in elections is encouraged. Núñez had no more support to rally, yet, once mobilised, significant opposition to him emerged.

Núñez controls the membership list, and invokes secrecy laws and privacy laws in Catalonia to prevent other members of the club gaining access to the list. He spends each of his terms of office currying favour with certain influential members. The whole of the membership cannot go along to the council which elects directors and, as with any elections, there is always a limit on the number of people who actually bother to vote. L'Elefant Blau members are ordinary people who are members of the club, yet are not allowed access to the membership list, and so are at an obvious disadvantage when campaigning against a president with the wealth and influence of Mr Núñez. To move a censure vote you must have 6,000 signatures. In order to obtain enough members' signatures we had to sit at a table on Las Ramblas, Barcelona's main thoroughfare, for a week and sign people up to petition the club. L'Elefant Blau believes there is no doubt of the opposition to Núñez, but it can be difficult to mobilise support as people think that there is no point in a campaign against him. That's why L'Elefant Blau is proud to be friends with supporters' groups all over Europe, who, as the Manchester United supporters have shown, can organise to oppose plans they believe to be against the best interests of their clubs.

FC Barcelona is in the hands of a kind of mafia, who are only interested in the club as a commodity. Football and FC Barcelona are a way of life for many Catalans. It is this tribal spirit that is so important to football. Without it, football means nothing. Businesspeople like Rupert Murdoch will kill football if they continue to direct its development. Football needs to maintain its local and tribal links if it is to survive. At the moment, however, our club is financing the Netherlands national team and their European Championship ambitions.

We believe that FC Barcelona should be careful about having so many foreign players in the club. Of course, the club has always had players from all over Europe, but it is possible that the fans will not identify with the club any more if the team lacks local players. L'Elefant Blau is not xenophobic, but there are problems here. It is important for any football club to develop home-grown talent for its long-term future – for the benefit of the club and the local community. There are also mysterious business deals around the sale and transfer of foreign players; we have evidence that the club paid more for one player than they publicly declared. It can be difficult to prove financial wrongdoings when there are offshore companies involved, but we see that there is a lot of money flowing out of the club in a not-always-transparent way. This is damaging to the future of the club, and this again is a general point, as Gordon Taylor argues elsewhere in this book.

The experiences of L'Elefant Blau have led us to believe that the creation of an independent, European-wide regulator of professional football is vital to safeguard clubs from irresponsible officials. The traditions of the game are at serious risk of erosion. Such a regulator should establish European-wide rules that apply to all football clubs. It should set standards of financial propriety and act as a watchdog over television deals, sponsorship and merchandising. The regulator should ensure that any club board of directors which fails to meet these standards receives substantial sanctions. It should also work to ensure the rights of democratic members at clubs where such a constitution exists.

L'Elefant Blau believes that a European independent regulator could be an important force in protecting football from predatory business interests. The regulator should not be anti-business, but should seek to accommodate the business side of football with the game's social, cultural and sporting traditions. Thus rules should be drawn up that prevent clubs from embarking on risky financial strategies that jeopardise an important community asset.

L'Elefant Blau will be pleased to develop links with sister supporter associations in other European countries where business interests have threatened the special nature of their clubs. There is a growing feeling among fans across Europe that collective action needs to be taken to protect the game we love. Thus, L'Elefant Blau would propose the creation of a European Association of Football Supporters that would act as a lobby group to defend the interests of supporters and their clubs and communities. This lobby would seek to include as many supporter groups across Europe as possible, and would establish a central secretariat and headquarters, with branches in every country. L'Elefant Blau believes that one of the first campaigns of such an organisation should be to prepare a manifesto addressed to the European Commission proposing the above-mentioned independent European-wide regulator of professional football.

Fans across Europe have drawn a line in the sand. The game belongs to all of us, and with collective action we can still reclaim the people's game.

PART V

FINANCING AND ACCOUNTING FOR CLUBS

16. The financial performance of football stocks
NIGEL HAWKINS

In recent years, many football clubs have floated on the London stock exchange; 21 clubs have either a full listing or were quoted on the Alternative Investment Market (AIM). In many cases, substantial funds have been raised, some of which have been used, together with money from the Football Trust, to modernise grounds, which the Taylor Report concluded was a real priority following the Hillsborough tragedy. In total, the 21 clubs are worth around £1.2 billion – a relatively small sum compared with the £93 billion valuation currently placed on British Telecom. Indeed, around half the football sector's entire value is accounted for by Manchester United.

Football shares have not performed particularly well over the last 18 months. Investors have been most concerned about the big increases in players' wages, which average 30% per year. Moreover, the progress in developing pay-per-view television has been slower than some investors had expected and has certainly fallen well short of the aggressive financial expectations that had been built up. Nonetheless, after the expiry of the BSkyB Premier League contract in 2001, pay-per-view television is likely to become increasingly important.

Relegation worries for some of the lesser lights of the Premier League also concern investors. Bolton saw the shares of its parent company fall by a third once relegation was confirmed at the end of the 1997–98 season. A similar trend was identifiable when Sheffield United were relegated in 1997.

For the more discerning investor in football stocks, there are several key issues to consider. First, the underlying level of operating profits is crucial. Consequently, gate receipts and attendance levels are very relevant. Secondly, television revenues are central, especially for Premier League clubs, which receive an average £8 million per year from the existing BSkyB contract. Analysts study carefully the annual cash flow of each quoted club, which should give a guide to future prospects. However, takeover prospects in the sector – and the accompanying likely share price rises – have been dimmed somewhat by the government's banning in 1999 of the proposed BSkyB acquisition of Manchester United.

In hindsight, much of the stockmarket glamour for the football sector faded after the Newcastle United flotation, which was generally seen as having been over-priced. One exception, though, is Manchester United, which is in a different class off the pitch – with a turnover now well in excess of £100 million. In fact, investors are increasingly focusing on the relatively few clubs which can guarantee attendances of over 35,000 for each home league match. Celtic, for example, with a stadium capacity of 60,000, has no problem in meeting this target.

Nevertheless, despite the boom in television revenues for Premier League clubs, real concern remains about the level of player wage increases, especially for those clubs with low gates. Consequently, the gap between the élite and the remainder is likely to widen. The prospects for clubs outside the élite members of the Premier League are, in some cases, rather grim. Even so, some clubs, which are currently unquoted, are pondering whether or not to seek a quotation. Moreover, within Europe, there are further moves, notably in Germany, to float some of the more successful clubs.[1]

In conclusion, it is apparent that the overall performance of football clubs is partly about the financial performance of the club and partly about footballing performance. These two areas are linked, but in a complex way. Injecting cash into clubs can help improve performance on the field without improving the club's immediate financial performance. In the medium to long term, better performance on the field is likely to improve financial performance. As the other contributions to this part of the book argue, good financial management is as essential to the economic future of the club as good football management is to a club's ability to win titles and cups.

All in all, the sector has provided excitement for investors off the field as well as on it – even if the financial returns have fallen short of some expectations.

17. Playing in a different league

TONY DART

There is widespread recognition that football has become increasingly commercialised over the past 30 years. The signs are there for all to see in terms of inflated ticket prices, escalating players' wages and increased transfer values. However, it would be wrong to conclude that just because prices, wages and transfer fees have gone up, those involved in supporting and running the game are *necessarily* worse off in real terms. This may well be the case, but in order to give a definite answer to this question it is necessary to look at the facts and figures regarding price and wage increases in football, and ask three interrelated questions. Firstly, if prices have gone up by more than the general rate of inflation, does this mean that supporters are worse off, or could it be that they are actually paying more because they are getting more in terms of quality of play, entertainment value and facilities at the ground? Secondly, given that the turnover of football clubs has increased dramatically and football has emerged as a significant industry in its own right, are clubs being managed (off the field) in a professional and efficient way that offers supporters value for money? And, finally, are the assets of football clubs – in particular, the players – properly accounted for in balance-sheets, or are clubs undervaluing themselves? These questions take on particular importance at this time as the government's Football Task Force is investigating the escalating cost of ticket prices and UEFA is considering imposing payroll or salary caps. Moreover, ownership structures are changing as a number of clubs have floated on the stockmarket and adopted plc status. At the same time, the government has recently announced a package of support to help supporters form shareholder trusts in order to give the fans a bigger say in how their clubs are run.

FOOTBALL INFLATION: TICKET PRICES, WAGES AND TRANSFER FEES

There is a popular perception that football has become more expensive over the years but is that impression actually true? Table 1 looks at changes over the past 30 years in three factors: ticket prices, players' wages and transfer fees. The data tell a story that will be familiar to many football supporters. First of all, it is evident that the actual costs of all three factors have increased much faster than general price levels. A ticket for an old

First Division match cost 2/6d in the 1960s. The average you would expect to pay for a Premiership match now is around £25 – a 200-fold increase. Also in the early 1960s, players' wages were capped at £20 per week (and many players were on £16 per week in season and £14 per week out of season). Now some top players can take home £20,000 per week or even more – a 1,000-fold increase. Manchester United won the European Cup in 1968 and its successor in 1999. The 1968 team had a transfer value of £110,000, while the 1999 team was worth £36.5 million – an increase of 330 times.

To put these increases into perspective, they must be compared with the general rate of price inflation. The general index of retail prices (the RPI index) rose by a factor of 9.6 (almost 10 times) between 1968 and the end of 1998, so all the increases quoted above must be divided by 10 – but this still means that in real terms football ticket prices alone have risen by at least 20 times.

1960 TO 2000: INFLATION?

	1960s	1990s	FACTOR
● Top-division game: price to spectator	2/6d	£25	200
● Top-division player: weekly earnings	£20	£20,000	1000
● Transfer values: (Man Utd 1968 and 1999)	£110,000	£36.5m	330
● Year end RPI ratio: (1968–98)			10

Table 1: Escalating Costs

VALUE FOR MONEY?
Given that the price of football has risen so sharply – has the value done the same? Management accountants try and answer this question by carrying out value-for-money (VFM) assessments – but there are some peculiar problems in applying these to football clubs. To begin with, VFM analysis makes implicit assumptions about the motivation of those running clubs and assumes that they are following some form of strategy

designed to realise their objectives. In particular, VFM assessments are undertaken on the assumption that owners and managers of clubs are rational in the sense that they have clearly defined objectives, such as profit maximisation and a management strategy designed to deliver those objectives. The problem is that football is not like any other business in that financial performance may be considered secondary to performance on the pitch. Many owners and managers of football clubs have multiple objectives, such as winning titles and trophies *and* making money, where the former may take precedence. Often these different objectives conflict, and often they are not linked by a coherent strategy. Instead, the business side of the club is run and managed separately from its football side. Moreover, customers (supporters) may continue to support their club even when the product provided is substandard. As a result there are only weak constraints on financial managers to manage well.

Despite the problems of weighing up the relative value of a football club's performance on and off the field, I would argue that VFM appraisals of football management can and should be used to assess four aspects of a club's performance: economy, efficiency, effectiveness and equity. Here, *economy* refers to the *price* of resources, such as wages, transfers, stadiums and merchandise. *Efficiency* looks at how *much* was produced by those resources, in terms of say, number of wins, profits, seat occupancy, sales and TV broadcasting. *Effectiveness* is concerned with how *many* targets were attained, such as promotion, trophies, share price and 'glory'. And equity looks at how fairly the rewards were shared and who gained most benefit, club or fans.

In terms of *economy*, we've already seen that prices and wages in football have increased much faster than the general rate of inflation. In short, it is clear that there has been a dramatic increase in the amount of economic resources going into football. However, the question remains as to whether this 20-fold increase in resources has been accompanied by increased value for money in terms of improved efficiency and effectiveness. In addition, it remains to be seen whether the increase in resources has been equally distributed or whether there have been clear winners and losers.

The *efficiency* and *effectiveness* of football are strongly influenced by the fact that most clubs are 'accidental businesses' – social outfits which incorporated only for their own protection – characterised by closed share-holdings and often undervalued property assets. Shortcomings in management are all too obvious in many clubs. These failures are all the more remarkable in an industry where customer loyalty is so strong that supporters will turn up to buy tickets and merchandise even when the club is performing badly. Indeed, there are many instances in football where the customers – the supporters – have bailed out their club financially rather than see it go to the wall. Despite the goodwill of supporters, the failure of many clubs to be run efficiently and effectively can be gleaned from a variety of indicators. For example, some clubs have failed by simple neglect of cash flow; others did not maintain basic safety standards; still others fell victim to property development and were forced into homelessness or even extinction. Supporters are all too often neglected. Trading in players is favoured over longer-term investments in ground improvements and holding the line on ticket prices. The balance-sheets of clubs often fail to capture fully the true value of the club (these accounting issues or balance-sheet valuations are discussed below) making clubs vulnerable to takeover and asset-stripping.

Notwithstanding these examples of the 'accidental business', financial mismanagement and neglect of their customer base, a few clubs have become enormously successful, with the result that the gap between rich and poor is yawningly wide and the competitiveness of the game may be weakened. Professional football in England has become a significant industry, with an annual turnover of over £800 million, but overall returns are low and very skewed towards a small number of major clubs.

This brings us on to the last factor determining value for money – *equity*. Who has gained from the enormous increase in revenue flowing into the game: owners, supporters, players? The benefits from increased resources are clearly not distributed evenly across the clubs or among the different stakeholders – owners, players, supporters, shareholders. In terms of the clubs, there has been a trend towards growing inequality. The top five Premier League clubs now earn more than all the Football League clubs combined and the biggest club in terms of assets – Manchester United – can earn more on one match day than some Football League clubs take in a year. In terms of the stakeholders, the largest increase in resources has gone to the players, who have been able to capture most of the increased income from higher ticket prices and income from TV broadcasting revenue. Players' true salaries have increased 100-fold over the last 30 years. In contrast, supporters have faced a 20-fold increase in the real cost of supporting their clubs. Football is certainly no longer the working man's sport it once was, but has moved sharply upmarket. The rich–poor divide is continuing to widen. The Taylor Report, the Football Trust and the Football Task Force have all brought about some sharing of benefit in the form of improvements in spectator safety and comfort, and a number of clubs have invested in completely new multi-purpose stadiums. However, it must be remembered that many of these improvements were financed by public money distributed via the Football Trust in order to allow clubs to implement the Lord Justice Taylor's recommendations regarding safety. Moreover, notwithstanding these improvements in the quality of facilities at the grounds, it seems unlikely that all of the increase in ticket prices has been matched by increased value, not least because, given a choice, some supporters would prefer to stand on the terraces (and many still insist on standing *in front of* their seats). In addition, similar improvements in facilities – in terms of sound quality, screen quality, seating and refreshments – have occurred at cinemas throughout the country for a relatively modest increase in ticket prices.

ARE FOOTBALL CLUBS PROPERLY VALUED?

If football is to be managed efficiently and effectively it is crucial that all aspects of a club's assets are properly recorded. This raises questions about how we should value players' contracts and transfer fees; how we should value home-grown players for whom no transfer fee has been paid; and how we should value the goodwill of the fans who may be crucial to the economic performance of the club. Accounting procedures allow companies to record monetary values for intangible assets, intellectual capital and goodwill. The issue of the balance-sheet recognition of players' contracts is a fascinating one. Does one really see (for example) Mr Vinnie Jones as an *intangible asset*? Or as *intellectual capital*? And does he exhibit *goodwill*? If you recognise the contracts of players, should you include other valuable contracted staff, such as the team manager? How should players be depreciated? Are football managements anywhere near sophisticated enough to understand the concept of a transfer fee as 'the *expected net present value* of future income to the club'? And should there be a corresponding liability for contractual pay? New accounting rules such as FRS 10 may help to give more accurate balance-sheet valuations of clubs – but, as a management accountant, I can see that they also bring new snags and problems. By far the most interesting problem is the anomaly of the home-grown player, who, having incurred no fee, does not appear in the balance-sheet. While this may make strict accounting sense under FRS 10, does it make management sense? Who could be worth more as a player: Dwight Yorke or David Beckham? But who would appear more valuable in a balance-sheet? Does discounting the value of home-grown players not conflict with the aim of youth training, for example through football academies? And will it tend to favour expensive foreign players over British talent?

Figures 1 and 2 illustrate this anomaly, using the team pages of two original Manchester United programmes. Figure 1 shows the Busby Babes team in January 1958. What would those players be worth in the balance-

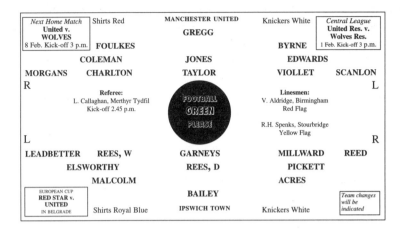

Figure 1: 25 January 1958

sheet today? £40 million? £50 million? Actually, they would appear to be 'worth' very little – the Busby Babes were home grown as a matter of policy. Figure 2 shows the team pages for the next home game played, on 19 February 1958. They look very different – in fact, the players' names are handwritten, because this was the first appearance after the Munich air disaster and the team was decided only at a late stage. Of course, this is a sad moment in history, but there is an important point that is relevant. Under FRS 10, had it existed in 1958, the players would not have been 'valued'. But their life assurance payments, being cash, would appear as assets. Similarly, any new player (such as Ernie Taylor) bought in to

Next Home Match United v. NOTTS. FOR 28 Feb. Kick-off 8 p.m.	Shirts Red	MANCHESTER UNITED	Knickers White	Youth International Match ENGLAND v. GERMANY Wednesday 18 March. Kick-off 7.30 p.m.
		Gregg		
	Foulkes		*Greaves*	
	Goodwin	*Cope*	*Crowther*	
R	*Webster* *Taylor (E)*	*Dawson*	*Pearson* *Brennan*	L
	Referee: A. Bond, London Kick-off 7.30 p.m.		Linesmen: F. Wain, Bakewell Red Flag / F.F. Clarke, Coventry Yellow Flag	
L				R
	FINNEY *Cargill* FROGGATT	~~SHINER~~ *Johnson*	QUIXALL WILKINSON	
	O'DONNELL	SWAN	KAY	
	Baker JOHNSON		MARTIN	
Team changes will be indicated by loudspeaker		RYALLS		Team changes will be indicated by loudspeaker
	Shirts Blue & White Stripes	SHEFFIELD WEDNESDAY	Knickers Black	

Figure 2: 19 February 1958

strengthen the team, would appear at transfer valuation. So the club might have lost a team – but its balance-sheet valuation would be *increased*. There's certainly a plot for a thriller in all this but does it aid management decision-making? And does it give true and fair guidance to investors and other stakeholders? We all know that any club's balance-sheet should be treated with care – this example illustrates how inappropriate accounting conventions can obscure the true financial position of a club. Recent developments in football and broadcasting illustrate that there is an urgent need to find answers to these questions. Until all the assets of a club are properly taken account of, football clubs run the risk of undervaluing themselves and becoming takeover targets for firms trying to purchase the clubs' assets on the cheap.[1]

POST-MATCH ANALYSIS AND CONCLUSION

There is no doubt that the resources flowing into football have increased dramatically over the past 30 years. Over this period the real price of football has increased at least 20-fold. This increase has been paid by the supporters, which begs the question: are they receiving a product that is 20 times better value today than it was in the 1960s? Both from the perspective of the match-going supporter and the management accountant's value-for-money analysis, the answer to this question would appear to be no. VFM analysis indicates not only that things do not appear to have got 20 times better, but also that there are serious weaknesses in the way many clubs are run. These include failures in business management and a tendency for clubs to undervalue their own assets. In addition, the gains from increased resources have been distributed very unevenly across clubs and stakeholders. Clearly there is a need to improve the management and accounting practices of many clubs and to ensure that gains are more evenly distributed across clubs and stakeholders. A first step to achieving this goal is for clubs to recognise the true value of all their assets, including the goodwill of their supporters.

18. Football club balance-sheets: fact or fantasy?
LEE MANNING

Much has been made in recent years about the influx of vast sums of money into the football industry. Stadiums have been modernised, transfer fees and players' wages have rocketed, and individual club owners have made millions by floating their clubs on the stock exchange. It is also the case that through the trend for many clubs to float on the stockmarket, a long overdue modernisation of football club financial practices has commenced. However, it is important to remember that while it is indeed the case that many clubs have started to modernise, the overall picture is distinctly patchy. The reason for this is very simple: buying a football club is not just like buying any other asset – it is in large part about emotion, and this blinds owners to the true value of their assets, and to what they can realistically spend. In this chapter I draw on my experience as a professional insolvency practitioner who has been involved in administrations at a number of clubs to present an alternative picture of the state of football clubs' finance. I want to illustrate that the peculiar nature of football clubs as tradable assets means that the clubs present special challenges if their finances are to be managed effectively.

THE STRANGE CASE OF CRYSTAL PALACE
The first point I would make is that a lot of what you see in football clubs' balance-sheets is meaningless. The reason why it is meaningless is because, to an even greater extent than a house, a football club is worth what someone is willing to pay for it. If you look at the 'market' values of football clubs and you consider their earnings, there is a stark contrast between notional value and true earnings. English professional football made a loss of £32.5 million in 1997–98. The Premier League and First Division clubs paid dividends of £8.7 million on a combined turnover of £744.5 million. From a straight business point of view this is an extremely mediocre performance: it does not make sense from a return-on-investment perspective.

The distorted reality which many clubs' financial statements demonstrate is very clearly illustrated by the case of the financial collapse of Crystal Palace FC. Mark Goldberg sold his information technology recruitment business for approximately £24 million. Suddenly he is a cash-rich man. He has been a Crystal Palace fan all his life and decides that he wants to fulfil his lifelong passion by buying the club. He approaches the owner of Crystal Palace, Ron Noades, who is an astute businessman. Mr Noades values the club at £25 million. They negotiate and arrive at a figure of £23 million. Mark Goldberg proposes that, as he already has £24 million he will give Mr Noades £23 million, £19 million up front together with a loan from Mr Noades of £4 million, enabling Mr Goldberg to retain the use of £5 million of cash, of which £1 million is his own.

Mark Goldberg's business advisors were appalled at the price he was prepared to pay for the club. Crystal Palace had just been relegated from the Premier League, with all the negative revenue implications that came in train with that. As is always the case with relegated clubs, there was no certain prospect of returning quickly to the top flight especially if there are no significant funds available to purchase and reward new players. In addition, excluded from the £23 million price tag was the club's freehold stadium at Selhurst Park in south London, ownership of which was retained by Ron Noades. That posed the question: what in fact was Mark Goldberg actually acquiring?

Goldberg believed that by having the appropriate coaching and management team with an exemplary record on the field he could secure a rapid return to the Premier League and be able to generate dramatically increased revenues from supporters enthused by the on-the-field success. The man he turned to was Terry Venables, former manager of Tottenham Hotspur and the England national team. Goldberg was prepared to offer extraordinary financial terms to get what he felt he needed, terms which raise serious questions about his business judgement once he entered the emotionally charged arena of football. For example, it is reported he paid Venables £130,000, in the first instance, just for the privilege of engaging in preliminary talks with him. Indeed, perhaps Mark Goldberg's biggest mistake was interfering so much with the day-to-day running of the club himself. Venables signed a four-year contract worth over £1.1 million per year and a number of expensive but not necessarily high-profile players were signed.

The consequences of Goldberg's actions soon became apparent. Within eight months of acquiring Crystal Palace the club had gone into administration[1] amidst a colossal financial crisis. The money that he paid for Crystal Palace went straight to Ron Noades. As the club owner and a businessman, Mr Noades was perfectly entitled to do this. Many supporters were not sufficiently astute to appreciate that virtually all of Mark Goldberg's fortune had been used to acquire Ron Noades' shares, which was of no direct benefit to the club's finances. Unrealistic expectations were raised regarding pending star-player purchases. In the period before the collapse, Terry Venables took up his position as team manager receiving £750,000 in cash up-front, a house and a Mercedes as part of a generous remuneration package. He signed a number of players from Australia and the Far East where he had experience as the manager of the Australian national team manager. The players were paid very large salaries, but were signed on very low transfer fees. It has been suggested that the reason for this was because, as an efficiency incentive exercise, Terry Venables was paid a percentage of any transfer money he did not spend. Rapidly the club's finances spun into disarray. Gates dropped from an average 23,000 to about 15,000 as supporters became disillusioned by poor results. It soon became apparent that Terry Venables did not have the heart for a First Division promotion struggle of this nature and the team's on-field performances were mediocre. Any chance of promotion to the Premiership receded. Then the club quickly began to run up arrears to PAYE, VAT and other trade creditors, which it financed through borrowing, until the whole business imploded.

The problem was that Mark Goldberg was chasing a dream. But he did not have quality in this organisation to help him implement that dream, and to help him guard against his heart when making critical financial commitments which overvalued assets. The saga at Palace has yet to be resolved and as of December 1999 the club's future remains uncertain.

MILLWALL: SPEND, SPEND, SPEND

Another classic example of how not to manage a club's finances is the case of Millwall. In November 1995, Millwall, the third football club to float on the stock exchange after Tottenham Hotspur and Manchester United, were riding high at the top of the First Division with promotion to the Premier League a realistic possibility. At that time they could realistically expect to generate, through gate money, season-ticket sales and TV revenues, approximately £2.5 million per annum. By winning promotion to the Premier League they estimated they could triple their turnover to £7.5 million. At this point the club board of directors decided to take an enormous gamble. They signed on loan two Russian internationals, Sergei Yuran and Vassili Kulkov. Yuran had scored a winning goal for Benfica knocking Arsenal out of the Champions League in a previous season. Both players received £150,000 each just to sign, together with a favourable monthly salary package. In addition, a number of other domestic players were signed. The club, which had always prided itself on its exemplary success in the transfer market, could really not afford this, but took a gamble and borrowed additional funds to cover its outlay, backed by a personal guarantee by the chairman. He was also the chairman of a very large advertising agency and one of the most respected and successful executives in that industry.

The gamble failed. The two Russians turned out to be unfit and disruptive. Of the 32 matches following their signing Millwall won only four and were in fact relegated to the Second Division at the end of the season. So facing the 1996–97 season, from bringing in £2.5 million, and investing in expectation of receiving £7.5 million in the Premier League, they were now facing an annual revenue of £1.25 million; but with the same cost base as a club playing in a division above. Millwall were facing financial disaster.

The club was able to get through the first six months of the 1996–97 season by spending the revenue from one-off seasonal income from season-ticket sales, executive boxes and so on; plus they sold a number of their best players – Kasey Keller to Leicester and Alex Rae to Sunderland – which managed to cover the £3 million operating loss for the first six months. A ray of hope emerged in November 1996 when they briefly topped the table and a swift return to the First Division seemed a real possibility. Then they lost their next seven games, were eliminated from the FA Cup by non-league Woking Town, and were knocked out of the Auto Windscreens Shield by Colchester. The possibility of any income-generating cup run was thus extinguished. At this point the club owed £750,000 VAT and slightly less to the Inland Revenue. Their bank overdraft facility was at its full limit. They had already mortgaged their ground to another bank, and had substantial equipment and motor vehicle leasing commitments. No financial institution was prepared to lend them any more money. The result was that they went into administration, a job which was carried out by Buchler Phillips.

INSOLVENCY, CVA AND 'FOOTBALL CREDITORS'
There are parallels between the way that Millwall and Crystal Palace imploded. Heart ruling head played a large part in both situations. At least because Millwall was a public limited company (plc) there was an escape route for investors, in that it is far easier to raise new capital with a fully quoted company than for a private business. The situation at Crystal Palace was and is far worse.

Crystal Palace, in financial terms, has nothing to offer and in fact resembles a financial black hole. It has now spent all its reserves and had borrowed in full against the next season's TV revenue; it does not own its own ground so it cannot borrow against the value of that asset; it has cannibalised its future revenue streams to such an extent that, for example, it has sold back the catering rights at the ground to Ron Noades for the next ten years. The club's only income is from season-ticket sales and regular gate money, plus small amounts of sponsorship. Yet they retained players who are on wages of up to £12,000 a week in Division One. A number of their players were on £5,000 to £6,000 a week. So, in terms of wages alone, the club is haemorrhaging cash to the tune of £2 million to £3 million a year.

The conventional way to approach a situation like this is to secure the protection of the insolvency process. A meeting of the creditors is called and what is known as a CVA is executed. This means that the administrator offers the creditors whatever percentage of what they are owed is available. Once this process is complete the administrator can then begin the process of hiving off whatever healthy parts of the old business remain, ridden of the unprofitable baggage. This process is complicated in the context of football clubs by the concept that is known as 'football creditors'.

The football creditor is a wonderful concept that was created out of the best of intentions by the Football League and the other regulatory authorities including the PFA to protect menber club interests. It basically means that where any football club becomes insolvent, for the club to retain its league membership those persons defined as 'football creditors' must be paid in full eventually by the defaulting company. This is a rule which goes beyond the definitions of what is a special category of creditor – as defined by the Insolvency Act or the Companies Acts. The special category of creditor places a very heavy burden on any financial rescue of an insolvent football club.

In total this did not present too great a problem with the administration at Millwall in 1997. The club owed £4.2 million to preferential and secured creditors. They had approximately £7 million of unsecured creditors so if you were going to offer them 10p in the pound you would have to offer them £700,000. They did have assets which they could potentially sell to pay off the secure creditors, but they needed another £2.5 million to settle with their banks. In total Millwall needed to find approximately £4.9 million, if this were a conventional CVA situation.

But unfortunately the football-creditor rule imposes an additional burden on the CVA situation. It covers debts to any existing or former player; any member club of the English and Scottish football leagues from the Premier League downwards; any manager on a player's contract; any debts to the Football Trust, to the Football League, the PFA; and any debts to European clubs (though this latter condition has proved to be something of a financial grey area). Unless these debts are paid in full, not necessarily on the first day of the CVA but paid in full nonetheless at some stage, the club in question loses its league status. As league status is one of the main (if not *the* main) source of value of a club, this imposes a very heavy sanction against not treating football creditors as preferential creditors, and thus increases the cost of any financial reconstruction of the insolvent club, greatly complicating the rescue process.

When Barnet were in administration they had football creditors of around £200,000. This was a comparatively small amount of money and was capable of being dealt with over approximately two years. Millwall, on the other hand, had football creditors of around £2 million; this included items such as player signing-on fees, unpaid transfer money and so on. So the administrators had to find an additional £2 million from a new investor to make the CVA work in a way that the club could retain its league status. Millwall own their ground and, as I have explained above, they needed to raise £4.9 million to make a settlement with all their secured and unsecured creditors; and a further £2 million to pay off the football creditors. So, for just under £7 million, Millwall as a business could wipe the slate clean and start again with a ground, team, and no creditors. Although in fact the total amount raised through a new share issue which brought in new investors was approximately £9.8 million, stock exchange rules required they also raise £2.5 million working capital as a listed company in order that they be allowed to continue to trade on the exchange. If they had been a private company the total bill for the CVA would have been £6.9 million.

Crystal Palace, on the other hand (before allowing for the question as to whether the European team creditors have a valid claim or not as football creditors), have between £5 million and £8 million potentially owed to football creditors. This places an enormous obstacle in the way of anybody considering trying to implement a successful CVA because of the sheer financial burden of having to take on these debts and pay them in full if the club is to retain its league status.

FOOTBALL'S FINANCIAL ASSETS – FANTASY FOOTBALL

What the Millwall and Crystal Palace stories illustrate in graphic detail is the fundamentally flimsy value of the asset base of most football clubs when these are exposed in the ultimate crisis situation. But such is the power of the romance of football that otherwise hard-headed businessmen completely overlook this central reality when considering the purchase of a club.

Crystal Palace does not own its ground; it has a lot of expensively contracted players; it has little reliable forward income (gate receipts, TV monies, merchandising sales – all are affected by performance on the pitch and ultimately promotion, relegation and the winning or losing of trophies); it has a potential £8 million in football creditors and another £2 million preferential creditors; it is not a marketable security because it is not a stock-exchange-traded share – so any purchaser of company shares has no readily available exit. But, despite this, Mark Goldberg was still prepared to pay £23 million for a company that arguably was worth nothing. In other words, he purchased goodwill, tradition and hope value, but with it a stream of trading losses. To compound matters, in trading terms, its situation had not changed all that dramatically since the previous June when he bought it – the club had already been relegated. So it was difficult for him to claim that he was the victim of some sudden surprising new information.

Millwall's ground cost £18 million to build. It is a modern, comfortable 22,000 all-seater stadium. Unfortunately, as the estate agents will tell you the world over, in property the three most important attributes are location, location and location. Millwall's New Den ground is in a deeply unfashionable part of south-east London. The club itself also suffers a reputation for hooliganism and football-related violence which is perhaps no longer deserved, but which still lingers in the public mind and has become the stuff of stand-up comedians' staple urban myths. So while the club have a licence to use the stadium for 32 outdoor events a year, it has been spectacularly unsuccessful in mounting any more than a handful of such events of a fairly low-publicity profile. Their most successful event to date was the World Marching Band Championship. People will travel to Wembley or Twickenham quite happily; but the 'intimidation' factor at Millwall has destroyed any prospect of it becoming a viable outdoor events venue in the foreseeable future. It is poorly serviced by public transport, has poor parking on dimly lit streets and negligible local catering facilities.

Millwall's New Den ground cost £18 million but who is really prepared to buy it? Realistically there was only one purchaser when Millwall collapsed, and that was currently groundless Wimbledon FC, who have been forced to ground-share with Crystal Palace. Blackheath rugby club, also based in south-east London, would find the stadium too large. Wimbledon in fact offered the administrators at Millwall £4 million for the ground; that was therefore its true worth because that was all anyone was prepared to pay for it.

Let us look at another example of the problem of valuing football club assets. Charlton Athletic's Valley ground, but not the club, was in receivership during the 1990–91 season. Charlton were ground-sharing at Crystal Palace. The club had spent approximately £3 million to modernise the ground to bring it up to Taylor Report standards. The obvious course of action with such a large inner-city site was to sell the land for development. But this was impossible. The lease on the land stipulated that not only was the land available only for the playing of sport, but this sport must be association football. Eventually, Charlton Athletic FC were able to buy the ground back for about £1 million, as a sale for development was impossible. This raises the key point that the worth of what is in a balance-sheet is dependent upon what you can do with it. Millwall's New Den, which cost £18 million when completed in 1993, had an unofficial forced sale value of £4.5 million when the club was in administration due to the absence of any purchasers.

The case of the valuation of players' contracts in the balance-sheet is another case of playing with mirrors. With the new accounting standards a club is obliged to amortise the cost of a player's transfer fee over the life of his contract. So if it is a £5 million fee the value of the player in the balance-sheet decreases by £1 million a year, roughly, over the life of the contract. Ironically, players who did not cost a fee therefore have no carrying value in a club's balance-sheet. But if a club is in financial crisis, like Crystal Palace, and it cannot pay its football creditors in full and in particular cannot pay its players' wages going forward, this has serious consequences. If clubs do not pay their players' wages on time the PFA could prevent a club from employing these players as the club is adjudged to be in breach of contract with its players. (This is why an administrator may be obliged to continue to pay all the players in full at a football club when in a conventional business administration there would have been no financial justification for doing so.) Automatically, if a club breaches a player's contract without his consent then that player becomes a free agent and can leave the club without the club receiving any compensation. In this context the balance-sheet carrying value of players' contracts becomes meaningless.

Similarly, where a club is in distress the capitalised value of its players' contracts to some extent is meaningless because, firstly, the value of the contract depends on what another club is prepared to pay to buy it out, which depends on the player's form, and the perceived desperation of the selling club, regardless of any hypothetical amortised value. And, secondly, if you are a potential purchaser and you know that a club is in distress and they have a player who originally cost them, for example £5 million, but they cannot afford to pay him and in two weeks' time they are going to lose him altogether because they will be in breach of contract, you are going to be in a very strong bargaining position and will come in with a fairly low offer for that player.

CASH IS KING

What clubs should really concentrate on is not hypothetical values in the balance-sheet, but what is happening with their cash-flow. You have to have professional management and a hard-headed business assessment, not management based on an inflated view of assets based on emotion. Both Millwall and Crystal Palace hit the financial wall sprinting. Management had lost all sense of financial reality and may have kept on spending on gambles until creditor pressure got the better of them.

Michael Knighton, owner of Carlisle, argues that there is no way his club can make a profit purely out of attracting spectators and their spending power to the club. The club needs an ancillary revenue arm and for Carlisle that arm is its role as what Knighton terms 'a football farm'. Carlisle breeds players for sale to bigger clubs and that is how they make a profit and have done so successfully for a number of years. Over the years that is exactly how most clubs outside the Premier League, and often some in the Premier League like Wimbledon for example, made their profit. Wimbledon are the only club in the Premier League who have had a net transfer fee income in the last five or six years. Newcastle had net expenditure on players between 1993–94 and 1997–98 of £45.6 million, closely followed by Liverpool with around £33.7 million net outlay on players. Manchester United had only spent approximately £13.5 million net over the same period, which is another good indication of how well they are managed as a business.

But, to return to my central point, what this illustrates yet again is how balance-sheets really are not that meaningful as guides to the financial health of football clubs. What will help a club survive is not attempts to build up the balance-sheet through inflated player and stadium valuations, but recruiting professional management who understand the importance of controlling a club's cash-flow and who do not just think about revenues; who control costs but recognise that clubs need ancillary sources of income other than just match-day-related income. The necessity to control costs is nowhere better illustrated than by the fact that virtually all the operating profit of Premier League clubs is immediately spent on buying players, often from abroad, on very expensive contracts. However, the knock-on effect is that because the Premier League clubs are no longer buying from lower-division English clubs, an important source of revenue is lost to these clubs, thus hastening the day when some of them will collapse.

CONCLUSION

I have to say that on the basis of my experience, I am not optimistic that more than a few football clubs can ever be truly profitable in the sense that we expect conventional businesses to be. So, if anybody asked me for advice about investing in a football club, I would have to tell them not to do it. If they asked me to advise about investing in a rugby club, I would refer them to a psychiatrist.

19. Business management issues

ROBERT MATUSIEWICZ

A review of professional football clubs reveals myriad management styles. Some clubs recognise that the multi-million-dollar football industry is complex and have appointed chief executives with an understanding of the issues involved in running a sophisticated leisure business. Others cling to the idea that 'football is different' and insist that usual business principles do not apply. This mistaken belief, held with varying degrees of self-delusion, is generally used to justify an archaic management style and a lack of understanding of the real issues facing football. I recall, for example, being advised by one football club chairman that, 'Unlike real business, in football having £1 million to spend allows you to buy a player for £2 million on the basis that the selling club would only require a down payment of 50%.' Having raised the question of the balance-sheet, I was told in all seriousness that that was next season's problem. Such views are no longer common but the fact they do still exist indicates the range of business sophistication.

The key management issue is understanding exactly what the business is and the environment in which it operates. This is, of course, no different from any other business. The real problem (and challenge) of the football industry is in coping with the rate of change, which is as rapid as in any high-tech industry. All-seater stadiums, Bosman, public ownership, telephone-number wage demands and transfer fees and an apparently insatiable appetite for the game by the world's TV companies – all are relatively recent developments. Is the business management of football clubs developing at the pace necessary to keep up with the increasingly sophisticated world of professional sport? What does the future hold for clubs that adapt (or fail to adapt) to the changing environment?

The environment in which professional football operates places a considerable strain on the ability of some clubs to survive in their current form. Even English Premiership clubs face an uncertain future if they ignore the consequences of current trends that have the potential to overwhelm their business. This chapter provides a brief overview of the nature of the football business, the emerging trends to be managed and how this translates into practical reality.

WHAT EXACTLY IS THE BUSINESS?

The answer to the question of what exactly the business is for football is that even for a club in the Third Division, it should be a multi-faceted leisure business with a range of income streams. Each income stream demands its own strategy and plan and should be co-ordinated to achieve the overall objectives of the business. The main business segments are:

Source	Revenues
Football team	Tickets and merchandising
	Development and sale of players
	Sponsorship and advertising
	Broadcasting rights
	Secondary spend
Premises	Conference facilities
Brands	Used to promote non-football goods, for example, credit cards, aftershave etc.

There is mutual dependency between the football and the commercial aspects of a club. Success on the pitch sells season-tickets and merchandise, providing of course that there is a well-run commercial operation to exploit the opportunities. A properly run business can increase the spending power available to a manager, which, if wisely used, should improve the success of the team.

THE EMERGING TRENDS

Having considered the business we now turn to the trends that clubs must recognise and take into account in managing their business strategies. In my view the most important are countering the pressures of short-termism; the globalisation of football; the implications (and wisdom) of stockmarket flotation; increasing solvency problems; the widening gap between clubs; and the continuing effects of the Bosman ruling. It will become apparent that these issues are linked and cannot be viewed in isolation.

COUNTERING SHORT-TERMISM

It is sometimes argued that there is a difference between a hard-headed leisure business seeking to generate a return on investment on the one hand, and a members' club seeking to raise money to plough back funds to increase success on the field on the other. However, in my view both situations require long-term commercial success and both require success on the pitch on which to build revenue streams.

A key business management issue is controlling the pressures of short-termism and in educating both managers and fans into the benefits of managing for sustained growth (or survival). Football managers, much more than managers in general, are usually judged by results on the pitch in a period that can be measured in a number of months. No other industry exerts this sort of pressure or creates the media circus that surrounds the manager of a struggling team. As a consequence, clubs can lurch from crisis to crisis, taking ever more expensive remedial action. Symptoms of this problem are evidenced by the signing of players in the twilight of their careers on long-term contracts with large signing-on fees and often a significant fee payable to the selling club. Such decisions are often justified on the basis of the need for 'an experienced head' to help a club avoid relegation or win promotion. This can often lead to conflict with the 'business' managers who may be concerned about the overall cost of employing a player and the financial burden he represents to the club.

From a commercial viewpoint, the long-term interests of a club may be better served by spending £2 million on developing a youth programme and scouting network. If, however, a manager is under pressure to produce immediate results, the prospect of buying an ageing star may be more appealing. With regard to customers, fans do not generally care about or understand the niceties of financial prudence and corporate governance. They just want a winning team. Radio phone-ins are inundated with calls from fans pleading for club directors to release the pursestrings to allow their team's manager to go into the transfer market and buy success. Successful business managers cannot ignore customer expectations but they must educate supporters of the need to manage for the long term.

THE GLOBALISATION OF FOOTBALL

The recent controversy concerning the decision of Manchester United to compete in a World Club competition has centred around claims of government pressure to compete in order to assist the FA bid to host the 2006 World Cup. In reality the real significance of the absence of Manchester United from the FA Cup is that it is the first step on the road leading to a devaluation of national competitions. It is now simply a matter of time before the introduction of a European club league competition, which in turn will be the precursor to a global league of some description.

Globalisation of competitions is only one factor to be borne in mind. There is, in addition, the existence of what will become a virtual global labour market. The expansion of the European Union with its associated rights of employment in the UK has seen an influx of players with EU passports from South America. This trend is set to continue. For example, within two years Poland is likely to become a member of the European

Union. As a consequence a new market for football talent will be open, offering relatively inexpensive players who no longer require a work permit. A number of clubs are already exploring this market in order to be in a position to move quickly when the barriers come down.

THE IMPLICATIONS (AND WISDOM) OF PLC STATUS

In years to come, business analysts will look back on the 1990s as the decade when football tackled the stock exchange. Football, with aspirations of massive pay-per-view opportunities, will be seen as having been the sexy sector. Football will be seen to have been moving away from the cloth-cap, pie-and-Bovril image and moving towards the business entertainer willing and able to afford a seat in a box or some other 'executive suite'. Everyone wanted to be involved with the latest boom in stocks. The market was frothy.

Things are now a little different. Pay-per-view has not developed as fast as some pundits expected, and the City has lost its enchantment with football. As a consequence, a number of clubs find themselves with a falling share price and the burden of stock exchange compliance and institutional shareholder expectations without any of the perceived benefits of a flotation or the ability to raise finance. The problems experienced by Leicester City are a case in point. Widely publicised board-room bust-ups are barely acceptable in private companies and they suggest a total failure to appreciate the responsibilities associated with running a public company.

With the exception of Manchester United and the other four or five major clubs in the Premiership, the stock exchange will not be the source of capital that clubs expected it to be. One can only speculate as to the reaction in the City if Southampton, Bradford, West Bromwich Albion, Nottingham Forest or Leicester City sought to raise funds from the market. The only people with an interest in these and similar clubs are the fans, not pension funds or financial institutions. Some clubs may attract a wealthy fan wishing to take a financial stake in 'their' team but a stock exchange listing may be more of a hindrance than a help as the rules concerning takeovers come into play.

INCREASING SOLVENCY PROBLEMS

The keys to long-term business survival are simple: do not spend more than you earn; if you borrow, do not borrow more than you can service and repay; and consider the cash cycle. Although football has had financial problems for decades, the amount of debt involved has been relatively small and has often been covered by a benevolent fan or a kindly bank manager content to wait for a player to be sold. As a consequence, few clubs have failed.

Circumstances are changing now that the sums involved in financing football have grown substantially. Transfer fees and players' wages continue to escalate; the Taylor Report resulted in major investment in stadiums. Although ticket prices and TV revenues have increased, the fact that administrators are controlling Crystal Palace (and other clubs have been through the administration process) indicate that not all clubs have been able to manage their financial affairs in a prudent manner. In addition to the clubs that have been through the administration procedure, there are persistent rumours that a Premiership club is in such financial difficulty that player transfers are governed as much by the club's bankers as by the coach.

It is perhaps appropriate at this stage to consider a model of the cash cycle as it applies to football clubs. An appreciation of the cash cycle is of critical importance because financial accounts can be manipulated and distorted by changing polices and pronouncements, but at the end of the day a bad business will run out of cash. The model uses the image of water for cash and of leaks in a bucket to signify expenditure; the secret of a successful club being one that can at least turn on the taps to an extent that matches the flow of leaks.

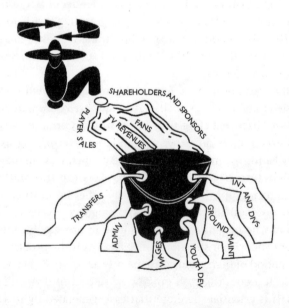

For simplicity, the model identifies cash as being received from five principal sources, namely: fans (season tickets, match receipts, pro-grammes, merchandise, hospitality); sponsors; player sales; TV revenues;

and shareholders and banks. Similarly, the outflows have been simplified to include players' wages (including signing-on fees); player purchases; youth development; ground maintenance and improvements; club administration; and dividends to shareholders and interest to lenders. Viewed in these simple terms, it is perhaps easier to appreciate why some clubs appear to be in a never-ending struggle to remain solvent.

When considering the sources of funds it is important to realise that with the possible exception of TV monies, many of the variables are within the control of the club. The business management of a football club requires a thorough understanding of the market in order to maximise the earning potential of these sources of revenue. Although few clubs can match the global appeal of Manchester United, much can be done to maximise the merchandising opportunities and secondary spending of supporters. Few clubs fully utilise their facilities on non-match-days. The extent to which this can become a significant income generator depends not only on the facilities available but also on the professionalism with which the task is tackled.

If a club adopts a squad management policy and seeks to manage player movements, cash generated by player sales is a controllable variable. Sponsorship is another source of cash although its significance depends on the overall value of the club's brand and success on the pitch. Shareholders and banks have historically been seen as the lender of last resort and as the people to whom a club's management have turned just before the bucket empties. There is no doubt that shareholders and banks remain important sources of cash although the limits and demands imposed are now becoming more onerous.

With the exception of a few multi-millionaires who can afford to indulge their passion for football, most clubs are coming under increasing scrutiny from backers before they inject funds. Certainly, raising cash on the stock exchange is an expensive and time-consuming exercise. Also, practically and to maintain credibility, business managers cannot continually return to the City or the bankers cap in hand every season asking for a top-up. In many respects the imposition of financial disciplines on football clubs is in the long-term interests of everyone, regardless of whether the fans react to it as an unwelcome intrusion.

Another issue with institutional investments is the problem of predators seeking a 'pound of flesh', and consequently as equity capital and bank debt increase, so too does the cash outflow in respect of dividend and interest payments. It is essential therefore that cash generated by new share issues or bank debt is used in a way that will help the future earning power of the club. Failure to recognise this creates a problem for the future when share-holders and banks may well refuse to advance funds merely to prop up a failing business. Unlike some of the cash receipts, all of the cash outflows are controllable, and successful clubs actively manage their expenditure and work to budgets and forecasts. Again, the fans may regard business planning as an unwanted intrusion by 'The Suits', but it is essential for every club to have some idea of the anticipated cash-flows for the season. Furthermore, such plans should be regularly reviewed and revised to take account of unforeseen developments. Prudent clubs will plan their affairs on the basis of early cup exits. In this way, if they embark on a money-spinning cup run, they can perhaps use the windfall receipts to reduce borrowing or buy another player. This is preferable to basing a plan on reaching the quarter-finals only to become the victim of a giant-killing feat in the third round.

THE WIDENING GAP BETWEEN CLUBS

There can be no doubt that there is a widening gap between football clubs. The financial clout of Manchester United is awesome and anyone looking at the Premiership table will see the increasing dominance of Manchester United, Liverpool, Arsenal and Chelsea. Clubs with limited financial resources such as Coventry, Wimbledon, Southampton and Leicester have done remarkably well to compete in the top flight for so long. The recent decision to allow collective bargaining of TV rights was essential for the 'smaller' Premiership clubs who struggle to compete with the global appeal of the Manchester United brand.

UEFA changed the face of the Champions League and UEFA Cup competitions in the 1999–2000 season but how long will it be before there is a European league running throughout the season? The stratification of football clubs goes beyond the Premiership. Some of the clubs facing the most challenging business dilemmas are the so-called 'yo-yo' clubs that are the serial promotion/relegation candidates. These yo-yo clubs are found at the top and bottom of all divisions but the effects of the yo-yo clubs are most keenly felt at the Premiership/First Division border. These clubs are faced with demands for improved terms from the players and, in all probability, the need to recruit additional players to compete at a higher level. Although playing in the Premiership does result in a slice of the Sky revenues, any club that enjoys a single season in the Premiership may find that on returning to the Nationwide it retains its Premiership payroll but with reduced TV and gate monies – an unpleasant combination.

THE CONTINUING EFFECTS OF BOSMAN

The effects of the Bosman ruling continues to have a detrimental effect on the financial health of all but the wealthiest clubs. Historically, many clubs survived by finding young players who were coached and given experience in the lower leagues before being sold on to a higher division. In many respects the *real* business of clubs was in the development and trading of players. Following the Bosman ruling, clubs can no longer rely on a successful youth policy to provide funds to ensure future survival. The argument that clubs facing this predicament can protect themselves by taking youngsters on long-term contracts is fundamentally flawed. No club is in a position to make long-term financial commitments to young and unproven players and, as has been seen, the minute a player at a lower-division club does show real potential, it is difficult for the club to compete with advances made by richer competitors.

Despite the effects of Bosman, an important element of the business may still be the development and trading of players. The Bosman ruling has complicated this aspect of the business, which now requires a conscious manpower plan that anticipates the end of a player's contract so that a decision is made about the player's future. Clubs need to consider the value of a player at all stages of his contract. This may result in attempts to negotiate a new contract, sell the player before the end of the contract, or retain the player in the knowledge that he will leave at the end of the season on a free transfer. Regardless of the club's preferred option, the player may not wish to be sold and he may want instead to see out his contract to benefit from being a free agent; however, it should still be possible to negotiate a mutually advantageous settlement.

THE IMPORTANCE OF BASIC BUSINESS PRINCIPLES AND DISCIPLINES

A visitor to the business section of a bookshop may well be overwhelmed by the number of books on the strategies for successfully running a business. Every author has specific ideas on what is needed but this is not the place to regurgitate the latest theories. However, no club can afford to ignore the basic business principles, namely: have a plan or strategy with clearly defined objectives; understand your financial position; do not spend more than you earn, but if you do, do not borrow more than you can repay. There is also an old proverb: 'If you don't know where you are going, any road will take you there.' A football club is doomed to failure if it does not have a business plan, budgets, financial forecasts and projections, manpower plan and strategic plans covering all aspects of the business. The days of being able to run a complex business without detailed planning and effective controls are long gone. At the very least a football club should prepare a strategic plan, annual budgets incorporating a teampower plan, profit and cash-flow forecasts, monthly management accounts, and variance analysis between actual results and budget showing the estimated outcome for the year on a regular basis.

STRATEGIC PLAN

The strategic plan should cover the objectives of each business segment and incorporate an assessment of the current position together with an action plan that is intended to take the club to where it wishes to be. This is more than an academic exercise and should be reviewed periodically and updated to reflect achievements and failures. The reason for deviations from the plan should be understood so that lessons learned can be incorporated into subsequent plans.

A key consideration to many football clubs is recognition of the need to build the value of the brand. As with any service or commodity, much can be done to protect the existing customer base and develop the next generation of supporters. Failure to acknowledge or manage customer needs and expectations can lead to a swift decline in turnover. It is essential that there is close liaison between the football and commercial operations and that tasks are carried out by the people most suited to doing them, and the strategic plan should also identify where departmental responsibilities lie and the way in which the business is to be managed.

It is becoming increasingly common for football managers to work within budgets for player costs. Also, although the manager will make decisions about player contracts, increasingly the actual negotiation of contracts is done by the chief executive. Viewed from a corporate perspective this is an important control. Furthermore, the segregation of duties in this aspect avoids the conflict that can arise for managers who have to motivate a player on the pitch having just told him that he is not worth a pay rise or that he is going on the transfer list.

ANNUAL BUDGETS AND MANPOWER PLAN

Following from the strategic plan it is important to prepare annual budgets for each income source and cost centre. Ideally the budgets should be compiled with the departmental managers so that there is accountability for the achievement of the targets. Although viewed on an annual basis, certain budgets should have regard to the longer term. This is especially true of the team budget. It is essential for clubs to understand their full financial commitments in respect of players over the length of the contract, particularly if there are escalation clauses, signing-on fees and other commitments that may trigger additional liabilities. For example, it is not uncommon for transfer fees paid to be based on the number of appearances, goals scored or the achievement of promotion. Monitoring the club's financial commitments in respect of the playing squad for the next two or three years will highlight potential problems and allow management to form a strategy for player retention. For the 'yoyo' clubs it will put into perspective the financial consequences of promotion or relegation and allow serious thought to be given to the merit of adopting a policy of augmenting the squad by the acquisition of players on long-term loan, with an option to buy.

PROFIT AND CASH-FLOW FORECASTS

These forecasts should be based on realistic expectations of the trading performance for the year. This in turn will determine the likely cash-flow position of the club. It is also sensible to prepare a range of forecasts based on different assumptions so that the sensitivity of the cash position can be established. The cash-flow forecasts will show the headroom available between the banking facilities available to a club and the cash requirements. Constant monitoring of the cash position should allow a club to identify problems at an early stage and take the appropriate action before a crisis develops.

MONTHLY MANAGEMENT ACCOUNTS

Management accounts should be prepared as a matter of course on a monthly basis showing the profit-and-loss account for the period, as well as a balance-sheet.

VARIANCE ANALYSIS

Although the production of accounts, budgets and forecasts is important, an essential feature of financial control is the explanation for any significant variance. If the actual results do differ significantly from the expected outcome, understanding the reasons for the variance could lead to a revision of the strategic plan or the adoption of remedial action to avoid financial crisis.

CONCLUSION

In the same way that the formation used by a club on the pitch is no guarantee of success, the club that adopts all of the planning and monitoring techniques may not prosper or survive. As with the team on the pitch, much depends on the skills and abilities of the individuals involved. What is certain, however, is that the implementation of good business practices promotes success and makes it easier for the management team to recognise the problems at an early stage and take corrective action. The successful clubs will anticipate change and regard a football club as a business with all of the basic financial and commercial controls in place.

20. Achieving best practice

STEPHEN MORROW

Much has been made of the dramatic changes which football and its clubs have undergone over the last five years. There is no doubt that the sector has been transformed in terms of its financial size, and in terms of its integration into other business sectors such as TV broadcasting. As is well documented in other chapters in this book, football *as a game* has been replaced by football *as a business*. Nevertheless, I would argue that in terms of accounting practice, the same underlying problems have been apparent throughout the game's history; the current dramatic transformation in the size and structure of the industry has simply thrown these into sharper relief. For example, consider the following quotes:

> The game of association football is attracting more public attention. All aspects of it are being discussed both in the media and at the highest levels within the game. The major area of interest currently is that of finance . . .

> Certainly the method of accounting for such transfer fees makes it difficult to evaluate the financial position of any particular club and the industry as a whole.

> Many clubs are now paying out as much in wages and bonuses as they receive in gate receipts.

> Whilst historically the success of a club has been measured by performance on the playing field, management's attitude is now changing by looking more toward success in realising income from commercial sources.

> . . . there are probably three categories of clubs: those at the very top which can always earn profits, those in the lower part of the League which are nearly always struggling to make ends meet, and a band of teams for which financial results will vary year by year with success on the field. The distinction between the various categories of clubs is even more noticeable currently with

some unsuccessful clubs in the lower divisions close to liquidation.

. . . in most cases the traded price of shares in football clubs is significantly in excess of the net asset value of the club as shown by its accounts. This indicates the difficulty of valuing a club's shares although there may also be special reasons for a particular share trading at a premium over its net asset value, e.g. the unrecorded value of its team.

As we approach the twenty-first century such observations are not likely to surprise most followers of football. What may, however, be significant is that these quotes are taken not from a contemporary source, such as the 1999 Deloitte & Touche *Survey of Football Finance*. Instead, the quotes are taken from a book entitled *The Financing and Taxation of Football Clubs* published as long ago as 1982 by one of the other global accounting firms, Arthur Andersen. *Plus ça change, plus c'est la même chose.*

ACCOUNTING FOR FOOTBALL CLUBS

It has long been argued that the use of traditional financial reporting practices obstructed full understanding and consideration of the causes and indicators of football clubs' financial difficulties. A particular problem was the difficulty in making comparisons between the financial statements of different clubs, owing to the very different accounting treatments adopted for items such as transfer fees, grants from bodies such as the Football Trust or sponsorship income. In recent years, however, there has been a notable improvement in both the quantity and, more importantly, the quality of accounting information provided by the clubs. Partly this reflects a widening of the concept of stewardship; an acknowledgement that stakeholder groups other than shareholders have legitimate needs for accounting information in forming judgements about how well the directors have used the resources entrusted to them, and about overall business efficiency. Other factors have also contributed to the improvement. These include more involvement of professional advisers in football clubs, greater financial awareness among football club directors, increased public and media interest in the financial affairs of clubs, a culture of best practice, the need to provide adequate information to potential investors and lenders, and improved, more relevant financial accounting standards and generally accepted practice.

Accounting problems still remain for clubs. Among these are the questions of whether and how clubs should revalue their specialised property assets (such as stadiums), whether clubs should depreciate such assets and, in view of the well-recognised loyalty of football supporters, whether clubs should be able to recognise their brand names as accounting assets. The most prominent issue remains that of how best to record the investment made by a club in its players.

The traditional practice of accounting for football players excluded any valuation of players from the balance-sheet, whether they were players bought by a club through the transfer market or those developed internally by the club. The first club to adopt an alternative treatment was Tottenham Hotspur. In its accounts for the year ended 31 May 1989 Spurs adopted an accounting policy that recorded the cost of purchased players' registrations as intangible assets on the balance-sheet. Prior to the Bosman ruling in 1995, similar accounting policies were adopted by a further 12 English and five Scottish clubs.

The introduction of Financial Reporting Standard (FRS) 10, *Goodwill and intangible assets* in December 1997 (applicable for accounting periods ending on or after 23 December 1998) means that some consistency has now been brought into this area. Under FRS 10, when a club signs a player through the transfer market, it is required to include the cost of acquiring the player's registration as an intangible fixed asset on its balance-sheet. In subsequent financial years this cost is then amortised (or written off as an expense) through the profit-and-loss account over the length of his contract. Notwithstanding this guidance, the debate is very likely to continue about how best to record the investment made by a club in its players. The issues to be addressed include the following: Is FRS 10 the best solution? In particular, is it appropriate to distinguish between players acquired through the transfer market and those who are home grown? How should costs incurred by clubs in respect of training and development be accounted for? Within the historical cost accounting model, should additional information on the likely market value of players be disclosed elsewhere in the financial statements, say in the Operating and Financial Review?

FOOTBALL CLUB FINANCE

The financing or funding of football clubs has recently been an area of dramatic change. Historically, football clubs were undercapitalised (that is, there was a disproportionately low level of equity funding compared to the asset base), restricted in their rights to pay dividends, had little or no retained profit and relied heavily on borrowings as a source of funding, often bank funding in the form of overdraft facilities (and hence short term in nature). But in recent years, more and more clubs have begun to recognise the possibility of using the capital markets, firstly, as a way of raising funds, and secondly, of subsequently providing a market for their club's shares. As of August 1999, shares in 21 British clubs were listed in London either on the Stock Exchange Official List or the Alternative Investment Market (AIM), while a further three clubs' shares are traded on a matched bargain basis through the OFEX market under Rule 4.2(a) of the London stock exchange.

The increasing numbers of clubs listing on the stock exchange has resulted in clubs coming under greater financial scrutiny than ever before. But, although football is a business, it is not just a business. In consequence, attention has focused not only on the business aspects of football but also on the nature of contemporary football clubs. A particular area of interest has been conflicts that arise as a result of the dichotomy between football as a sport and football as a business.

Among the issues that need to be addressed by all those involved in the game – directors, shareholders, institutional investors, bankers, supporters and others – when considering the financing of football clubs there are four main points. Firstly, there is the nature of investment in football clubs, in particular the potential for conflict between conventional financial investors and emotional investors or stakeholders such as supporters (irrespective of whether such supporters actually own shares in a particular club). Secondly, there is the issue of accountability to small shareholders (and to stakeholders more generally). Thirdly, the issue of thin trading or illiquidity in the market for most football club shares.[1] Prices of thinly traded shares are likely to exhibit greater variability as the market seeks to match supply and demand. And, fourthly, there is an issue of more concentrated ownership of shares in clubs. Concentrated ownership exists where one or a few individuals or institutions own a large percentage of shares in a company. Concentrated ownership may bring risks for clubs, particularly with regard to the possible exploitation of small or minority shareholders and with regard to the possibility of majority shareholders cashing in on their investment.

Some of these issues are addressed in other chapters in this section, and have been discussed by myself in detail elsewhere.[2] However, the debate on how these four issues might satisfactorily be addressed is still embryonic.

BEST PRACTICE

It is clear that there are a number of mainstream accounting practices for football clubs, which need to be developed further. Many of these relate to what might best be described as best practice in the mainstream accounting areas and their continued significance in the context of football clubs is a reminder that while clubs have undoubtedly become more sophisticated financially in recent years, much work remains to be done.

In addition there are large and important sets of non-financial factors, peculiar to the football sector, which need to be accounted for when it comes to the business of football. The debate on how to address these factors is still truly in its infancy. But I would argue that unless they *are* addressed, the essential 'sporting' quality of football, which has made it the cultural and social asset that it is, might well be lost.

PART VI

....

THE RESTRICTIVE PRACTICES COURT CASE
AND LEAGUE BALANCE

21. The Restrictive Practices Court case, broadcasting revenues and league balance

PETER SLOANE

Professional sports leagues pose a particular problem for competition policy. Unlike a conventional industry, clubs must combine together to produce a product and have a vested interest in the economic health of their rivals. Organisation into leagues in which each club must play the others provides for the possibility of a championship. Attendances are influenced by uncertainty of outcome and this requires that the league should not become too unbalanced. Leagues must have rules and a governing body which controls the activities of the individual clubs. That the Premier League is a cartel cannot be in doubt but, given the special circumstances of the industry, is it better simply to regard the league as a multi-plant firm which competes for consumer expenditure with other sporting leagues and leisure pursuits? The question of the definition of the market then becomes critical.

Within this context broadcasting has become extremely important to the well-being of the league. The four-year deal between the Premier League and BSkyB covering the period 1997–2001 was, at £670 million, Britain's largest sports contract. This, however, is dwarfed by the US National Football League's $15 billion sale of its broadcasting rights over an eight-year period. It is estimated that by 2005 television income will account for roughly half of all English league clubs' income, making it more significant than gate receipts and similar to the situation in North America.

What is at issue is the collective sale of league broadcasting rights with the fear that this will lead to a monopoly restriction of output (fewer televised games) and higher prices for viewing them, though it has to be said that there are more games shown live on television today than has been the case in the past. Indeed, the TV purchaser has a vested interest in ensuring that the output of games is as large as possible and what may be of more concern is the duration of contract when there is no competition other than for edited highlights. The defence of collective negotiation is that this helps to maintain uncertainty of outcome and enables the league to organise the fixture list so that televised games do not clash with the fixtures in the rest of the league, thereby reducing any negative effect on attendances. A study in 1996 by Bainbridge, Cameron and Dawson of the impact of satellite television on live coverage in 1993–94 found that live transmission of matches on Monday evenings reduced attendances by over 15%.[1]

It is noteworthy that collective negotiation is a common feature elsewhere. In North America collective negotiation has been usual for national broadcasting rights, but in addition clubs have generally reserved the right to market local broadcasts of games which are not within the national contract. Furthermore, there are blackouts of matches in the geographical area in which the game is being played and the banning of the broadcast of any other game in an area in which a live game is taking place. Such arrangements came into conflict with the US anti-trust legislation, resulting in Congress passing the 1961 Sports Broadcasting Act, which in effect exempted the four major team sports from the anti-trust laws in relation to broadcasting activity. This was perceived to be in the best interests of viewers, spectators, competitive balance and league health.

The US football authorities even extended blackouts to games which were already sell-outs on the grounds that television would result in some no-shows and therefore in fewer ancillary sales and some loss of atmosphere. However, in 1973 legislation was passed to ban blackouts in the home area of clubs whose games were due for network TV, where all tickets offered for sale were sold out 72 hours before the game.

In Germany the competition authority successfully challenged the centralised sale of broadcasting rights to games of German clubs in the UEFA and Cup-Winners' Cup competitions on the grounds that there were no compensatory benefits to the consumer or the sport itself. Subsequently, however, the German government passed a specific law exempting the German football authority from the relevant cartel laws on the issue. In the Netherlands, Feyenoord successfully argued in court that it should be allowed the right to negotiate its own TV contract despite the fact that the Dutch Football Association had negotiated the collective sale of TV rights and the Dutch Minister for Economic Affairs confirmed that the collective selling of rights was in breach of competition laws. The position in Europe is, therefore, much less clear than in the US.

The situation is also complicated by the advent of pay-per-view television. Following the rejection by the Premier League of a proposal from BSkyB to show pay-per-view on a regular basis, the experiment so far has been limited to six games in the Nationwide League. It seems likely in the long run that clubs will show their own games on digital television following the North American pattern of local televising of games. But that brings us to the question of revenue-sharing.

If the defence of the protection of uncertainty of outcome is used with regard to collective negotiation of television rights then the division of television income should be equalising, and this becomes even more important as the share of television in total income rises. Currently the Premier League contract shares half of the contract value equally among the clubs, 25% on the basis of the actual games televised and 25% on the basis of league performance. This results in the top club receiving about double the amount received by the bottom club. This does not look particularly equalising. An alternative would be to reward clubs inversely in relation to league position along the lines of the North American player draft system. It should be noted that in North America national TV contracts in all sports uniformly involve equal sharing of revenues by all league teams (with negotiated temporary exclusions for expansion franchises). It is argued that this has no effect on competitive balance because payment to clubs is independent of each club's win-percentage. But that is not the case in the Premier League allocation system.

It is, however, the advent of pay-per-view television which is the major threat to competitive balance, if clubs are free to negotiate their own contracts and have widely differing revenue potentials. Using a mathematical optimisation model, Rodney Fort and James Quirk have shown that the rational choice for a league as a whole is to have the same rules for gate and local TV revenue sharing, since this is likely to lead to a distribution of playing strengths that maximises league-wide revenues in the absence of a salary cap.[2] Without local TV income sharing the concentration of playing talent in the rich clubs is likely to be more extreme than that which maximises league-wide revenues. A similar distortion will occur if gate-sharing were increased without an increase in local TV income sharing, as this would place more importance on local TV income in club decisions.

In the event, Mr Justice Ferris, together with two colleagues in the Restrictive Practices Court, dismissed the Office of Fair Trading's claim that the Premier League's exclusive broadcasting agreement with BSkyB and the BBC was unlawful on the grounds that it reduced consumer choice and increased the price of viewing games on television. He found that the benefits which occurred from the agreement in terms of reinvestment in the sport and the share of income that is redistributed to the smaller clubs outweighed any potential detriment through a reduction in competition. However, this does not end the matter since any new agreement to follow in 2001 will come under the 1998 Competition Act, which will require the approval of the OFT before it can come into force. In addition the advent of pay-per-view television may lead to individual clubs negotiating their own contracts on top of any collective agreement. Thus, the Premier League may need to rethink its strategy under such circumstances, perhaps by imposing a tax on this revenue for redistribution to the financially weaker clubs. Further, if the Fort and Quirk model is applicable to the Premier League case, a similar tax may need to be imposed on gate receipts or more equal gate-sharing encouraged.

22. Football rights and competition in broadcasting
MARTIN CAVE

The link between the football and broadcasting industries has been the subject of two recent competition law proceedings in the UK. In the first, a proposed merger between BSkyB and Manchester United was referred to the Monopolies and Mergers Commission, which recommended that it should be prohibited, a recommendation which the Secretary of State then followed. In the second, the director-general of Fair Trading undertook proceedings against the Premier League, BSkyB and the BBC over the manner in which Premier League rights were sold on an exclusive basis – live rights to BSkyB and terrestrial highlight rights to the BBC. In this case, the respondents were able successfully to argue that the arrangements in question conferred advantages and were in the public interest. Unless this judgement is successfully appealed by the Office of Fair Trading, the arrangements will be allowed to stand, and – possibly – to be renewed when the current agreements expire in 2001.[1]

These cases are representative of a range of competition issues which have arisen throughout the world in relation to sports rights. As an illustration, the broadcasting rights to Formula One racing are currently under investigation by DGIV of the European Commission. In the United States, too, there is a long history of regulatory and legislative actions relating to rights to broadcast both professional and college sporting events.[2]

Many people regard it as inappropriate that sporting events – activities which involve a combination of co-operation and competition, where providers are traditionally guided by a variety of both commercial and non-commercial motives – should be subject to the full rigours of competition law. In many ways, this attitude is understandable, and it is unlikely that a competition authority would take a close interest in a sporting activity which was not of great financial significance, even if its fans attached great importance to it. However, the nexus between sport and broadcasting gives much more prominence to sports rights in the competition authorities' minds. If rights to broadcast the matches played by a particular group of teams have a major impact upon competition in the much larger broadcasting industry, the competition authorities may have to do something about the situation.

This 'tail wagging the dog' situation applies in the relationship between the Premier League (whose clubs have an annual turnover of about £500 million), and broadcasting in the UK, where the annual turnover is over £5 billion.

This chapter reviews the two recent competition proceedings relating to Premier League rights in this light. Section 2 gives a brief account of the legislative framework within which the proceedings occurred. Section 3 discusses the debate over the relationship between the organisation of sports competitions and the collective sale of rights. Section 4 discusses the market definition question. Section 5 considers likely future developments, while Section 6 concludes.

2. THE LEGISLATIVE FRAMEWORK OF THE TWO PROCEEDINGS

In September 1998, BSkyB and Manchester United announced a recommended offer under which BSkyB would acquire all the shares in Manchester United in exchange for shares in BSkyB, with a cash alternative. The offer, which valued Manchester United at £623 million, was referred by the government for consideration by the Monopolies and Mergers Commission. The Commission's report recommended that the merger be prohibited, and in April 1999 the Secretary of State for Trade and Industry acted on this recommendation. The referral took place under the Fair Trading Act, 1973, which allows the Secretary of State to refer mergers when the value of assets to be taken over exceeds £70 million.[3] The legislation is broadly worded to allow a variety of public-interest issues to be taken into consideration, including – but not confined to – effects on competition in any of the industries involved.

The proceedings taken by the director-general of Fair Trading in relation to the sale of Premier League rights were begun in 1996 under the Restrictive Trade Practices Act, 1976. The Act provides for agreements between firms which involve restrictions of specified kinds to be registered with the director-general of Fair Trading. The director-general can then apply to the court for a declaration of whether any restrictions are contrary to the public interests. The underlying assumption in the legislation is that restrictions are deemed to be contrary to the public interest unless the Court is satisfied *both* that the restrictions pass through one of the gateways mentioned below *and* that the restrictions are not unreasonable having regard to the balance between their benefits and their costs. In the Premier League case, the gateway around which most of the argument revolved was gateway B. In order to pass through this gateway, the Court must be satisfied that:

The removal of the restriction . . . would deny to the public as users of any services . . . specific and substantial benefits or advantages . . .

The provisions on which the court was required to rule were three:

i) A rule of the Premier League (D.7.3) which provides that no Premier League match can be televised without the consent of the board of the Premier League, which in practise is never given. Under this rule the members of the Premier League bind themselves not to sell television rights of matches on an individual basis, but solely through the Premier League.

ii) A clause of the agreements between BSkyB and the Premier League, relating respectively to the years 1992–1997 and 1997–2001 (clause 2.2) under which the Premier League agreed with BSkyB that, in return for £191 million under the first agreement and £670 million under the second, the Premier League would allow BSkyB to broadcast 60 live matches per season and would not allow anyone other than BSkyB (or the BBC under its own separate agreement – see below) the right to broadcast live any Premier League matches. In effect this gave BSkyB a monopoly of the broadcast of live Premier League matches.

iii) A clause in the agreement between the Premier League and the BBC, which gave the latter exclusive rights to attend certain Premier League matches to record them for the purpose of broadcasting a programme of Premier League highlights, *Match of the Day*. For this the BBC paid £22 million under the first agreement and £73 million under the second agreement.

The analysis below is confined to the Premier League/BSkyB agreements in view of their greater commercial value and impact upon broadcasting markets. It is clear that they require not only that the broadcaster have exclusive rights to one given live match (so called 'narrow exclusivity'), but that, once the Premier League has contracted with BSkyB for the live broadcast of 60 matches per season of the 380 matches played, no other match can be broadcast live (so called 'broad exclusivity').

3. IS THE COLLECTIVE SALE OF SPORTS RIGHTS EQUIVALENT TO A CARTEL?

One of the bolder claims made in the OFT's case before the court was that the Premier League was acting like a cartel in deciding to market its sports rights collectively. A cartel operates through an agreement by firms in the industry to raise prices or, alternatively, to restrict output. The benefits of the arrangement are allocated among the participating firms either by dividing up the market, so that each firm gets a preordained share of profits, or by a system for redistributing revenue or profit.

Most cartels face considerable hostility from their customers. If the Premier League were a cartel, it would thus be surprising if its customer, BSkyB, supported the arrangement. However, in present circumstances this could be explained by the claim that BSkyB itself benefited more than it suffered from the arrangement, through enhanced market power in the downstream pay broadcasting market.

The argument that a sports league is not a cartel relies upon special features of the relationships among its members. In most industries, a firm would benefit from eliminating or weakening its competitors. A member of a sports league, in comparison, clearly requires the participation of its competitors to make the competition possible, and, given the evidence that spectators are attracted by competitive balance within a league,[4] it is not in any team's long-term interest to unduly weaken its competitors. Moreover, interest in any Premier League match is based in part upon interest in the competition as a whole. According to this view of the matter, the combination of competitive and co-operative arrangements distinguishes members of a sports league from the members of an industrial cartel. The court accepted this.

Against this, it can be argued that it is possible to separate the various activities undertaken by a sports league and its members into those which have to, or can beneficially, be undertaken collectively, and those which, in the public interest, should be organised competitively.[5] Agreement on a set of rules and a fixture list clearly comes into the first category. However, other associated activities need not. Premier League teams derive their revenue from three main sources – gate receipts, television rights and marketing turnover. Although there has been gate-revenue-sharing in the past between the home and the visiting club, under current arrangements the home team keeps all the revenue. This provides it with incentives to improve the quality of the spectators' experience and to compete in relation to ticket prices. A possible alternative arrangement, in which the seats sold at all matches were restricted by agreement among the clubs to increase overall revenue, would not generate the same incentives. A similar position applies to fixing the prices of marketed goods such as replica shirts.[6]

The question then arises as to the category – necessarily co-operative or beneficially competitive – into which the sale of television rights should be assimilated. Collective selling is not a necessary requirement, in the way that collective acceptance of a set of rules and a fixture list clearly is. It does, however, clearly facilitate exclusive selling.

In his argument before the court, the director-general made it plain that he had no objection *per se* to the collective sale of matches by the Premier

League. Indeed he suggested that two or more packages of rights might be sold to separate broadcasters, each granting narrow exclusivity over the matches in question. This could be supplemented by giving clubs the right to sell further matches on an individual basis. In the director-general's view, this would combine the benefits of a degree of certainty for the broadcaster for the package over what rights it had available, with a constraint on the price of such packages resulting both from the fact that there was more than one and that further matches could be sold separately. In other words, the OFT objected not to a degree of central organisation of sales, but to the cartel-like output restriction implicit in broad exclusivity.

In the event, for reasons noted below, the court did not take up the option of this compromise, which would have combined the transactional advantages of collective selling with the competitive disciplines of individual selling.

4. MARKET DEFINITION

As is common in competition proceedings, some of the arguments before the RPC and much of the analysis in the MMC report revolved around the question of market definition. This is relevant to competition in the broadcasting industry because if Premier League broadcast rights were a product for which, in viewer's eyes, there were many substitutes, then an arrangement under which they were sold exclusively to one broadcaster would not confer upon that broadcaster significant advantages in the pay TV market; if, on the other hand, actual and potential buyers of pay TV regard Premier League live matches as a product for which there was no substitute, or a limited range of possible substitutes, then a broadcaster with exclusive access to those rights would be placed in a position where it could exploit market power in pay TV.

It is useful in this context to make a distinction between markets at the wholesale and at the retail level. Given the very limited development of pay-per-view broadcasting, the relevant retail market is likely to be framed as one for broadcast channels, and the question at issue to be whether premium sports channels constitute a separate market. At the wholesale level, where owners of rights sell them to broadcasters for packaging as channels, the question is whether Premier League rights constitute a market or a significant part thereof, or whether broadcasters have available to them a variety of competing programming, which may include or go beyond the sports programming. The retail and wholesale markets are obviously linked because, if viewers have a strong and irreplaceable demand for live Premier League matches at the retail level, that will confer significant market power on the seller of such rights at wholesale level.

The standard form of test for defining whether a particular set of services constitutes a market is to ask whether, if a single firm managed to corner the supply of that set of services, it could raise their price significantly above the competitive price for a sustained period.[7] The smallest set of services which has this characteristic is defined as the market.[8] This way of addressing the question leads naturally into the second stage of a competition analysis, which involves asking whether a firm is in fact in a position to exercise dominance in a market thus defined, and whether it does so.

The MMC,[9] and the director-general before the RPC, cited a range of data which, in their opinion, bore upon the question of market definition. These included:

i) The higher prices per match paid at wholesale level for Premier League matches than for Football League matches, FA Cup matches and matches involving overseas leagues. (This argument was to some extent undermined by the rate – about £2.2 million per match – roughly equivalent to £2.8 million per match under the Premier League contract, paid by Carlton and ONdigital for European Champions League rights, with effect from the 1999–2000 season.)

ii) The fact that television audiences for Premier League matches exceeded by a significant margin those for Football League matches or matches involving overseas leagues, whether the comparison is made between current pay TV audiences or (based on earlier data) comparative audiences on free-to-air television.

iii) The fact that such a high proportion of the annualised costs of BSkyB's current rights to sporting events was accounted for by Premier League rights – 53% in 1997–98 out of a total expenditure on football rights of 76%.

iv) A survey of pay TV subscribers carried out by NOP in 1996 suggested that the Premier League and the FA Cup were regarded by respondents as the most important football competitions on Sky Sports, followed by European matches involving British clubs, Worthington Cup matches and England internationals.

v) The predictable weekly availability of televised live Premier League matches was acknowledged to provide subscribers with a regular weekly 'appointment to view' on Sunday afternoons, and Monday evenings, which was not available in the case of other competitions.

The argument that Premier League matches form a separate wholesale market and underlie Sky Sport's dominance in a premium sports channel is subject to the criticism that other matches which involve Premier League clubs, in domestic competitions or European competitions, are equally popular with audiences and, in the case of the European Champions

League, equally expensive. One way of addressing this issue is to include within the market definition European matches involving Premier League clubs. Even with the expansion of televised European Champions League matches in 1999–2000, Premier League matches account for over half of this larger set.

This definition and the conclusion that the Premier League and BSkyB exercise considerable market power in, respectively, the market for 'top-quality' live football matches and the market for premium sports channels can be attacked on a number of grounds. The most fundamental of these is that market definition is unnecessary and/or impracticable.

A first way of making this argument is to note that, because rights to Premier League live matches have never been bought competitively, there is no 'competitive price benchmark' against which any observed price can be compared.

More generally, it can be argued that broadcasting is an industry characterised by product differentiation. As a result, any channel faces competition from many others, and any sports channel could draw on a large range of sports material. On this view, it would be impossible to draw a line at any point in the chain of substitution and to identify a clearly defined wholesale or retail market. Moreover, the relative lack of importance of Premier League rights is shown in a variety of ways:

i) Only a small fraction (about 3%) of sports programming shown on Sky1 is devoted to live Premier League football.

ii) Subscribers to Sky Sports1 only watched a minority of the matches broadcast.

iii) The share of Sky Sports1 viewing in television viewing in pay TV homes was only 4%.

From this perspective, the chief manifestation of competition in broadcasting is not price competition but product differentiation. In these terms, broad exclusivity is a means of enhancing differentiation and sharpening competition, rather than a means of exploiting monopoly power.

In the event, the MMC and the RPC took diametrically opposed approaches to the question of market definition. According to the MMC:

> We have not found it necessary or appropriate to choose between a definition of the relevant football market based on Premier League matches only or one based on all matches involving Premier League clubs, and even in the latter case the great majority of matches would be those of the Premier League. We do not, however, see grounds for a wider definition involving the

whole of football as it does not seem credible to us that matches involving clubs drawn exclusively from divisions other than the Premier League would be acceptable substitutes for matches between leading teams (para 2.24).

To summarise, we conclude that the relevant broadcasting market for our purposes is the market for pay TV sports premium channels. We see this market as being one level in the hierarchy of broadcasting markets (para 2.51).

The conclusions of the RPC in its judgement were, by contrast:

The considerations set out in the previous paragraph seem to us to cause great difficulty both in identifying the appropriate market (because the risk of concluding that any differentiated product forms its own market) and in identifying a competitive price level (because competitive price levels can only be readily determined in homogenous markets, page 125).

While it is clear to us that Sky enjoys a very strong position in the provision of specialised sports channels, and that this position is attributable in part to its possession of the rights to Premier League live matches through the period of the two contracts, the arguments that this had improved, sharpened or enabled competition seems [sic] to us to be more convincing than the arguments that it has distorted or discouraged it.

The significance of this divergence of view is that the MMC was able, on this foundation, to anticipate a reduction in competition in broadcasting resulting from the proposed merger. The RPC, by contrast, concluded that BSkyB's exclusive access to Premier League live rights has enhanced competition in an (implicitly) wider broadcasting market.

5. THE FUTURE

The decision of the RPC has placed the Premier League in a position where (subject to the provisions of the Competition Act, 1998, which comes into force in March 2000) it can continue to sell its rights on a collective and exclusive basis. This does not necessarily mean a repetition of the two Premier League/BSkyB agreements already concluded. In particular:

i) BSkyB may face more significant competition than it has in the past, from a variety of sources, including both broadcasters and others. The latter may include financial institutions and the Premier League itself, which could provide its own football (or sports) channels.

ii) The Premier League may choose to sell its rights not to a single wholesaler (which in BSkyB's case is also a direct-to-home retailer), but on a platform-by-platform basis. This would involve negotiating separate deals with cable operators, the digital terrestrial television broadcaster, ONDigital and a satellite broadcaster (which is likely to be, but need not necessarily be, BSkyB). Such an arrangement would present significant practical difficulties over pricing the deal, but would put the Premier League in a position where it would negotiate direct with all operators, rather than via BSkyB.

iii) The question of pay-per-view rights will acquire much greater prominence in the next negotiation than it has to date. Developments in and the spread of digital television make pay-per-view much more practicable. The larger and more popular clubs will be reluctant to submit the pay-per-view revenues associated with their matches to redistribution, as is now the case with the BSkyB contract.

iv) The issue of mergers or takeovers involving broadcasting firms and football clubs is likely to recur. The MMC report on BSkyB's proposed merger with Manchester United does not appear to rule out other such mergers, and a ministerial statement on this issue is awaited.

From the OFT's position, the replacement of BSkyB as exclusive buyer of Premier League rights by another exclusive buyer would have a relatively limited effect upon the market for premium sports channels, although the consequential effects in the rest of the premium pay TV market would be mitigated if BSkyB maintained its strong role in film channels. The development of pay-per-view would increase opportunities for households to get access to matches additional to the 60 now available, but if these were sold on an exclusive basis then they too would be subject to monopoly pricing. This means that, although more games might be available to the public, the pricing of each would be set with an eye to its impact on demand for the others. The outcome would thus differ markedly from what would emerge under competitive pricing.

6. SOME TENTATIVE CONCLUSIONS

This chapter has argued that, because of the impact which sports rights have on broadcasting, it is both inevitable and desirable that the way in which they are sold comes under the scrutiny of the competition authorities. In the UK this has happened twice in recent months, as the MMC has examined and recommended the prohibition of the takeover by BSkyB of Manchester United, and the RPC has concluded that the arrangement under which Premier League rights are collectively and exclusively sold to BSkyB (live rights) and BBC terrestrial (highlights) confer benefits and are in the public interest. It is, however, apparent from a comparison of the MMC report and the RPC judgement that the framework of analysis adopted by the two bodies has been significantly different. The MMC has undertaken a standard analysis aimed at defining markets at the wholesale level and the retail level (premium sports channels). It has then gone on to investigate the likely impact of a merger within that analytical framework, reaching the conclusion that the merger would further restrict entry into the sports premium channel market and cause retail prices to be higher than would otherwise be the case. This would feed through into reduced competition in the wider pay TV market.

The RPC, by contrast, concluded that market definition in relation to broadcasting was infeasible, in part because competition took place on the basis of differentiation. On this footing it concluded that the current restrictions conferred specific and substantial benefits because *inter alia* they encouraged, rather than impeded, competition among broadcasters.

The RPC set against this benefit the fact that the restrictions do cause less Premier League football to be shown on television than would be the case in their absence. But it did not attach much weight to this detriment. As a corollary, if the restrictions were struck down there would be a greater choice of programmes comprising Premier League matches. However, the court concluded that it could not prescribe an alternative régime which would improve matters *vis-à-vis* the continuation of the restrictions. The choice it had to make lay between the restrictions in the current agreement or no restriction at all. Given the benefits that it perceived as flowing from the restrictions (including both enhanced competition in broadcasting and other benefits relating to football) it concluded that the restrictions were in the public interest.

This analysis lays bare two particularly interesting aspects of the UK competition law approach to the relationship between sports rights and broadcasting. The first is that the MMC and the RPC reached diametrically opposite conclusions on the applicability to the broadcasting industry of the market analysis standard in competition cases. The second is that the RPC interpreted the Restrictive Trade Practices Act, 1976, as constraining its freedom of action to seek a solution which best furthered the public interest.[10] The alternative, which it compared to collective and exclusive selling, was universal individual selling. Intermediate solutions, such as those proposed by the director-general, could not be taken into account. Because of its interpretation of the Act, there is no way of knowing whether the court believed that such a beneficial intermediate solution existed. However, the court's recognition that the restrictions limit choice and reduce the amount of Premier League football broadcast suggests that an alternative way forward could be found.

In other words the Restrictive Trade Practices Act, as interpreted by the RPC, invites an answer to a question which, in economic terms, is of little relevance. What is required, in the public interest, is a much more nuanced approach to evaluating restrictive agreement. Fortunately, from 2000, this will be available in the form of the Competition Act, 1998, Chapter 1 of which, relating to agreements between firms, will allow the OFT to negotiate undertakings designed to retain any benefits they may have but also to eliminate any anti-competitive features.

23. Hearts, minds and the Restrictive Practices Court case

STEFAN SZYMANSKI

In footballing terms, the Office of Fair Trading (OFT) lost 5–1. Under the 1976 Restrictive Trade Practices Act (RTPA) the OFT can ask the Restrictive Practices Court to decide on whether a restrictive agreement between business organisations operates in the 'public interest'. When such cases come to court the OFT on one side presents arguments as to why any agreement in question operates against the public interest, and the companies involved (the respondents) explain why it is. In 1996 the OFT referred to the Restrictive Practices Court three agreements entered into between the Premier League and its member clubs, British Sky Broadcasting (Sky) and the BBC. These were:

(a) Rule D.7.3 of the Premier League rulebook that requires any club wishing to broadcast a match to obtain permission from the Premier League board;

(b) Clause 2.2 of the broadcasting contract between the Premier League and Sky that gives Sky the exclusive right to broadcast 60 matches;

(c) Clause 2.3 of the broadcasting contract between the Premier League and the BBC that gives the BBC the exclusive right to broadcast a highlights programme (*Match of the Day*).

In practice, any request by a club under rule D.7.3 is refused as a consequence of the exclusive broadcasting agreements. The OFT claimed these agreements operated against the public interest because they restricted consumer choice to only 60 televised matches when in practice there would be considerable demand to watch the remaining other matches (currently 320 in a season). The OFT also argued that restricting choice raised the price of the rights by creating an artificial scarcity. Lastly the OFT argued that exclusivity restricted competition among broadcasters, since Premier League football is an important driver of demand for pay TV services using new technologies.

The court ruled that the restrictions as a whole do operate in the public interest. The court identifies five specific and substantial benefits flowing from the agreements:

The ability to market the championship as a whole, not just parts of it	1–0
The ability to spend on players and stadiums	2–0
The ability to share TV income fairly	3–0
The ability to subsidise non-Premier League football	4–0
The maintenance of competition in broadcasting	5–0

If one is charitable one might say that the OFT scored one goal:

The agreements did place some restriction on consumer choice	5–1

Overall the judgement represents a fairly thorough victory for the Premier League, Sky and the BBC.

In the rest of this chapter I will give my views as to how the OFT came to lose. I must at this stage declare an interest, since I was employed by the OFT in the case to analyse issues of football economics and appeared as an expert witness for the OFT on those issues. In my analysis I will concentrate mainly on the football issues as distinct from those issues relating to competition in the broadcasting market. These are dealt with in Chapter 22 by Martin Cave (the OFT's expert witness on broadcasting) in this book, which should be seen as complementary to this chapter.

My argument is that the OFT lost for two reasons. In legal terms, the OFT lost on a technicality. The judgement states the court must under the terms of the RTPA evaluate the benefits flowing from the agreements in comparison to a world where there existed no broadcasting restrictions of any kind. This, it was admitted on all sides, would lead to chaos. The court rejected the argument of the OFT that the relevant comparison was with a world where some restrictions exist, but do not have the adverse consequences identified by the OFT and recognised by the court. The current law is to be replaced on 1 March 2000 by a new Competition Act whose interpretation may be more in line with the OFT's approach to the Premier League case. Having lost the away leg, the OFT might do better with the home advantage.

The second reason for the OFT's heavy defeat was the almost complete absence of any support for its action among the wider public. In particular a number of football supporters' associations, most members of the Football Task Force as well as a majority of journalists in the national press argued that a victory for the OFT would not be in the interests of the game. Apart from the representatives of Premier League clubs and broadcasters who appeared as witnesses in the case, the Premier League was able to produce a whole string of independent witnesses to support their case including Graham Bean, then chairman of the Football Supporters Association, David Mellor, chairman of the Football Task Force, the well-known referee David Elleray, the journalist Bryon Butler, and even Kenneth Clarke, former Chancellor of the Exchequer. Such widespread support, coming as it did from those who might be thought to be the very consumers whom the OFT was trying to defend, clearly influenced the court's decision. However, in supporting the Premier League, many of these individuals expressed strong reservations about the way football has developed in recent years. Many expressed regrets about the game's commercialisation and indicated support for root-and-branch reform of the game.

In the next section I will discuss the legal and economic reasoning that underlay the court's ruling. In the following section I will discuss in more detail the tensions underlying the qualified endorsement of the Premier League by the supporters.

2. THE REASONING BEHIND THE RESTRICTIVE PRACTICES COURT JUDGEMENT

The essence of the RTPA is the balancing of benefits and detriments arising from a particular set of restrictions to determine the public interest. In the Premier League case the court decided that the five benefits mentioned above outweighed the three detriments which the court said could reasonably be said to exist (the three can more easily be treated as one, namely the restriction of choice implied in the limitation on broadcasting).

The pivotal issue in the case turned out to be the way in which the balancing act is to be conducted. To say that a benefit arises from a restriction the court has to imagine what the world would be like if the restriction were removed. If the alleged benefit could still be produced in a world without the restriction, then the benefit cannot reasonably be said to be caused by the restriction. The court took a firm view on the limits to its imagination. 'What the court has to compare is, on the one hand, a world in which the relevant restriction exists and is given effect to and, on the other hand, a world in which no restriction at all is accepted' (Judgement, p.136). In particular this would mean comparing the current state of affairs with one in which Rule D.7.3 was 'abrogated and not replaced' (Judgement, p.139).

What this meant in practice was that if Rule D.7.3 were struck down by the court no collective agreement of any kind among the clubs to sell broadcast rights in the UK could be legally enforced. For instance, if the clubs agreed to sell a package of 60 live matches over the season, to provide a broadcaster with a coherent series of broadcasts, then there would be nothing to stop a club offering to sell any of its matches that were part of the package to another broadcaster. Obviously no broadcaster would be prepared to pay very much for a package of matches that might end up being simultaneously broadcast on other channels. In all probability collective packages would not be sold in such a world.

It was as a result of this reasoning that the court identified its five benefits. For example, it is clear that many consumers would like to see not just one-off matches in the Premier League but a whole sequence of matches following the ups and downs of the Championship leading to the end-of-season climax. Many of these people would be 'floating voters', not committed to a particular team but interested in the competition as a whole. If the existing rules were abrogated and not replaced, it is hard to imagine a package of matches that a single broadcaster would be willing or able to provide. Not only would broadcasters be wary of buying rights to individual matches over which they did not hold an exclusive right, but the clubs themselves might sell their own exclusive packages (e.g. a club channel) so that certain clubs could not be covered at all in any collective package. It would be hard to imagine an attractive package that completely excluded, say, Manchester United.

This comparison was made even less attractive by the court's view that in the absence of Rule D.7.3 the court could not reasonably speculate on who might actually own the broadcast rights to individual matches. The court viewed a régime of 'individual selling', the state of the world that would ensue on abolishing Rule D.7.3, as operating through 'a series of trilateral deals between home and visiting clubs and particular broadcasters' (Judgement, p.101).

This was not the comparison which the OFT had in mind. It argued that the only obstacle to a new set of agreements which preserved any benefits found in the current arrangements, while enhancing consumer choice, would in practice be the continued opposition of the OFT, and that in practice the OFT would not obstruct a reasonable arrangement. The simplest example of such an alternative arrangement would be to continue with the existing Sky contract for 60 matches while permitting any remaining matches to be sold individually by the clubs. The current contract effectively gives Sky the first option on all 380 matches played in a season – it can select any 60 subject to providing at least six weeks' notice of the matches it intends to broadcast. Presently when Sky does not exercise its option no one else can buy the rights instead. If Rule D.7.3 were rewritten so that clubs could not broadcast matches without prior permission of the Premier League, *but such permission could not be refused for matches not taken up under the option contract,* the most likely outcome would be that Sky or another broadcaster would be prepared to buy the option contract, while the remaining games could be sold on an individual basis or broadcast on club channels. The option contract would most likely be worth less to most broadcasters than the current contract, but this would also mean that a terrestrial broadcaster might be able to afford to compete, with obvious benefits to viewers, or the subscription for such a package on pay TV could be lower reflecting the lower cost of acquiring the rights. The main beneficiaries would probably be those fans interested in watching a club channel, mostly those committed fans who either could not afford a season ticket or were unable to travel to away matches.

Clearly, if one compares the existing arrangements with the kind of alternative world envisaged by the OFT the former yield far fewer benefits than they appear to generate when the alternative is the kind of chaotic world imagined by the court. From the legal point of view what matters here is what the law requires the court to imagine, and the court made clear its opinion. However, from a practical point of view it seems obvious that one should compare the current arrangements to the kind of régime that might actually exist in practice (indeed this is standard applied by, *inter alia*, the US Supreme Court and the European Court of Justice). The chaotic world would not be likely to occur simply for the reason that all the parties to the case, including the OFT, said they would not wish for such an outcome and collectively they would have had it in their power to produce an alternative. Thus the one régime that the court considered was one that was unlikely to occur in practice. The kinds of alternative régime that would be likely to occur were simply not considered, or given any weight, by the court.

If a coherent series of matches could have been produced in the alternative world then the existing arrangements produced no benefit on this count, removing entirely one of the five specific and substantial benefits identified by the court. As far as the remaining four are concerned, the effect of considering a plausible alternative world would not have eliminated entirely the benefits perceived by the court, but would have substantially reduced them in size. For example, in the chaotic world the income generated by TV contracts would have been substantially lower since broadcasters would have been unwilling to pay much for products (matches) that might end up being sold again by someone else. Further-more, putting together a package of matches on the basis of tripartite agreements for every single match might be difficult and it might prove impossible to create attractive packages. With much less income there would be much less to spend on players and stadiums, spending which the court considered to be an unmitigated benefit. In a more plausible alternative world the clubs might still generate less income than under the existing package, because there would be some competition between the clubs for the sale of rights, but the fall of income would be much less precipitous because it would still be possible to put together attractive packages.

The court also held that the best way to redistribute income is through collective packages. The existing agreements allocate the income from the collectively negotiated contracts on the basis of 50% allocated on an equal share to each club, 25% on the basis of merit (league position) and 25% in proportion to the number of televised appearances. If a collective package were still sold then it would continue to be possible to redistribute income from this source (as well as redistributing income in other ways such as gate-sharing and levies that have traditionally been employed in football). Finally, the court held that the Premier League would be much less likely to subsidise non-Premier League football if its collective broadcasting income were lost. If the loss were less substantial in the real world, the potential loss of subsidy would also be smaller.

When the 1998 Competition Act replaces the RTPA on 1 March 2000 the OFT will be able to challenge restrictive agreements on the same basis as under European law. The Competition Act was modelled on articles 85 and 86 of the Treaty of Rome (now articles 81 and 82 of the Treaty of Amsterdam). The article that relates to restrictive agreements is rather different from the RTPA. It prohibits agreements between undertakings, unless such agreements provide benefits for the consumers *and are indispensable for the attainment of these benefits*. Indispensability implies that the same effect could not be achieved by a less restrictive set of agreements, rather than in the absence of any agreements at all. While not impossible, it seems much less likely that Premier League agreements would pass the test of indispensability. Whether or not the OFT does choose to challenge the broadcasting arrangements of the Premier League in 2000, it is widely agreed that the new Competition Act provides a much sounder basis for dealing with restrictive agreements. Indeed, this seems to have been the view of the court, which spoke at one point about 'anomalies' created by the RTPA. 'We think that these are the inevitable consequence of an attempt to promote competition by striking down commercial provisions which have to be identified by applying the highly technical provisions of the 1976 Act. No doubt this was one of the reasons why Parliament has now repealed the 1976 Act.'

3. THE FANS

Few of those who applauded the outcome of the case were interested in the highly technical procedure that led to the court's decision. As far as they were concerned, the decision was victory for common sense, and that was all that mattered. The views expressed by the Football Task Force seem representative of a broad stream of opinion on this issue. Set up by the Labour government, it includes representatives not only from the Premier League and the Football League, but also from the PFA, the Sports Council, the League Managers Association, the Association of Premier League and Football League Referees and Linesmen, the Football Supporters Association, the National Federation of Football Supporters Clubs, the Disabled Supporters Association, from local government, the Commission for Racial Equality and Rogan Taylor of Liverpool University's Football Research Unit. One might have expected that such a disparate group of interests would find it hard to agree on anything, but in fact they managed to produce a unanimous denunciation of the OFT. In its report *Investing in the Community*, coincidentally published the day before the RPC hearings began, it declared: 'The Football Task Force is united in the belief that this outcome [victory for the OFT] would have a negative impact on English football.' David Mellor QC, chairman of the Task Force, was even more direct and described the OFT's approach as 'fat-headed'.

The Task Force assumed that, had the court agreed with the OFT, it would have meant individual selling of *all* matches, rather than the ability to sell matches individually that had not already been sold through collective agreements. The Task Force argued against the OFT on two counts. Starting from the premise that there would be no collective income left to share out, they argued that, if the OFT won its case, 'there is a strong chance that it would spell the end of redistribution of income within football'.

Second, they argued that clubs in the Football League might face bankruptcy because (a) there would be less Premier League income available as subsidies and (b) income from Football League collective agreements would also disappear. This second point seems completely erroneous since the Football League had been specifically left out of the OFT's reference, because the income generated by and level of interest in live Football League matches was not great enough to warrant a challenge on grounds of the public interest. Thus Football League clubs would have become relatively better-off compared to Premier League clubs whose TV income would be expected to fall somewhat.

As far as subsidies are concerned, the Premier League has since 1997 paid £20 million per year to the Football League clubs for player development, equivalent to £280,000 per club (compared to an average turnover in 1998 of £7.3 million for First Division clubs, £2.8 million for Second Division clubs and £1.1 million for Third Division clubs). Clearly such a subsidy could in some instances provide a substantial boost to some clubs. A further £5 million a year goes to the Football Trust (although some of this may be retained for ground developments at Wimbledon and Southampton). Furthermore, the court pointed out that the Premier League has received far more in subsidy from the Football Trust (£88.5 million) than the £12.7 million it has so far paid out. The Premier League also pays £7.5 million a year to the PFA.

Perhaps more importantly, Richard Scudamore, then chief executive of the Football League and at the time of writing (September 1999) having been offered the post of chief executive of the Premier League,[1] stated in evidence to the court that the two Leagues were interested in jointly negotiating a broadcasting contract and sharing the income. If all Premier League matches had to be sold individually, a joint contract would no longer have been possible.

Once it is agreed that redistribution would end and smaller clubs would go bankrupt as a result of a ruling in favour of the OFT, it is not hard to reach the conclusion that it would be bad for football. However, even if the decision of the court had prevented any collective selling of Premier League rights, there are grounds for caution about the Football Task Force's conclusions.

Firstly, it seems unlikely that redistribution would end if there were no collective sale of broadcast rights. Redistribution takes place in professional team sports because all the teams perceive that it is in their collective interests to ensure a degree of competitive balance. Where the players are hired in a competitive market each player attracts a salary that reflects his talents. Sharing income can promote competitive balance by equalising the purchasing power of the clubs. As long as shared resources are used to buy players (rather than to pay dividends to shareholders) redistribution will tend to create a balanced competition, and therefore a more interesting competition. The clubs support redistribution not out of goodwill, but because of their regard for their own self-interest. During the case all the club representatives that gave evidence were asked in court whether or not they would support income redistribution if collective selling of broadcast rights ended, and every one said that they personally would support it. If all the Premier League clubs supported redistribution then it would surely come to pass, and in fact under Premier League rules a redistribution scheme would require the support of only 13 clubs to become compulsory.

Whether or not redistribution were to occur, it is wrong to exaggerate the benefits of income equality among clubs. One of the notable features of the development of football over the last 30 years has been the growing inequality between clubs. At every level the income gap has widened. For example in 1967, compared to a Fourth Division club an average First Division club generated nearly four times as much income, a Second Division club over twice as much and a Third Division club around 60% more. In 1997, compared to an average Third Division club, an average Premier League club generated 21 times the income, a First Division club five times the income and a Second Division club more than double. At every level of the game, both within and between divisions, inequality has grown. The foundation of the Premier League has not stopped this trend. In the last year of the old First Division, Tottenham generated the largest turnover of any club (£19.3 million), nearly six times as much as Coventry with the lowest turnover. In 1997, Manchester United generated an income of £88 million, almost ten times as much as Southampton on the lowest income. Yet, despite this, the Premier League has been a success and top-division football in England has enjoyed unprecedented popularity. Match attendance has grown fairly consistently in all four divisions over the last ten years. If competitive balance were so critical to creating an attractive competition, we should have seen a decline in interest in recent years, not the growth we have actually witnessed.

The second reason for being cautious about accepting the Task Force's apocalyptic scenario is that the Football League clubs would be unlikely to be bankrupted even if they received smaller subsidies from the Premier League. Football clubs are businesses, and have been for over a century. They pay wages to players to entertain fans who provide the club with income through ticket sales and related expenditures. If clubs obtain income from an additional source such as a subsidy they may increase their expenditure on players. If the subsidy is withdrawn and expenditure on players is maintained then the club may be bankrupted. But the directors of the company would be negligent if they allowed this to happen. Responsible directors would ensure that expenditure on players fell so as to bring expenditure into line with income. The highly publicised cases of club bankruptcy in recent times have had more to do with irresponsible behaviour on the part of club directors, in part fuelled by the lure of Premier League TV money, rather than inequality in income distribution.

Of course, many fans would argue that even if the loss of subsidies did not lead to bankruptcy, it would be regrettable if clubs in the lower divisions were less able to finance investment in players and therefore to compete with the Premier League teams. However, this view arises from a fallacy. If my team suffers a loss of income while the income of all the other clubs remains unchanged then my team is disadvantaged. But if all the clubs suffer an equal loss of income then no one team is disadvantaged relative to another. Assuming that the effect of lost income would be greater for the Premier League clubs than the Football League clubs (since over 90% of the money goes to Premier League clubs), the relative position of the Football League clubs would actually be improved.

The losers, of course, would be the players, whose salaries would fall because there was less money available to pay them. Partly this would make England less attractive to foreign stars. This argument was endorsed by the court but notably omitted by the Task Force, since most fans realise that for every £1 million spent on attracting international talent, £10 million has gone on paying the same old players more money.

In many ways this was the real issue in the case, at least from the footballing point of view. The spiralling cost of watching football, either at the ground or on TV, has financed staggering increases in the salaries of players. Whether one begrudges the players their salaries or not, there is no obvious reason why clubs should be permitted to enter into restrictive agreements that simply have the consequence of fuelling player wage inflation. While it was reasonable for the clubs and the administrators to defend the positions that they have created for themselves, it is regrettable that so many of those who claim to represent the fans have refused to acknowledge the underlying economics of the situation. Many of these individuals bemoan the increasing cost of going to matches and the fact that many traditional fans have been priced out of the grounds. Some argue that player salaries are unreasonable and should be capped or taxed or shared out in some other way for the greater good.

Yet had the OFT won its case both the cost of watching football and player salaries would have been likely to fall. If clubs could sell individual matches not selected for a collective deal there would certainly be more broadcasters and there would follow some competition on price, and possibly even a return of top-division live football to terrestrial TV. At the grounds, some clubs already discount tickets for matches broadcast live, and if more matches were broadcast this discounting would become more widespread. One wonders why supporter groups placed so little value on this probable effect, particularly given the fact that so many matches are sold out and tickets are so expensive. One reason may be that most of the supporter groups represent fans actually going to the matches. In many cases fans who attend matches despise those who stay at home to watch, and certainly do not think that the interests of such people should be given any weight. 'Couch potatoes' do not appear to have a voice in football.

This is unfortunate, given that, depending on the match, there are as many as 20 million couch potatoes in the UK interested in football.

Perhaps a second reason for the Task Force's view was that many of the supporter groups want a far more wide-ranging restructuring of football. Many of these groups have been calling for a regulator. For example, Adam Brown, a member of the Task Force and member of the Football Supporters Association, drafted a proposal to create a 'semi-independent regulator' who would:

> establish a code of conduct for football clubs; establish binding rules for clubs; set performance targets for football clubs on a variety of issues . . . call any club to account at any time for alleged breaches of the code or rules; gain access to any evidence from clubs, including financial and ticket records; carry out spot checks; issue reports on the performance of clubs in relation to the code of conduct and make recommendations, in conjunction with the clubs, for any failure to meet standards; undertake a series of measures where the regulator has the power to enforce rules, including imposition of new club governance structures, fines and points deductions.[2]

These concerns go well beyond the notion of maintaining free and fair competition between the clubs. Because the OFT is only concerned with competition issues, rather than root-and-branch reform, many fans saw its action as at best irrelevant to the main agenda. The problem with this approach is that no government is ever likely to impose a régime as draconian as that suggested by Brown and others on what is, after all, a branch of the entertainment industry. Brown's catalogue of functions and powers is reminiscent of the kind of wartime restraints imposed on essential national industries. Even during the Second World War, when every aspect of national life was closely regulated, football was largely left to devise its own way of contributing to the war effort.[3] It hardly seems credible that such an approach would prove acceptable in peacetime.

The justification for regulatory intervention usually rests on one of three supports:

(i) natural monopoly;

(ii) income redistribution;

(iii) asymmetric information.

Asymmetric information refers to the situation where consumers have much less information about what they are buying than the sellers – as in the case of mis-selling of pensions. This problem does not seem to have any relevance to football.

Many fans have advocated regulation for the purposes of income redistribution. One justification for providing an NHS and a free education system is that if consumers had to pay out of their own pockets the poor might not be able to afford a reasonable standard of either service. Public provision through taxation is thus seen as an acceptable method of income redistribution. Many people argue that football should be treated in the same way, keeping ticket prices down so the poor can afford to attend matches. There are dangers in extending what may be a reasonable principle too far. Football is a form of entertainment rather than an essential service like health or education. It would seem ludicrous if the government tried to regulate the prices of the many forms of entertainment available on income-redistribution grounds. If the government believes that income redistribution is desirable it can achieve its aims more easily through the tax system. In cases of health and education there is a concern that redistribution through the tax system might still lead to a situation where not enough is spent on the 'merit' services. It is hard to see how this argument extends to football.

Natural monopoly is a situation where competition is not feasible since only one firm can reasonably supply the market. In most cases this is on the grounds of cost (for example, water, electricity). Economic regulation prevents the firm from exploiting consumers by restricting the prices that can be charged. Some have tried to apply the natural monopoly argument to football but there are several problems with this approach. A football club such as Manchester United is not a monopoly on grounds of cost, but because to a true United fan no other team is an acceptable substitute. Yet there is unquestionably competition among football clubs, and while committed fans may have unswerving loyalty, every club has to compete at the margin to attract floating voters and new fans entering the market. It makes no more sense to treat Manchester United as a monopoly than it does to treat the soft drink Coca-Cola as a monopoly. The Coca-Cola Corporation has only faced competition policy attention as it has acquired rival soft drinks such as Dr Pepper, just as Manchester United would not be allowed to buy up all the other teams in the Premier League.

All those who support the natural monopoly argument should also be concerned about the broadcasting arrangements since this amounts to a collection of monopolies acting in concert. However, this point does not appear to have been appreciated by any of those opposing the OFT on behalf of the fans. In any case, as long as the clubs are viewed as competitors, what is required is to ensure that competition is effective.

4. CONCLUSIONS

The direct cause of the OFT's defeat in the Restrictive Practices Court[4] was a technicality involving the way in which the court evaluated the benefits derived under the current régime. The court held that the only yardstick of comparison was with a world in which no restrictions whatsoever existed on the broadcasting of matches. Had the OFT known before the case began that the court would apply this standard it would in all likelihood have dropped the case. What the OFT envisaged was an alternative, less restrictive set of arrangements that would preserve some collective selling while permitting the individual sale of club matches not selected for the collective package. The consequence of such a ruling would have been to increase the number of matches available for broadcast and therefore to increase consumer choice.

Some commentators have argued that this outcome is likely in any case because of the developments of broadcasting technologies such as digital TV which will enlarge broadcasting capacity so as to make services such as dedicated club channels more attractive. While this may be true, it is already clear that the technology has developed more slowly in the UK than in other countries such as France, Italy and Spain, and that in the absence of competition the incentives to innovate are likely to be dulled.

The broadcasting arrangements may become more liberal in future because of the desire of the clubs to stave off further intervention from the competition authorities. Under the new Competition Act the OFT may choose to challenge the restrictions again, particularly since the standard of comparison required would be more likely to produce the result the OFT wanted. Furthermore, there have already been some indications that the competition authorities in Brussels are concerned about the anti-competitive structure of football broadcasting and could challenge the Premier League on its arrangements. These threats may provoke the clubs to widen access to broadcast matches.

If that were to happen, supporters' groups should welcome it. More generally, supporters might be better served if their representatives recognised the contribution of competition policy. Once it is accepted football is not going to become a nationalised industry or a closely regulated utility like water or electricity, it becomes clear that the supporters' main allies are the competition authorities. The aim of competition policy is to prevent the exploitation of consumers either through the abuse of market power and a dominant position or through restrictive agreements among competitors. Although the competition authorities need to recognise the peculiar economics of sport that can make activities such as income sharing pro- rather than anti-competitive, their role is ultimately to ensure full and fair competition. Competition is the best defence for the fan from increasing prices and restricted access to the game they love.

This defence cannot operate without the support of the fans. Part of the reason that the OFT lost in court is that it was not perceived to have any supporters among the fans, many of whom were prepared to testify in favour of the Premier League. In the long term, competition authorities can have little effect if they are not perceived to command public support. Of course, it may be that the OFT was wrong and that fans are better served by cosy deals entered into by the commercial directors of the clubs and the broadcasting executives. However, this does not sound like the typical opinion voiced by representatives of the fans. In the Manchester United/BSkyB takeover and subsequent MMC inquiry the fans took the opposite view from that of the clubs (the Premier League took no view and, while Arsenal, Leeds, Newcastle, Southampton and Tottenham all supported the deal, no Premier League club publicly opposed the deal). When the next Premier League broadcasting deal is announced everyone will be able to take a clearer view of the impact of the current selling arrangements. If the OFT is right, the deal will signal yet further increases in the price of watching football and continued limitations on the access to broadcast matches.

Author's note: I am grateful to Steve Ross, Martin Cave, Daniel Beard and Jon Turner for helpful comments. The views expressed, however, are entirely my own.

24. The Restrictive Practices Court case: implications for the Football League

RICHARD SCUDAMORE

BACKGROUND TO THE CASE

In 1996 the Office of Fair Trading initiated proceedings against the Premier League which challenged the legality of the Premier League's collective sale of television rights on behalf of the 20 clubs that make up the league.[1] Despite the fact that the Football League (of which I was chief executive at the time) was not formally indicted in the subsequent Restrictive Practices Court case, in many ways the Football League could be viewed as a co-defendant in the case. To begin with, the Football League operates an almost identical system of collective selling as the Premier League. Hence, the central charge of the OFT – that the Premier League's collective sale of TV rights represented a restriction akin to a cartel – applied equally to the Football League's contract for the sale of its TV rights.[2] Moreover, there is redistribution of revenue from the Premier League to other parts of the game, including the Football League. Although such redistribution is not directly part of the broadcasting rights contract, it is nonetheless influenced by the income of the Premier League and thus by the amount of revenue the Premier League attains from the sale of its TV rights.

Despite the obvious parallels with the Premier League's sale of TV broadcasting rights, the Football League was extracted from the case and the proceedings and subsequent court action were directed solely at the Premier League. Of course, one can only speculate as to the reasons underlying the OFT's decision to extract the Football League from the case, but one possibility is that the OFT may have expected the Football League to act as an expert witness on its behalf. If it could have been shown that the Premier League's contract for the collective sale of television rights operated to the detriment of the (larger) Football League, it would have clearly weakened the Premier League's defence that the contract did not operate against the public interest. Clearly, in order for the Football League to be free to act as a witness for the prosecution it could not be indicted alongside the Premier League. Initial soundings from one or two Football League clubs who had not fully understood the nature and extent of the implications of the proceedings may have given the OFT the mistaken impression that the Football League *would* act on its behalf. However, once the nature of the proceedings and the case became fully apparent, there was agreement within the Football League that ending collectivity would be detrimental to the Premier and Football Leagues alike, and in the event the Football League acted as a witness for the Premier League and the broadcasters – BSkyB and the BBC.

While many of the arguments surrounding the case apply equally to the Premier and Football Leagues, this chapter focuses on the implications from the perspective of the Football League. In particular, it argues that ending the collective and exclusive selling of television rights by the Premier League would have had three main adverse effects for the Football League. Firstly, it would have also signalled the end of collective selling and associated redistribution of income in the Football League and threatened the very existence of the league. Secondly, the end of exclusive selling in the Premier League would most probably have led to a greater number of live matches being broadcast on television which, in turn, would have reduced attendances at Football League grounds as supporters stayed at home to watch Premier League matches. Finally, an end to collectivity and exclusivity would have signalled not only the end of redistribution within the Premier and Football Leagues but also the end of redistribution from the Premier League to other parts of the game including the Football League. The rationale for these arguments is discussed below.

THE CASE FOR COLLECTIVITY AND EXCLUSIVITY

The main arguments in the RPC case centred around two inter-related aspects of the current contract for the sale of live broadcasting rights between the Premier League and BSkyB, namely collectivity and exclusivity. These two aspects are also features of the Football League's contract with BSkyB for the sale of its television rights. The Football League currently sells the live TV rights to broadcast its matches collectively on behalf of 72 member clubs. The objection raised by the OFT to such collective selling by the Premier League is that by acting collectively on the part of all member clubs, the League is restricting output (so that fewer matches are screened) and raising price. However, this objection misses the point that the League adds significant value to the quality of the matches it co-ordinates via two mechanisms.

Firstly, the League organises the matches in the form of a coherent contest for the championship operating an open system of promotion and relegation. When they form part of such a contest, individual matches generate significantly more excitement and interest than they would as a series of unconnected matches between teams. Hence, the co-ordinating role played by the League generates significant value-added in football. Secondly, the League redistributes the income it receives from the sale of TV rights from the leading to lagging clubs. The Football League is a large league comprising 72 clubs across three divisions with an average of 36 games played each week. At present about 30% of clubs have significant broadcast value, in that they are capable of attracting a TV audience that is highly valued by broadcasters. However, it would be virtually impossible, as well as undesirable, for all the matches involving the leading clubs to be screened live each week on national TV. There are clearly constraints both on the total number of matches that can be screened and the balance of matches involving leading and lagging clubs. Focusing on an élite band of leading clubs runs the risk of overexposing those clubs and diminishing interest in smaller clubs. At the same time, screening too many matches would have the adverse effect of diminishing gates and would run the risk of overexposing the league on television and reducing TV audiences.[3] In addition, there are significant scheduling problems.

The income that the Football League receives from the sale of TV rights constitutes approximately 60% of the Football League's central income and is redistributed to all clubs according to the League's redistribution rules. About 70% of clubs are net beneficiaries of TV revenue in the sense that they receive significantly more from the current scheme than they would if they sold the rights to screen their matches individually. The significance of income from redistributed TV revenues should not be underestimated. Such income can account for up to 25% of club turnover and is crucial to the economic viability of many clubs. Without this redistribution it is doubtful whether the current Football League structure of 72 clubs and three divisions could survive. Moreover, by strengthening the lagging teams, redistribution closes the gap between the leading and lagging clubs and makes the outcome of any game more uncertain. Increased competitive uncertainty makes for more exciting matches and increases interest in the game.

The above arguments illustrate the importance of collectivity for the very existence and survival of the Football League and constitute a direct argument in favour of the collective selling of TV rights. However, there are also a number of indirect arguments for collectivity. In particular, collective selling provides an efficient and effective vehicle for redistribution of income. Under the present system the League does not have to collect any monies from TV revenue from individual clubs, it simply redistributes the income it receives centrally from broadcasters. There are, therefore, no problems of clubs defaulting or reneging on payment. Other methods of redistribution that rely on collection of income from 72 individual clubs are not practical. Here, it is important to remember that the current system of collectivity and associated redistribution is agreed on a democratic basis between the clubs and is written into the rules of the League. Payments by clubs to the Football League are simply deducted from their share of broadcasting revenue. Shifting from the current system to a new system based on raising payments from individual clubs would be likely to be complex, costly and unmanageable.

The other aspect of the current contract for the sale of broadcasting rights that was central to the case was exclusivity. Under the current system, the rights to broadcast Premier and Football League matches are sold by competitive tender, for a fixed term. During this term, the broadcaster that holds the contracts has the exclusive right to screen live matches. The OFT argued that this aspect of the contract restricts competition. However, exclusivity brings a number of benefits and solves a number of problems that would otherwise beset the league. First of all, as with the performing arts, literature and music, entertainment value is associated with the uniqueness of the performance. If live performances, music and literature can be freely copied their value or saleable price falls – for these reasons property rights (in the form of copyrights) are assigned to artists to ensure that they earn some income from their art. If a football match is available through a variety of channels its price or value will fall and for some matches it will fall below the cost of providing the match. The reduction in value associated with removing exclusivity will therefore make it impossible for clubs, particularly smaller clubs where values are in any case lower, to earn any income from the sale of broadcasting rights. These problems are particularly acute in a bidding situation where each broadcaster does not know how many other broadcasters may gain the rights to screen matches. In such a situation, uncertainty over how many viewers the broadcaster can hope to attract to watch a particular match may deter broadcasters from bidding and make it impossible for clubs to realise any value from their matches.

There are also considerable scheduling and co-ordination problems associated with non-exclusive deals. Even under the current system with a single broadcaster problems are not to be underestimated, as any football fan will tell you. Moving to a system of individual selling, with each match available via more than one broadcaster, would signal the end of the centralised co-ordination provided by the current system and would exacerbate scheduling problems. But perhaps the greatest problem with calling for an end to exclusivity is the threat this would pose to attendances at the grounds. At the moment there are a limited number of live matches screened each week. If two or more broadcasters had the rights to screen matches simultaneously, it is likely that the number of matches screened each week would increase, threatening attendances at the grounds as football fans stay at home to watch games on TV rather than support their local club.

THE THREAT TO ATTENDANCE

The Football League has seen attendance at its matches grow for 13 consecutive seasons. This growth has occurred, despite the negative impact of live broadcasting, for two main reasons. Firstly, the introduction of the playoffs in 1987 contributed greatly to competitive uncertainty and boosted attendance in the latter stages of the season. Secondly, following the Taylor Report, the introduction of all-seater stadiums, better facilities at the grounds, improved access for disabled spectators and concerted action to kick racism out of football, the game has attracted a wider audience. The importance of match-going supporters to the viability of football cannot be overestimated. Gate revenue accounts for 46% of the turnover of the clubs making up the Football League. In direct terms, therefore, attendance at the ground brings in almost half of clubs' total revenue. However, to focus only on this direct effect of gate income on revenue would be short-sighted. No club would be viable for long without the support of match-going fans. Indirectly, attendance accounts for all of turnover. Any threat to attendance at the ground is a threat to the very existence of a club.

In the RPC case, statistical evidence was presented by expert witnesses for both the OFT and the Premier League regarding the impact of live televised matches on attendance. Despite its 'sophistication', the evidence of the expert statisticians was discounted by the court, partly on the grounds of its complexity but mainly because each side produced conflicting evidence without offering the court any conclusive way of deciding whose evidence was correct. For its part, the Football League chose to present a more straightforward analysis of the impact of televised matches on attendance. While our evidence may have lacked the statistical sophistication of that presented by the expert econometricians, it had the triple virtue of being intelligible to members of the court, persuasive and difficult to refute.

Our analysis compared attendances at the ground for the 1998–99 season with those of the previous season for every match that was screened live in the 1998–99 season but not in the previous season. There were some 38 matches that fell into this category of being televised in 1998–99 but not televised in the previous season. The results of this comparison are shown in Table 1. The first thing to note is that for the season as a whole, attendances were up by 2% in 1998–99 compared with the previous year.

However, for the matches that were televised in 1998–99 (but not in 1997–98), attendances fell by 12.4%. If these matches had followed the average rate of increase of attendance, then instead of falling by 12.4% their gates would have risen by 2%. Hence, the real effect of televising matches on attendance at the grounds was to reduce gates by 14.4%.

Table 1. Attendance at Grounds: 1998–99 Season v. Corresponding Fixture in Previous Year*

Nationwide games

	Percentage change in attendance
Nationwide game screened live 1998–99	–12.4
Season average	+ 2.0

Real effect	–14.4

Sample 38 matches

Attendances are also affected by live TV broadcasts of Premier League matches and European matches as supporters may choose to stay at home and watch these matches rather than go to their local ground. Table 2 shows the change in attendance compared with the previous season's fixture when Nationwide Football League matches coincided with the live televised screening of Premier League and European games.

Table 2. Attendance at Grounds: 1998–99 Season v. Corresponding Fixture in Previous Year*

Nationwide Fixture Head to Head with live Premier League or European game

	Percentage change in attendance
Premier League or European game screened live	– 7.7
Season average	+ 2.0

Real effect	– 9.7

Sample 90 matches

It can be seen that the effect of Football League matches clashing with televised Premier League and European games was to reduce attendances at the ground by 7.7%. Again, given that on average attendance was up by 2% on the previous season, the real impact on attendance at the ground was a reduction of almost 10%. In short, it can be seen that increasing the number of televised matches – which is the inevitable outcome of removing the collectivity and exclusivity of the current broadcasting contract – would reduce attendance at the grounds and undermine the long-term viability of the Football League.

THE IMPORTANCE OF RETAINING COLLECTIVITY AND EXCLUSIVITY

If the OFT had won its case against the Premier League/BSkyB contract, there would no doubt have been pressure to break the existing Football League broadcasting contract and move to a system of individual selling. This would have raised four main threats to the Football League. Firstly, it would have led to league fragmentation as the top ten or so clubs would have been able to secure individual deals, while the smaller clubs would have experienced difficulty selling the rights to their matches. Secondly, it would have signalled the end of the current system of redistribution which is crucial to preserving a degree of balance within the league. If the current redistribution mechanism had been swept away it is not clear whether it would have been possible to reach agreement between the 72 clubs over an acceptable and workable new system. Thirdly, ending exclusivity would have resulted in the market for live football being flooded, reducing the value of the rights and reducing attendance at the grounds. Moreover, while the total number of televised live matches would be likely to go up if exclusivity and collectivity were removed, the number of slots available to the Football League could actually fall as more and more slots might be filled by Premier League matches, or as Football League matches were used only to top-up Premier League packages.

Finally, there is the question of the redistribution of income between the Premier League and other parts of the game, including the Football League. At present, there is a variety of mechanisms whereby the Premier League makes payments to the Football League. Clearly, the size of these payments is affected by the amount of income the Premier League generates. If the system of collectivity and exclusivity had been brought to an end, the value of the broadcasting contract would have been adversely affected and the Premier League would have had to negotiate a new form of revenue collection from its member clubs. It is likely that both of these factors would have put downward pressure on the amount of monies available for redistribution from the Premier League to other parts of the game, including the Football League – monies that are essential to fund programmes that are vital to the future of the game, such as youth development.

THE JUDGEMENT AND THE FUTURE

In the event, the weight of the above points and of similar arguments presented from the perspective of the Premier League won the day and the

OFT lost its case. The significance of the arguments outlined above, and in particular the importance of the collectivity of the leagues, is perhaps reflected in the fact that this was the first time the OFT had ever lost a case in the Restrictive Practices Court. What remains for the future is to ensure that collectivity is preserved both within and between the Premier and Football Leagues.

PART VII

....

NURTURING THE GRASS-ROOTS:
LOCAL CLUBS AND COMMUNITY INVOLVEMENT

25. *Partners for progress*

TOM PENDRY MP

It is a pleasure to be invited to contribute to this important book on the governance and regulation of professional football. The reputation of Birkbeck College continues to grow. Indeed, one only has to look at the book's contributors to see how highly people throughout the world of football regard Birkbeck's reputation. My primary purpose in this chapter is to set out the goals and activities of the Football Trust. Before turning to that, though, there is one specific issue that requires some comment.

THE FA CUP

As most of you will know I have since the general election kept – I hope – a dignified silence on matters relating to sport which emanate from Whitehall. However, I trust that readers will not think ill of me if I break that silence in print – writing not as chairman of the Football Trust or as chairman of the All-Party Sports Group but as one who is and has been concerned with the issues facing our national game over the years. I refer to the somewhat odd decision by Manchester United to pull out of the greatest national football competition in the world – the FA Cup.

There are mixed messages coming out in the media about who has been responsible for the decision. Initial reports suggested that as a result of discussions with representatives of Manchester United the FA offered to exempt them from the competition because they were keen for the club to participate in the World Club tournament in Brazil. United decided to accept this offer. However, revelations in a national newspaper have since suggested that it was in fact a proposal first put forward by Martin Edwards that United should drop out of the FA Cup.

Whoever was responsible, one thing is clear: this decision could sound the death knell for the oldest and most important club football tournament in the world. All those teams from the Nationwide League and below will be denied their ultimate dream draw – United at Old Trafford.

Defenders of the decision for United to sit this year out say that this is a one-off situation, and that they will be back next year. But surely this sets a dangerous precedent. The damage has been done. The image is irrevocably tarnished.

THE FOOTBALL TRUST'S VISION

I am grateful for this opportunity to outline the Football Trust's vision for the future of the game, and to set out how we intend to refocus the activities of the Football Trust. I must state at the outset that when I applaud the achievements of the Football Trust, I am not slapping myself on the back. Most of what has been achieved took place before I became chairman.

Let me begin by stating clearly that our vision is one of a united game, a game where there is a common strategy for football, drawing on the good work of the football authorities and the government for the benefit of our national sport at every level.

There is a clear need for a much more unified approach to funding, a much greater sharing of good practice and for more opportunities to develop new initiatives. I have opened discussions with the Football Association, the Premier League and Sport England on how best we can achieve this.

One area, which is crying out for such an approach, is grass-roots football. By this I mean youth, women's, feeder league and parks football along with educational initiatives and community and social-inclusion projects. It is in this key area that the vital work of the Trust has never been more needed. There are a number of investment initiatives already in place, for instance, Howard Wilkinson's Charter for Quality – a comprehensive strategy for the development and nurturing of excellence in youth football.

Underpinning the Charter is the FA's National Facilities Plan for Football – an assessment of the facilities required to realise its goals. The FA cannot fund the plan alone and will rely on county FAs, Sport England and, crucially, local authorities and our help to implement it.

The FA Premier League should also be applauded for its investment of some £20 million in the development of Schools of Excellence at professional clubs. But much more needs to be done for the rest of the game.

The more equitable distribution of football's new-found wealth is a major issue in the game. There is money aplenty at the very top of the game but many Football League clubs still struggle to survive. There is compelling evidence that grass-roots facilities, at schools and in the parks, are in a desperate state of repair and are crying out for investment.

Over 70% of organised football takes place on local-authority facilities. County FAs are assessing the needs in their area but it is clear that substantial investment will be required to meet the need for small-sided pitches and to improve facilities to the required standard. Pressure on local-authority finances by central government and a disinclination by government to stop them in the late 1980s and early 1990s led to the sale of pitches and the decline of remaining facilities through a combination of over-use and under-investment.

Some 10,000 sports fields, mostly but not all schools pitches, have been sold in the last 20 years. The government has put in place important measures to halt the sale of school playing-fields. However, many primary schools in inner cities no longer have access to grass pitches. In 1996, local authorities estimated that there would be a maintenance backlog of £255 million in school sports facilities by the year 2001. Is it any wonder that our sports people struggle at international level?

With the government's initiative to encourage local authorities to buy up brown-field sites for conversion into playing-fields, the Football Trust will be ideally placed to help fund the building of vital ancillary facilities. Furthermore, thanks to the commitment of the government – ensuring that the pools companies are able to continue their annual contribution to the Trust until March 2003 – we are able to make our contribution to tackle these new investment priorities and broaden the Trust's remit.

The extension of the Trust's present Reduction in Pool Betting Duty (RPBD) income will, I hope, spring funding from the football authorities, notably the Premier League, enabling the Trust to return to being a major player in developing primarily the grass-roots and to continue where possible in providing essential support to the Football League, Conference and national lower-league system for safety and improvement work.

Chris Smith, the Secretary of State for Culture, Media and Sport, underlined the government's commitment to the Trust by asking us to turn our attention now to improving facilities at the grass-roots level and in schools in line with the FA's Charter for Quality. This Charter sits comfortably with the government's ideas on mass participation in all sports and should be commended and taken forward.

Chris Smith also pointed to the success of the Trust as a role model for other areas of sport when he stated:

> This is the kind of partnership that we would like to encourage with all the main governing bodies of sport. The government will continue to back sport – but in return we would expect all sports to invest in their own grass-roots development.

One of the Trust's greatest strengths is that it brings all of football's major players together round one table. The FA Premier League, the FA, Sport England, pools companies, the Football League and the PFA *are* the

Trust. Each has made and continues to make a vital contribution to football through us. We are the established vehicle for aiding football through grants that brings together government and football in a unique and meaningful partnership. As the Secretary of State rightly pointed out, this is surely the way forward.

With government support and the continued commitment of our funding partners we can create a long-term partnership and strategy for our national game. With future television deals reportedly to be worth £1 billion there are widespread calls for more investment in our game to provide the right facilities for all, and Chris Smith's announcement that a levy on the next broadcasting deal will help fund the grass-roots is warmly welcomed. It is all very well talking about the Michael Owens of the future, but they need teams to play in and pitches to play on. To get the best we have to provide for the rest.

Further consideration could also be given to introducing a new levy on football betting with the proceeds flowing to the Trust. The pools companies continue to face stiff competition from the National Lottery, whereas the now booming bookmaking industry is making substantial profits from football. In 1998 the Horserace Betting Levy Board received some £58 million from the bookies and are lobbying hard for a 43% increase in this figure to yield £80 million. The bookmakers themselves identify football as the growth area of the sports betting market and are effectively using it to subsidise betting on other sports. Currently the only money that the industry gives to football is a licence fee of £275 per shop with no correlation to turnover. The time has surely come for them to put more back into the game.

The Trust has made an important contribution towards nurturing the grass-roots in the past with some £50 million invested, but much more needs to be done. The Football in the Community programme owes its very existence to the Trust and our investment of some £5.5 million. Substantial investment has been made in training facilities and youth development but we were forced to limit our contributions due to the pressure on our finances.

Our record remains a proud one. In 1999 alone the Trust made over 150 grant offers. This funding went to a wide range of initiatives and facilities such as the Kick Racism Out of Football campaign, the Learning through Football initiative, and women's football as well as towards the important area of work related to the Taylor Report at clubs. Our grant awards, large or small, play a fundamental part in the future of football. The Trust gets the money efficiently and effectively to where it matters most.

Our main focus has been overseeing the successful implementation of the Taylor Report. That, I am proud to say, has been virtually completed and we can boast some of the finest grounds in Europe, if not the world. These are grounds fit to grace the 2006 World Cup and I am sure that Tony Banks and his team are using that fact in their quest for us to host that event. The Trust has played a huge part in this success story.

We are ready to broaden our remit into player development and education and to ensure greater investment in the grass-roots, including community-based facilities, schools, building links between clubs and communities, supporting inner-city schemes, encouraging the development of education centres at football and support for park teams. The Trust can play a significant role in these areas especially in countering social exclusion and I know that the government is anxious that we do so. Social exclusion encompasses members of our society that have been disadvantaged. Most people consider the term social exclusion to mean poverty alone whereas in reality it engulfs a whole range of issues including low incomes, ill health, unemployment, poor skills, poor housing, high crime environments and dysfunctional or broken families.

Personally, I think of it as coming down to one core characteristic: alienation. Football can be used as a motivator for those affected. We have already seen a number of key educational initiatives springing up at professional clubs – pioneered at Middlesbrough and funded by the Trust. Children love being involved with the schemes and results suggest significant improvements in the literacy and numeracy of the participants. The professional clubs already involved in such projects are to be applauded and this work should be built upon to resolve the problem of alienation and disaffection amongst our youth. My colleague the Parliamentary Under Secretary of State for the Department for Education and Employment has been particularly impressed with the clubs' positive influence, commending them wholeheartedly for their efforts.

From a purely footballing perspective the following may appear obvious, but nevertheless it is worth pointing out that contact by clubs at this stage may often prove to be an investment in securing the clubs' next generation of supporters.

One aspect of these schemes that has been brought to my attention on several occasions – and does have serious cause for concern – is that take-up rates continue to be the lowest for the poorest groups in society. There is a clear need for research to be undertaken amongst all participants in these educational schemes to identify how and why certain individuals participate and to use them as a model for those that do not.

In recent weeks we have heard many opinions on the role that competitive sports can play in school and I wholeheartedly support the

£60 million initiative that the Secretary of State has launched through the National Lottery and New Opportunities scheme to create a team of 600 Active School Co-ordinators. I believe that exposing children to competitive team-sports is a vital component of their learning. For years there was a misconception that the Labour Party was against such activity – as Labour's spokesman from both the front bench and back benches for some 15 years I can assure the reader that this was never our policy. Some local authorities may have taken that stance, but that is a different matter, and in my view such policies were mistaken.

The government is committed to improving the understanding of the characteristics of social exclusion and the promotion of solutions to it. Sport impacts on government policies, bringing huge benefit to the country and the community. Football has a role in the economy, the environment and national culture, in health and well-being issues, in combating crime, drug abuse and unsociable behaviour.

CONCLUSIONS

I am not alone in thinking that sport, and football in particular, can play an enormous role in fulfilling these objectives. There are many fine social-inclusion projects being run up and down the country all in desperate need of finance, projects which use football as a means to tackle youth crime such as the Divert Trust or the National Association for the Care and Rehabilitation of Offenders (NACRO), and Salford Football Community Link Project which was famously visited by Eric Cantona as part of his community service.

Wolverhampton Wanderers FC are seeking funding for a pioneering scheme involving the creation of midnight leagues for teenagers in high-crime areas. There are many other schemes in need of help and the opportunity is there for us to help promote, fund and where necessary launch new initiatives in these areas.

Football is currently riding the crest of a wave of popularity and has risen from its darkest days of the 1980s to once again truly capture the imagination of the nation. Now is the time to embrace this mood of optimism and create a long-term partnership and strategy for our national game. With the continued commitment of government and our funding partners, I can assure you that the Football Trust will be working flat out to achieve that goal.

26. Kick Racism out of Football

PIARA POWER

This chapter opens with a brief overview of the campaign to rid football of racism – how we came about as an organisation, and what our activities consist of.

I think sometimes people are confused about the name 'Kick It Out' and the title of the campaign which is the 'Let's Kick Racism out of Football Campaign'. Broadly speaking, the campaign was launched in the season 1993–94 as a partnership between the Commission for Racial Equality and the Professional Footballers Association. That partnership managed to build a fairly comprehensive grouping of representatives from across the game, including the Football Association, the Football Trust, the leagues – the FA Premier League and the Football League – and organisations representing supporters' groups, the safety officers, the referees' groups and so on. In 1997 the footballing organisations decided that it would be a good idea to set up a campaign as an independent organisation with financial support from the Football Trust, the FA Premier League, the FA and the PFA.

The development of the campaign into one being run by an independent organisation has meant that we are now able to do some of the harder work – reaching out to clubs, local authorities, local supporters' groups, local ethnic minority communities and so on to try and redress some of the problems of racism. People often tell me that the problem is not as acute as it once was, that you do not hear, for example, racist abuse and chanting on the same scale as you once would have done even five or six years ago within football stadiums. It is certainly true, as I am sure many readers will recall, that even fairly recently it was not uncommon to hear 200 or 300 people singing chants that were overtly racist, directed at black players or ethnic minority communities of certain towns. It is true that this has diminished to some extent. I think this is partly due to the development of the modern football ground through all-seater stadiums and undoubtedly through the gentrification of supporters at the higher levels of the game within the Premier League.

Having said that, there is still a great deal to be done. There are still many incidents of racist abuse and chanting at football matches and some of the harder work that we are looking to do is indeed to take the campaign down to the grass-roots, to work with organisations such as county FAs and local authorities who own most of the pitches on which amateur teams play, to try and challenge the problem at that level. It is a massive problem and it is incredibly difficult to make sure that every single base is covered. But we are hoping that over the next three or four years we will see some real changes in the way that amateur football is being governed and a reduction in the number of incidents of racist abuse that we see at that level.

ETHNIC MINORITY COMMUNITIES

Turning to some of the other elements of our work – and this is the key insight that this chapter can hope to contribute to the current volume – we are increasingly working with professional football clubs to try and over-come historical exclusion of ethnic-minority communities as supporters, as players, and as employees within football clubs, not to mention as directors and owners.

The starting point has to be that until very recently most football clubs have had a poor record at doing any sort of community work. This was the case until perhaps three or four years ago. The work that was done was focused around the 'football in the community' schemes. And unfor-tunately those schemes were often hindered by a lack of support at boardroom level. We are hindered by clubs failing to see the importance of such schemes. Most have to raise the funds themselves; they have to go out and earn the money to spend on balls and other equipment. This is done largely through offering middle-class children coaching courses in school holidays, after school hours in areas that are often far removed from the localised support for a professional football club, but also from the location of a football club.

There are clubs in London, for example – I shall not name them because my task in this volume is not to name and shame – who have football in the community officers that go as far away as Guildford and Brighton to deliver courses to youngsters for which their parents are paying £30 a week, or even sometimes £10 or £15 a session. Clearly this can only be done by drawing on the appeal that only a Premier League football club will have. This does not constitute community work in the proper sense of that term.

In a geographical sense, at least, the local communities for football clubs are often ethnic-minority communities. Most football clubs in this country are based in areas that were once inhabited by what might be termed 'traditional working-class populations' and as those white working-class populations have moved on, ethnic minorities have moved in. West Ham is a good example of this, in the Upton Park area. Arsenal, likewise, and I suspect that in some ways Tottenham are an even better example. In Manchester you have the example of Manchester City in Moss Side. In Birmingham you have a similar picture with Aston Villa and Birmingham City, and so on. We could draw up a chart of top football clubs in this country and probably find that most of them are in areas where there are high ethnic-minority populations. Historically the problem has been that those ethnic-minority populations have felt a dislocation from the game. This has come about for various reasons. The most obvious one is because of the racist abuse and chanting that was heard within football stadiums, as well as the sort of behaviour that we saw outside the stadiums when supporters would often be openly racist. This led ethnic minorities to think that football, professional football at least, was not for them. They might observe it from a distance, watch it on TV, and perhaps even hear the roar of the crowd from their houses, but they were not going to venture into unwelcoming and even dangerous football stadiums.

There is a very real and important connection that most football supporters have with their clubs. David Conn has referred to it being in your blood.[1] But unfortunately the fact is that for many ethnic minorities, football is not in our blood in the same way in which it is for traditional white working-class football supporters, simply because we have been excluded from being able to take part in the rituals and the tribalism, which are important parts of the experience of being a real football supporter. It is worth spelling out the problem in these terms, I think, as it illustrates the distance that needs to be travelled if the effects of racism in our game are to be truly overcome. It is not just a question of preventing racist chanting and abuse. Until all communities in Britain are able to feel that their support for their team is really in their blood then it suggests that the legacy, at least, of racism in and around football in Britain remains to be overcome.

One of the problems that we have in the campaign against racism is that whilst many clubs would pay lip service and say 'Well we're anti-racist, we don't want racists at our club', actually getting clubs to agree to a programme of work that delivers' is a different thing altogether. Even making sure that action is taken against anybody who is caught engaging in racist abuse and chanting is an uphill struggle. Too often, stewards simply ignore it. Until recently it was not even an arrestable offence to be guilty of racist abuse – provided you were just an individual racist, not a collective. The work of the Football Task Force has had a positive impact here, with an amendment to the Football Offences Act having been passed. It is now an arrestable offence to be engaged in racist abuse whether collectively or individually. This is a measure that is fundamental to civil liberties. If I am walking down the street and am abused by somebody, I think I have the right to report it to the authorities, and to expect that the authorities will take action on that.

The more proactive element is the way in which football clubs can use their considerable voice amongst supporters to send out an anti-racist message. This is being done increasingly effectively. Clubs like Charlton Athletic and Leicester City are working with their players in anti-racist campaigns, exploring how these players feel about abuse when it is directed at them, to try and challenge some of those attitudes over a long period of time.

One of the other positive developments that football has seen over the past few years has been the development of educational work. I think that, through the Department for Education and Employment government initiative alongside the Premier League, we are now going to find more and more professional clubs, particularly Premier League clubs, setting up classrooms and educational facilities at their grounds. They will have educational programmes with a classroom based at the club with a focus on excluded children coming into the stadium to take lessons in literacy, numeracy and IT skills. This opens up possibilities for us to pursue anti-racist work at an incredible level. We are now finding teachers coming into those posts and working with children at football clubs, using players, trying to work with the management of professional football clubs to make them understand some of the issues that we are dealing with. A great example of this is Leeds United who have developed something called Community United. This is based on an educational initiative but it looks at all other areas in which the club could have an influence on. It considers bullying, anti-racism, sexism in schools and so on. There really is the opportunity for clubs to play a major role in working with local communities to try and overcome some of the historical problems that have existed around racism, using football as a force for good.

I will conclude the chapter with this final point, that football clubs have untapped markets sitting on their doorstep. For example, we do not in this country have a single Asian professional footballer at the moment, within any of the professional football leagues. This is astounding when you look at the demographics of the Asian community, which has the highest number of under-30s of any ethnic group. The Asian community also has amongst the highest levels of participation in football of any ethnic group. Despite some of the stereotyping that goes on of young Asian footballers, there are definitely some good players out there. In an age where football clubs are looking to build academies in Australia, South America, Ireland and South Africa, failing to tap into footballing talent at home is not just a moral question; it is a question of economics. Clubs are failing to reach out and draw on the talent that is there. They are failing to market themselves to communities that should be providing the supporter base, should be getting a stake in football. Until this exclusion is overcome, the real loser will be football itself.

27. The future of football: safe in whose hands?
TONY CLARKE MP

Not a day goes by without the national media passing comment on the off-field dramas affecting Britain's football clubs. It would seem that at any one point in time, there are a number of clubs on the brink of administration or closure. At other clubs, boardroom unrest causes friction. In addition, fans of clubs up and down the country launch protests against their chairmen, and local councils are lambasted (usually when planning permission is denied for that promised new ground).

Reporting the politics of football has become as commonplace as reporting the outcome of games played. No club however highbrow or humble is exempt. Whether it is the question of Manchester United's refusal to defend the FA Cup or Barnet's battle against the planners regarding a new home, the behind-the-scenes goings-on are reported to the fan base and then discussed at great length amongst supporters in clubs and bars across the country.

This outpouring of information and debate has in the main been welcomed by fans across the country. The previous diet of clandestine dealings and boardroom silence only led to unrest amongst supporters who had become used to being treated like second-class citizens. After all, what other business in the world would treat its customers as abysmally as football clubs treated their supporters during the 1970s and 1980s? Considering that a club's income stream has always been, and still is, so reliant on its fan base, it is difficult to understand why we were ever treated so badly – or why we put up with it.

Thankfully there have been improvements. Grounds and the facilities therein continue to improve, information through clubcalls, fanzines and the internet keep us much more in touch with the day-to-day happenings at the clubs. More importantly, independent supporters associations, trusts and supporter-shareholder groups are playing a growing participatory role in the running of football itself.

The example of supporter involvement within the boardroom at my own club, Northampton Town, together with the slightly different but equally interesting supporters' revolution at Bournemouth are well recorded, and give hope to all those frustrated fan groups out there that see a brighter future for their own clubs with the promise of greater supporter involvement. But on their own they do not represent the whole picture as to the future of football within Britain. To understand the future of football across the whole spectrum we have to reflect on how clubs at all levels operate with differing management structures, and perhaps even differing priorities as to their purpose and existence.

To do this I would like first to divide football clubs in to three main groups and categories. Each is easily definable and probably instantly recognisable by supporters in respect to where their own club would fit.

1. THE CORPORATE MONSTERS

The first group consists of those clubs which will increasingly become the corporate playthings of multinational industries and business. Institutions such as BSkyB and NTL have already made their move into the market, but these will soon be joined by others, not necessarily restricted to the media field. The fact is that the Manchester Uniteds, Chelseas and Arsenals of this world are seen less as football clubs by potential investors and more as income streams and useful share portfolios.

These markets are not just domestic; they are global. As long as Manchester United continue to perform at a reasonable level on the European and world stage then their corporate owners will continue to take delight in their ability to peddle produce across the globe at unsuspecting individuals who have never, and probably will never, visit the British Isles let alone come close to attending a match at Old Trafford.

Is it too late to stop this corporate monster? It now has a life force of its own. Even if the local communities whom these clubs used to serve were to turn their back on them a new stream of ready-made supporters will be on hand to take their place. And it is not just the Manchester Uniteds of this world that aspire to this golden future of share options and virtual-reality fan bases. Even the likes of Wimbledon FC have suggested through their approach to move to Dublin, and their continued absence from the Wimbledon locale, that where a club is based plays second fiddle to the potential for increased profits.

Manchester United now spend more time in Europe that they do at home in Manchester. Why not move them to London to make travelling that much easier and bring them into closer contact with their fan base? I jest, of course, and true supporters of the club will be horrified at the thought, but are nevertheless aware that unless their corporate culture is somehow checked then they will continue to leave their community roots even further behind.

2. THE PERSONAL FIEFDOMS

The second group of clubs fall into the category of personal fiefdoms, the playthings of individual chairmen who always wanted to own their own football club, in the same way as little boys who always wanted their own train set. Their open, philanthropical attitude is not, however, to be ridiculed, as their desire is often born out of real love and affection for their respective clubs. The potential progress of such clubs is really only limited by the size of the cheque book. Of course the agenda of all individual owners is not always so well intentioned. Supporters should ask themselves some deep questions as to the amount invested by the individual against any potential return from the assets owned by the same clubs. Inner-city building land is hard to come by and extortionately priced. The intended move to a green-field site – releasing the original ground for redevelopment – can be a big money-spinner for an individual owner.

The other concern for this group (or perhaps not, as some may welcome it) is a sell-off to the above group of corporate clubs. Surely the most worrying and of course exciting time of any supporter's life within these clubs must be those heady days of potential and promised promotion to the Premiership and the concern as to what life will be like on the other side?

3. LOCAL PARTNERSHIP

The final group are those clubs which survive on the back of differing partnerships between local businessmen, local authorities and well-off (but not necessarily hugely rich) individuals, the vast majority of whom are true supporters of their respective clubs.

As an example, Northampton Town has a board of six voting members and one observer. The six members include five local businesspeople (all of whom are devoted to the future of Northampton Town) and myself as the elected representative of Northampton Town Supporter Trust. Each of the six, including the trust, own shares in the club. In rounded terms these shareholdings (which do fluctuate as new investments are made) are above 10% but usually less than 30%. The local authority, Northampton Borough Council, own the ground, and derive a rent from the football club. As a result they have an observer who sits in on board meetings but has no vote. The right of the supporter trust to be represented on the board is of course clear as a major shareholder, but in addition the place is protected as of right as part of the lease agreement with the local council. At Bournemouth all the directors are part of a supporter group as well as being local businessmen. Quite unfairly, other supporters have suggested that having become directors they are now not truly representative of the view of fans.

Having met the chairman (and indeed played football in a charity game with him) it would seem that their devotion to Bournemouth FC is as great today as it was on the day they took over the reins. Perhaps it is simply a matter of improving communication channels between the terrace and the boardroom.

NO TAXATION WITHOUT REPRESENTATION

Having defined the different types of club, and the variety of management styles and ethos, how will the future of football shape up over the coming years? And can the community-based clubs, mentioned as the last example of the above three, ever compete with the bigger clubs? Perhaps more importantly, can the supporters' revolutions experienced at the lower levels of the league ever translate into boardroom representation at the highest level of the game? The answer, I firmly believe, is yes. The final report of the Football Task Force (eagerly awaited as I write) is widely expected to broach the sensitive subject of supporter representation at all levels of the game. At the same time financial and legal support for the formation of supporter trusts across Britain has been promised by the government.

Hopefully, clubs throughout the country will welcome the positive contribution that supporters and their organisations can make to the running of football. However, such groups should not simply await an open invitation to the boardroom. They should seek representation on equal terms, raise funds and become shareholders in their own right.

As a director, I often meet groups of fans at grounds (sometimes even in boardrooms) who contribute vast sums towards the running of their respective clubs. Sometimes known as vice-presidents clubs or maybe golden sponsors, what they all have in common is that their cash input buys very little other than a hot sausage roll and a padded seat. It is high time that supporters' groups asserted their right to access to the decision-making process as a prerequisite for the continued financial investment in their clubs over and above the money paid through the gate.

If anyone believes that the above model cannot be transferred into the bigger club world, then look no further than the mutually owned FC Barcelona as a role model of what is possible. Even the Manchester United board, through its share issues and recent attempt to sell the club, must accept that all shareholders have a role to play in the wider decision-making process. Just imagine what could be achieved if all of those individual shares came together within a trust which could then elect a representative to the plc board.

SUPPORTERS UNITED

Football still faces some stiff challenges over the next few years. Wages continue to spiral, TV contract payments still fail to be distributed fairly to clubs at the lower levels, and the need for a football regulator becomes more and more urgent. However, football's future can become a whole lot brighter provided clubs and supporters grasp the opportunities that wider supporter involvement can bring.

So where in the above descriptors does your club fit at present: Corporate monster? Personal fiefdom? Or local partnership? And what opportunities currently exist to enable supporters at your club to have a real say in day-to-day decision-making? These are the questions all true football supporters should ask themselves. And at a time when support funding is becoming available, there has never been a better time to act. Forget that televised Champions League game (there will be another along in a minute) and start organising that first public meeting. Football Supporters of Britain Unite! You have nothing to lose but your subservience.

28. The Football Task Force and the grass-roots
CHRIS HEINITZ

The Football Task Force, of which I was a member, looked beyond the glamour of the English Premiership to the grass-roots of football through-out the country. And, as detailed in our published reports, we found a very different and disturbing picture from the one that the increasing broad-casting revenues usually cast in people's minds.

The selling-off or disposal of playing-fields has led to the over-use of the remaining ones. In addition to – or, perhaps we should say, despite of – this process of disposing of playing-fields, there has also been a vast reduction in the level of maintenance of these playing-fields. For example, during the work of the Football Task Force, the North West Authority that we talked to reckoned that it had a backlog of £2.8 million of maintenance of its football fields. The changing facilities on those football fields consisted of steel containers. Then there was the very wealthy London authority that had a £500,000 shortfall on maintenance of its playing-fields and had no hot running water at any of the changing-rooms. There is a similar picture all round the country. In certain areas there is the additional complication – and problem – that traditionally a large amount of the recreational facilities were provided by an organisation called CISWO, the Coal Industry Social and Welfare Organisation. The closure of pits has resulted in a vast number of CISWO schemes either being closed outright or sold off.

All this is against the background of the Taylor Report. We estimated that £78 million of public money in the form of grants and interest-free loans was provided to the Premier League clubs alone via the Football Trust to implement Lord Justice Taylor's recommendations, with further funding to the Football League clubs. The wealth that people talk about as if it were being generated by the Premier League has actually been totally dependent on that investment of public money in those Premier League clubs. The boom in football, the middle-class fashion of football, would never have happened without that public investment in football grounds. One of the things we in the Football Task Force were saying in our *Football in the Community* report is that it is now payback time. One of the key proposals from that report was that for the foreseeable future a proportion of the television income for the Premier League ought to be invested in grass-roots football – in actually tackling the business of facility development, of changing facilities and all those other areas that desperately need investment. What is now a very rich game ought to be paying back the grass-roots community of football.

This proposal from the Task Force has now been accepted by government and will be implemented. This was spelt out by Chris Smith at the 1999 Labour Party conference at the same time as he committed government to support greater fan involvement in their clubs. Both announcements are to be warmly welcomed.

What I would describe as the threat to this progress from the Office of Fair Trading is dealt with elsewhere in this volume, but it should be said here, in the context of funding the grass-roots, that the proposal to break up the collective bargaining on television rights is indeed just that – a threat to the integrity of the game collectively, not just to the right to organise collectively in leagues, but also a threat to redistribution between leagues. The entire proposal for creating this investment in the grass-roots from a proportion of the revenues from the Premiership television rights deal would be destroyed if the Office of Fair Trading were successful. Of course, the OFT lost their 1999 case in the Restrictive Practices Court case, and this decision was a victory for football in general and for football fans in particular. But as can be seen by reading Chapter 23 in this volume by the OFT's own expert witness, Stefan Szymanski, the threat is still there. They have not necessarily accepted defeat.

The other important proposal from the Football Task Force in this regard is our recommendation that there should be a single pot for development of grass-roots football rather than all the different pots we have at present. In particular, we need to find a way of putting together the television money, the Football Trust money, the Premier League and lottery money and so on, to allow a coherent strategy for the development of the grass-roots of the game. Again, progress on this front is being made by government and, with the Football Trust's remit ending in April 2000, the proposals for funding and organising these sorts of developments will, it is to be hoped, be brought together within a more coherent and progressive strategy.

The final point to make in this chapter concerns the question of stadium development. This is another way in which local government is involved in professional football. It is the area in which local government usually gets all the worst headlines. Everything regarding stadiums tends to be portrayed in the media as being the fault of local government. If a stadium is not developed, the local authority is blamed, while it is rare indeed for local government to be praised when a stadium is successfully developed.

We need a spirit of partnership that understands that local government has far more of a role than just supporting directors of a football club. I had dealings a few months ago with one of our member authorities who was being criticised in the press, with vicious attacks from a developer who wanted to sell off two rugby grounds plus the football ground and build a new stadium on the prime site in the city centre which was the major site for economic development in the city concerned, which was an area of high unemployment. The city council had to say to the club and to the developer, quite properly, 'We very much want to help you but we cannot possibly consider you without considering the 17 other bids for this site.'

Another example of irresponsible reporting would be the demands being put on Islington as a local authority regarding Arsenal's desire to redevelop their Highbury ground on its present site. Reading some of the coverage, you would not realise that just to give the go-ahead would involve the demolition of at least 500 houses. Local government does have to play an overall role on behalf of the local community.

A more positive example is the magnificent development of the McAlpine stadium at Huddersfield. This was a wonderful example of the local authority being the instigator of partnership between two sports clubs and developers in order to look at the regeneration possibilities. They looked not just at the possibilities for the clubs, but also at how the development would actually help redevelop an important part of Huddersfield that was economically and socially deprived.

There has been a lot of good work and constructive proposals arising from the work of the Football Task Force. Government is now acting on this in a positive way. It seems that the high-water mark of irresponsible profiteering at the top, with disgraceful neglect of the grass-roots, has happily been reached. There is a growing recognition that we need a coherent strategy for the entire game. And to see that strategy through successfully we need a broad coalition working together, and this must include both the local authorities and the fans.

PART VIII

THE FOOTBALL TASK FORCE

29. The Task Force and the future regulation of football

ANDY BURNHAM

It is now ten years since Hillsborough and the subsequent publication of the Taylor Report. The game has changed a great deal in that time – partly for the better, partly for the worse. Facilities have improved beyond recognition and, on the whole, supporters are treated more decently than was the case in the 1980s. But the game's increasing commercial success has brought into sharp focus other concerns: spiralling ticket prices; the cost of merchandising; lack of supporter involvement in clubs; and the conflict created by plcs. The government was, and is, concerned about these issues and others such as racism, access for disabled people and the game's relationship with the wider community. It set up the Football Task Force to bring forward recommendations in these areas.

Essentially, these issues boil down to questions of regulation and governance. At the time of writing, the final report of the Football Task Force had not been completed and I cannot pre-empt what they will say. But I hope to give you a flavour of the government's thinking on the future regulation of football and our hopes for the resolution of the work by the Football Task Force drawing on my experience as a special adviser at the Department of Culture, Media and Sport.

One of the historical problems of football has been its turf wars and division. For all its difficulties, what the Task Force has achieved is to bring all the parties involved in the game – including supporters' representatives – around the same table to discuss issues of common concern. And it has produced three reports to date – *Eliminating Racism from Football, Improving Access for Disabled Supporters* and *Investing in the Community* – that have had the backing of all the major bodies in the game.

It is easy to be cynical about the Task Force – but consider some of its achievements: a Parliamentary Bill to change the law on racist chanting at football matches to make it a criminal offence for an individual to shout out racist abuse, which has now received Royal Assent. As we all know, that kind of abuse is now more of a problem than the mass chanting of racist abuse that was commonplace throughout the 1970s and 1980s. The government hopes to back up this change with a letter to every club asking them to alert all stewards to the change in the law.

The Football Trust has changed its grant-giving policy so that all clubs applying for funds have to sign up to the objectives of the excellent 'Kick It Out' campaign,[1] implement its action plan on an on-going basis and introduce an equal opportunities policy.

A number of clubs – Bradford City, West Ham and Leicester City amongst them – have now acted on the Task Force's recommendation that clubs buy copies of the excellent video produced by Show Racism the Red Card to distribute to local schools. Small beer, you might say – but nevertheless hard evidence of the game giving something back to the local community.

On access for disabled supporters, the government plans to act on a recommendation to amend the Building Regulations so that all new stands include the minimum number of wheelchair spaces recommended by the *Green Guide*. We have also accepted a suggestion that there should be guidelines on provision for visually and hearing impaired supporters and people who are ambulant disabled. Again, the Football Trust has amended its grant-giving policy to require that all newly built facilities comply with guidance on best standards. It should be a source of shame to the game that new stands have been built at Premier League grounds in the 1990s without including any wheelchair spaces. The changes recommended by the Task Force will prevent this happening again at any sports facility. And, perhaps most symbolically, the designers of the new Wembley Stadium have accepted all of the Task Force's recommendations in terms of the facilities it offers to disabled fans. (Facilities for disabled people at the existing Wembley stadium are disgraceful. I know this as I went to a match there in a wheelchair to find out for myself.) The new ground will offer 400 wheelchair spaces and outstanding facilities in terms of view and comfort.

The Task Force has also succeeded in putting other issues onto the agenda, such as the involvement of players in the local community, supporter involvement in clubs and the governance of plcs. Indeed, the key issues discussed in this book would not be so high on the agenda were it not for the work of the Task Force.

But the Task Force's crowning achievement to date was securing the commitment from the Premier League to invest substantial resources in grass-roots football. The Premier League has agreed to invest 5% of the next TV deal in the lower reaches of the game. This is a substantial and landmark commitment by the game's professional clubs. It is the first time that professional football has directly acknowledged its debt to the grass-roots and amateur game.

Football facilities in some of our inner cities are in a poor state and far behind some of those in the rest of Europe. It is an important principle that those people who are working to support the game at its foundations – from the schools and parks up to the Conference – should also benefit from the wealth now being generated at the top. The Premier League deserves real credit for responding to calls to invest in the improvement of these facilities and implement all of Howard Wilkinson's Charter for Quality. It is a recognition of the eloquent case made for the grass-roots game by David Conn and others.[2]

The government intends to add in its own resources to create a substantial fund that will be able to bring about real improvements and change in the game at its lowest level. I sometimes read sneering comments in the press about the Task Force. But the fact is that it has successfully addressed unfashionable but important issues in football, and produced results.

But, clearly, for the vast majority of supporters, the report on which the Task Force will stand or fall is the fourth and final report on the commercial issues in the game. During my time on the Task Force, I heard the refrain many times – and not just from chairmen and directors – that football clubs are just like any other businesses. We all know in our hearts that this is not true – but this argument doesn't stand up even on a purely business analysis. What other businesses depend upon their rivals for their own survival? What other businesses would lose money year after year and not close down? And what other businesses band together to sell their product and then share out the proceeds?

Football and sport are different from other industrial sectors. This is not to say that clubs should not be run to the high standards of accountability and transparency that the business world expects: they should. But without special regulation the game would face market failure.

In the US, the major sports leagues are exempted from anti-trust legislation. Special measures are used to balance the resources and the talent between the clubs. For example, they have the draft system where the bottom club has the first choice of the new crop of young players and top club last. These measures are intended to preserve a degree of parity between the clubs, and have a degree of competition and uncertainty of outcome. Maintaining a vibrant and competitive league is seen as essential to capturing the interest of TV viewers and thus to get and maintain high ratings. The Americans believe that uncertainty of outcome is crucial to the product known as professional sport. People will not turn on if the result is a foregone conclusion. These rules prevent a handful of clubs from dominating American sport. But we are now seeing the scenario that the Americans fear emerging in English football.

The year after Watford were last promoted to the top division – the

1982–83 season – they finished second. It is absolutely inconceivable that the same thing could happen again in the 1999–2000 season when Watford are back in the Premier League. That is a telling measure of how the game has changed.

For many football fans, our interest in the game and our club was forged at a time when there was a realistic chance of any club winning the First Division title or the FA Cup. Of course we will be there again next season even though outcomes are becoming less and less uncertain. It is an odds-on certainty, for instance, that, come the end of next season, Everton will be engaged in a desperate relegation battle – yet I have still renewed my season-ticket. For many supporters, football is becoming a question of relative success – staying up, promotion, a decent cup run – rather than the silverware itself.

After Charlton were relegated, Alan Curbishley talked of the Premier League having a league within a league. In fact there are probably three leagues within a league: one competing for the title; one for the European places; and one to avoid relegation.

But the dream factor is important – particularly for young fans. Today's youngsters are being introduced to the game at a time when six clubs have a realistic chance of winning the Premier League. This means that, for the vast majority of young fans, their home-town club has no genuine prospect of success. This should be a matter of genuine concern for the game's authorities. If football wants to retain mass popularity in the long term, more thought must be given to how the game is distributing its resources.

The Premier League and the Football League are part of the same competition yet most of the promoted Football League clubs simply do not have the resources to compete in the top flight. Equally, parachute payments give relegated Premier League clubs more resources than their Division One rivals and a better chance of being promoted. Sport's essential quality of uncertainty of outcome is draining out of English football year by year. There is a real danger that if the gap between the Football League and the Premier League becomes too wide, the game will start to lose its cohesion and appeal. Maintaining balance and parity is a matter of effective regulation. So are the range of other issues identified by the Task Force.

So, do we need an independent regulator of football, an OFFOOT? I would argue that we need better regulation of football – there is no question about that – but that does not mean that the government is best placed to deliver it.

In setting up the Task Force, the government has asked the game to take a hard look at how it is regulating itself, as all the issues in the remit are essentially a matter of regulation. But the government's preference is for the game to get its own house in order and develop modern and efficient systems of regulation. People in football know more about running the game than do the government. We accept that and are encouraged by the moves that are now being made to address these important issues. Better regulation of football means two things: modernising the rules to reflect today's circumstances; and then having proper procedures in place to ensure that the rules are rigorously and robustly implemented.

The FA's Rule 34 (which restricted the payment of dividends by clubs and the payment of salaries to directors in order to help preserve clubs' sporting ethos, as opposed to their commerial ethos) had a distinct and valid purpose, but there is little point in it being retained if it is no longer implemented.[3] I would argue that the principles behind Rule 34 were right, and the rule needs to be redrafted to reflect changed circumstances in the game – not dropped or ignored. If they did that, the game's authorities would find that they had a rule they could implement. We also need to update the rulebook to reflect new issues that have come into sharp focus in the commercial age, such as ticket prices and merchandising.

The FA has a unique opportunity to reinvent itself as the guardian of the game in the new commercial age and reposition itself as the friend of the supporter. There are numerous examples of industries that have suffered from lack of public confidence and have sought to address that by introducing codes of practice and new forms of self-regulation. I am thinking here of the banking and insurance industries which have both drawn up codes of practice that have been implemented by independent panels.

Getting the rules right is one thing. Implementing them is another. Take the example of a man close to my heart, Peter Johnson – a supporter of the second club on Merseyside (Liverpool) but who for some reason bought the premier local club (Everton) and the third club (Tranmere). If it is against football's rules to own a majority share in two professional clubs then club takeovers should be stopped. Four years on, the situation is being tackled with Everton and Tranmere facing expulsion from the FA Cup. But, while action is welcome, it is unfortunately the fans of both clubs who will suffer most if this course is followed.

Football has rules for good reasons – but they are useless unless people know that they will be implemented. The regulation of football has failed to keep pace with the commercial development of the game. The government wants the football authorities to take up the agenda and develop new systems of regulation that are in tune with the modern circumstances of the game. We hope that they will respond to this in the final Task Force report process.

But central regulation cannot be held up as the answer to everything. I think the future for football lies in better self-regulation coupled with better management of individual clubs. And the best way of achieving the latter is through more supporter and community involvement and ownership of clubs.

The movement towards supporter ownership of clubs is gathering pace. The thinking behind it has been set down in an excellent pamphlet by Professor Jonathan Michie – the latest in a series on the 'new mutualism' from the Co-operative Party.[4] Football offers fertile ground for the expansion of mutualism. Supporter trusts and community ownership offer answers to a number of issues in the game. They are the best way of ensuring that clubs are properly run, sensitive to the concerns of supporters and taking proper action on the issues identified in the Task Force's remit.

I do not think that the idea of a fan-on-the-board works if it is not backed by a proper financial base. That is what the supporters' trust option provides. And, like any other movement, this one has its own pioneer. This is a new kind of football hero. He does not wear sarongs or own a yacht, but Brian Lomax from Northampton Town has led the way for others to follow. The story of the Northampton Town Supporter Trust is truly inspirational and is providing supporters all over the country with a model.[5] Similar ideas have been implemented at Bournemouth and are being considered at clubs across the country, including Luton and Manchester City.[6]

I think this is where supporters should focus their attentions and where groups can have a real influence. I hope the Task Force will give real impetus to the move towards supporter ownership, along with proposals to improve the governance and regulation of the game.

30. Facing football's future: the Task Force and beyond

NIC COWARD

The Football Association has been, I think it would be generally agreed, a key participant in the work of the Football Task Force. In this chapter I present our assessment of the Task Force's activities in my capacity as the FA's company secretary under three headings: the good, the bad and the future.

THE GOOD

Firstly, I think it was a significant achievement to have brought together the various and varied groups within the game – as members of the Task Force, through the evidence-gathering sessions, and at the public meetings. This was the first real, and long overdue, opportunity for everyone involved in the game at all levels to share their knowledge and experience. What struck me particularly – and this is contrary to public perception – was the high degree of agreement that was frequently achieved between these supposedly very different groups. The game is, I think most people would agree, currently in a generally healthy state. There are certainly some problematic issues on which the Football Task Force, quite rightly, focused. However, we must not lose sight of the fact that participation and involvement in the game are currently at their highest levels ever, and in this I include playing as well as spectating.

There are, though, issues that we do need to tackle. The Task Force's published reports into race issues, disabled access, and football in the community were very challenging and presented many items on which immediate action was required. By the same token these first three reports also highlighted many of the good things already happening in the game, such as the anti-racism Kick It Out campaign,[1] and the many 'football in the community' schemes that clubs operate. Broadly, the FA's view is that to date the Task Force has successfully tackled many important issues whilst also highlighting many of the real successes of the game, particularly in terms of grass-roots activity. In this it has served as a useful clearing house of knowledge and experience with which to inform future policy development.

THE BAD

The fundamental weakness with which the Task Force has had to grapple with from day one is its extremely unwieldy structure. Given the very broad brief that was given to the Task Force at its inception, it was always going to be difficult to organise a focused exploration of the key issues. At times this led to a failure to communicate to the public exactly what the Task Force was about, and what it was intended to deliver. Perhaps this was also due in part to the fact that the Task Force's agenda tended to shift as new issues emerged during the day-to-day scrutiny of this initiative itself. This effect was amplified by the fact that the sheer range of (often passionately held) opinion reflected on the Task Force meant that discussions on even rather minor issues often became protracted; in such an environment it can prove rather difficult to secure a consensus on key issues quickly.

BEYOND THE TASK FORCE'S FINAL REPORT

The Football Task Force is due to end its work after the publication of its final report. There is a strong view at the FA, though, that some successor body will be needed to pick up the reins at this point. It is hard to say at this point what form such a body should take, but it seems to me that it would certainly be appropriate for the FA, as England's main governing body for football, to take on the administration of such an enterprise which could then tackle emerging issues as and when required.

With regard to the Task Force's final report on commercial issues, the government's requirement that such a report be issued has clearly meant that the FA, the Premier League and the Football League have had to look into the issues involved in some detail. As a result of this exercise, it is our shared belief that best practice, of which there is much throughout the football industry, has never been sufficiently articulated formally. There is now a recognition that this needs to be done, to cover issues such as ticketing, merchandising and supporter and community involvement, with the results then widely disseminated. Where objectively justified rules with sanctions for breach can be identified, the creation of a regulatory framework to ensure that these standards are complied with would certainly be appropriate. For example, charging one set of supporters more for the same service than another set of supporters is clearly wrong. However, it would be a mistake to try to apply such a régime to all commercial activities, as clubs are entitled to retain some management autonomy in what are key areas of their businesses.

A football club is a business, albeit a unique one, which should play a vital role in the community and in the lives of its supporters. For the latter, the club is far more than just a business from which to buy goods and services. The key objective, then, has to be to promote best practice within clubs, to promote confidence that the club is being run properly in the interests of *all* the stakeholders. Customers need to be at the heart of any business strategy. This is particularly true for clubs, bearing in mind the unique nature of supporters as 'customers', with their special emotional attachment to their teams. Supporters and directors should certainly be ambitious for success on the field, but not to the long-term detriment of the club.

There is no ideal economic model that the football authorities have yet encountered which can be applied to all clubs at all the various league levels, not even all clubs within a league. If you look at the FA Premier League, you might be examining 20 different economic models for clubs, such is their heterogeneity in the way they organise their business affairs. This is something which proponents of a statutory pricing regulation for tickets and merchandising, which would constrain clubs' ability to maximise revenue from these sources, need to consider seriously when arguing for an all-embracing regulatory framework. Ticket prices are a very good example of the problems that such a policy could raise. For this is likely to be at the heart of any club's business plans, at least for the present, and it is the view of the FA that such decisions are best left to the club.

Having said that, the FA recognises that clubs do need to be sensitive and long-sighted when deciding their ticket-pricing strategy. Each club needs to look at ticketing not only as a revenue stream, but also as a means of introducing the club to new supporters, and as a way of maintaining the club at the heart of a community. Rewarding the loyalty of season-ticket-holders needs to be balanced against the need to promote accessibility to home and away games for those who cannot afford a season ticket. Clubs should perhaps look at new ticket policies. The FA, the Premier League and the Football League believe that more sophisticated marketing can actually deliver what fans want. Perhaps the prices in the bottom category should drop, and the prices in the top categories should rise to compensate. Perhaps there should be more price categories. Even very successful clubs, which can sell out every game, need to have a ticketing strategy which is sufficiently flexible to continue to attract new fans who can come in to experience professional football, and who will then go on to become new 'supporters'. However, I would emphasise again, the FA would see such a policy developing largely on a voluntary basis, perhaps with guidelines provided by the appropriate football governing body, but without any statutory regulatory body enforcing fixed rules.

The FA believes that the Task Force's final report has to address the following key issues. Placing 'supporter satisfaction' at the heart of football club commercial strategies, but recognising that ambition comes at a price, and that the long-term financial health of a club has to be the priority. Directors must be allowed to make the difficult decisions and not have to operate within an obtrusive and inflexible over-arching regulatory framework which tries to impose 'one-fits-all' solutions on what is a very heterogeneous industry. Expertise and investment need to be encouraged into the businesses, and should be allowed to make a proper return on this investment. But a club must always make sure that it takes seriously its responsibilities to its customers, its supporters, and to the community in general.

31. The Football Task Force: a Premier League view

MIKE LEE

The work of the Football Task Force is, at the time of writing, nearing completion. Set up in July 1997 under the auspices of Chris Smith's Department of Culture, Media and Sport, the Task Force has thus far produced three reports, centred on: the elimination of racism in football and the encouragement of wider participation by ethnic minorities; improvements in disabled access to spectating facilities; and the strengthening of football's links to local communities and improvements to funding the grass-roots of the game. All three of these reports have helped stimulate an important discussion within football, involving fans, the media, the governing bodies, clubs, and government. And, since publication, many of the proposals have either been reflected in the development of policy within the game or have played a role in shaping the debate about the best way forward. These three reports are generally regarded as being reasonably balanced and based upon an attempt to find a sensible set of solutions to some of the most important issues facing English football.

The fourth (and final) report on the major commercial concerns of the modern game, including ticket pricing, merchandising and the rise of plcs, has proven to be a more difficult and complex challenge. In particular, from the point of view of the FA Premier League and its member clubs (for whom I am a spokesman), there has been, at times, a sense of a sustained attempt by some members of the Task Force to force through an agenda which fails to take any account of the enormous cost pressures within football and the need for robust commercial strategies to help sustain the future of the game. However, as the Task Force has worked through the issues set out in its brief from government, progress has proved possible.

To help aid the Task Force's deliberations and shape the drafting of the final report, the three English football authorities – the Football Association, the Premier League and the Football League – produced a joint report which can be seen as a major statement of their view of the current state of the English game. That report was also a summary of their proposals for maintaining progress into the first decade of the new century.

Our report recognises that football is, and has to some extent always been, an expression of different sporting, social and cultural characteristics. It is, among other things, a worldwide sporting experience; a tribal and community focus; an expression of athleticism, skill and passion; a source of great loyalty, joy, disappointment and commitment; an industry with significant revenue and cost demands; and a sporting business in a modern leisure market. Any attempt to examine the future of the game has to understand each of these, and, at the same time, appreciate the international marketplace in which professional football now operates.

In addition, in looking at the question of fans' interests and concerns, it is important to recognise that supporters are a diverse and varied group of people. There are armchair supporters who have no affinity to any particular club but have an interest in football, or sometimes just in sport generally. They tend to watch football on TV and will never buy merchandise. There are passive supporters who have a club affinity but rarely attend games, casual supporters who pick and choose matches, regular fans who attend consistently and buy merchandise. And there are committed supporters who attend home and away games, buy club kits and perhaps even name their children after the 1973 Cup-winning team. Then there are also those fans who participate in and perhaps even help run the various supporters organisations. In short, an effort to categorise 'the fans' as a single homogeneous group of people with identical needs is a mistake. Fans, like the rest of society, are a diverse group with many and varied interests and opinions.

This is reflected in the shape and structure of the professional game itself in that there is no single or simple model of a football club on which the modern game is based. Clubs vary enormously in their size, potential, revenue, ambition, ownership and outlook. It was ever thus and long may it remain so. As a result, efforts to summarise crudely the 'needs' of fans or impose a singular view of the 'ideal' club are doomed to fail. However, it is surely right that the fans' concerns do need to be understood and heard and that steps should be taken to encourage good corporate governance and customer responsiveness at all levels of the game.

To this end the football authorities have attempted to remind the Task Force of the many excellent things that go on in the English game and to suggest ways in which these can be built on and made the basis of best practice for others to follow. Thus, on the sensitive issue of ticket pricing and distribution, while recognising that each club is an individual business with differing demands and pressures, there is a need to highlight best practice on price ranges, concessions, imaginative marketing for young people and families, and sensible discount schemes in order to encourage better access policies at all clubs.

The football authorities are also keen to see clubs keep back 5% of tickets for general sale on a match-by-match basis to ensure some access for non-regular attenders and to help widen the experience of a live game.

On merchandising there is much evidence from the survey work conducted for both the Premier League and the Task Force by John Williams of the Sir Norman Chester Centre at Leicester University that fans, on the whole, welcome many of the developments of recent years. However, there are clearly some concerns in relation to kit pricing and cycles, which do merit attention. The first issue will be helped by the agreement reached recently between the football authorities, the leading clubs and the Office of Fair Trading. To address the second concern, the football authorities have recommended that all clubs should have a published, well-communicated kit cycle policy with all fans being aware of kit change dates.

In general, the football authorities support moves to promote greater liaison with supporters via supporter forums or panels, questionnaires and focus groups to improve communication around club policies. Furthermore, we would propose that every club look at the development of a customer charter stating what fans can expect from the club, how the service will be delivered, how feedback can be given and what recourse is available if there is a failure to meet published standards.

This sort of approach, based on codes of conduct and the encouragement of best practice is much more likely to be genuinely effective than crude threats of intervention from outside of the game. Certainly over recent years all three governing bodies, fully supported by the professional clubs, have taken steps to modernise the rulebooks; improve the quality of regulation; ensure consistency; improve independent scrutiny; introduce new codes of conduct; and promote best practice. This sort of regulation is allied to the significant amount of statutory and other regulation governing the game on issues ranging from spectator safety to business conduct which emanates from government, stock exchange scrutiny (in some cases) and competition regulation from the OFT and the Competition Commission.

In our view English football is not an undergoverned sport, and nor by comparison with other sports and business is it badly governed. The English game is in fact one of the healthiest, exciting and most buoyant football cultures in the world and one of the most successful aspects of modern Britain. There can, however, be no room for complacency. We recognise that football is an essential part of our society's culture and those who govern the game have a duty and responsibility to help nurture the game for future generations.

Much has been said about a new football 'regulator' but the football authorities cannot accept that the overall well-being of the game would be helped by new layers of regulation or bureaucracy. Nevertheless, the governing bodies do want to see improved self-regulation and more obvious public accountability in the process. To achieve this end, the football authorities have proposed two key measures. Firstly, best practice guidelines should be established in key areas such as ticketing and merchandising. Secondly, an independent scrutiny panel should be set up to conduct a regular health check, or audit, of governance in the game. This panel should be made up of independent people with relevant skills and expertise, with membership and terms of reference to be agreed with the Secretary of Sate for Culture, Media and Sport. To ensure the efficacy of the panel, mechanisms should be put in place to ensure it works closely with the football governing bodies to evaluate progress and make recommendations for improving performance.

Taken together, the football authorities believe these steps will improve the quality of self-regulation, while also enhancing the accountability and transparency of decision-making in the game. They represent a sensible and balanced approach that provides the right framework for the development of English football, culturally, commercially and socially.

32. The Football Task Force and the 'regulator debate'

ADAM BROWN

This chapter explores how the issue of the overall regulation of football rose up the agenda of the government's Football Task Force. It argues that by focusing on some 'coal-face' issues of public concern, a wider problem of the game's administration and the ability of the football authorities to regulate for the long-term health of the whole game was called into question. This chapter argues that an examination of the commercial issues in the Task Force's remit, in particular, highlighted the problems the football authorities have in regulating within the context of the new corporate governance priorities of many clubs. This perceived inability on the part of the football authorities led many, including fans groups, MPs (including the former Minister for Sport, Tony Banks) and others to conclude that a new, independent regulatory régime is required for football. The chapter outlines how this came about and describes the response from the football authorities and government. The chapter concludes by suggesting that a common perception of regulation – the 'big stick' approach – needs refining if football is to get more effective and democratic regulation than it has enjoyed to date.

Football, like all sports, has always had a set of rules governing not only competition on the field of play but also the organisation of the game off it. These have included rules about the ownership of clubs, how transfers are conducted, the structure of competition and the structure of this governance – how the rules are themselves constituted and enforced. This regulatory function within England has been undertaken historically by the Football Association. Whilst the English game is subject to the world governing body, FIFA, particularly in relation to rules of play and refereeing, the structure of domestic competitions and other questions such as club ownership have been left largely to the national associations. It is this role which is now under scrutiny.

The Football Task Force was established by the incoming Labour government in July 1997 as a fulfilment of its election pledge to create a body which would suggest solutions to a series of perceived problems in the game.[1] Its genesis lies in Labour's Charter for Football, itself a response to a loss of confidence in the administration of English football in the mid-

1990s. As argued elsewhere,[2] whilst the Charter promised a wholesale re-evaluation of the way football was run, and whilst it pointed to a unification of football's authorities as one solution to the crisis in administration, the Football Task Force's remit was considerably narrower. Thus, despite the then Sports Minister's description of the Task Force's work as being to answer the question of 'how can clubs avoid alienating the less-well-off from the sport that they love?' the body was instructed, for instance, that it was not to consider the role of broadcasters. Given the increasing importance of television revenue to the financing of the game[3] as well as subsequent events (the BSkyB/Manchester United merger and MMC enquiry; the Restrictive Practices Court case)[4] this seems an incredible omission.

However, the government was clearly determined to focus the Task Force's work around the coal-face issues as they are publicly perceived. These were racism, disabled access, football in the community, ticket policies, the particular problems of plcs, fans' involvement in the running of clubs, and merchandising. Some of these issues, such as ticket prices, were of central concern to fans; others, like merchandising, less so. What is ironic, however, is that even though the body was given a narrower focus than most would have hoped for, by considering each of these issues the more structural problems of football's governance still came to the fore, not least the subsidence of the FA's regulatory role. We shall look at each of these in turn.

One example was racism. During the Task Force's ten regional visits, local football teams and football fans complained vociferously about the continued presence of racist abuse both on and off the pitch. At a legislative level, the Football Offences Act of 1991, which outlawed racist chanting but only if it involved one or more people acting in concert, was clearly unsuitable for dealing with individuals racially abusing players or other fans. One of the recommendations of the Task Force's first report, *Eliminating Racism*,[5] was for this legislation to be altered so individuals could be prosecuted. Although a minor change, the implementation of this recommendation illustrated how the Task Force's work could feed into policy and alter common practice, however piecemeal on this occasion.

More significantly, though, were the verbal testimonies of several amateur teams and those of some of the FA County officials. Whilst the former told the Task Force of routine and sustained racial abuse of players and complete inaction by match officials and local FAs, the latter greeted Task Force enquiries about how they dealt with racial abuse with quizzical expressions and declarations that their County FA had 'no problem with the ethnics'. It should be conceded that the national FA officials present with the Task Force were dismayed by such comments, but there was clearly a breakdown between the existing rules of the game which outlawed serious abuse and the implementation of them throughout the whole game. Obviously, a complete lack of awareness and knowledge of the problem did not help, but for an organisation which was centrally involved in establishing the 'Kick It Out' campaign[6] to have officials and structures seemingly unable to deal with the issue or even the complaints we were hearing, suggested a deeper malaise. Thus, another alteration to how the game is governed came in the recommendation to make racism a specific red-card offence with disciplinary sanctions to be implemented by County FAs. An assessment of how this, and other recommendations, are affecting the situation on the ground is now needed.

When considering the remit of increasing disabled access to football, the Task Force found that many grounds did not meet the requirements for disabled provision set out in the *Guide to Safety at Sports Grounds* (Green Guide). Given that many of the country's stadiums had been rebuilt with considerable sums of public money, that criteria on disabled access were not being met was a major mistake and again illustrated a failure in enforcement. Following the Task Force's second report, *Improving Disabled Access*,[7] football clubs building new grounds or stands must now demonstrate how they will meet Green Guide specifications before they receive any public finance. However, disabled fans also complained about their treatment by clubs' administrators, ticket offices and stewards with a rampant inconsistency in the way fans were treated across clubs. Thus, not only had the authorities failed to be forward-thinking enough when distributing grants for all-seater stadiums to be built, but there was also little guidance and even less enforcement of a reasonable standard of provision in a whole host of areas for fans. The Task Force's response was to recommend sweeping improvements in how clubs treated their disabled fans from the moment they contact the club to buy a ticket to the time they leave the stadium. This is fine as far as it goes, but without a determination by the football authorities to get clubs voluntarily or by force to change their day-to-day practices, prospects for wholesale change are slim. Again, the issue of enforcement, of regulation, moved to centre stage.

The third report the Football Task Force issued was in January 1999 and related to clubs' roles in their communities. Although the remit was originally worded with players as role models in mind, the report was far more wide ranging and covered such areas as the formation of supporter trusts as well as support for the Premier League in defending the collective sale of TV rights in the RPC. However, even on the specific area of what community work players undertook, the Task Force found that often players did not fulfil their contractual obligations of two to three hours of work with community schemes per week. The PFA has been instrumental in the establishment of community schemes and encouraging players to commit time to working with them. Given top players' commercial activities and increased bargaining power *vis-à-vis* the clubs, it is perhaps not surprising that many do not meet their 'paper' obligations, but it suggested a failure on the part of clubs to take their work in the community seriously.

The Task Force found that community schemes were often under-funded and given low priority, with the lack of player involvement only one symptom of many. This amounted to a failure of the football authorities to ensure that their clubs took their roles in the community seriously, let alone developing new ways of establishing links between the club and its locale. Indeed, as the debate on community work moves from players' roles in providing 'sport for all' to broader issues of involving fans and local residents in the club, the focus is already moving to the roles of supporters and supporter trusts. Within the Task Force's *Investing in the Community* report,[8] therefore, are calls for backing to be given to fans wishing to establish supporter trusts, especially at those clubs facing financial difficulties.[9]

This has led to potentially the most significant recommendation of the Task Force so far. We shall return to this example later, but once again it is an issue which traditionally should have been the responsibility of the football authorities. Maintaining the health of the game means main-taining the health of individual clubs and, short of the kind of financial compliance unit called for in Sir John Smith's report,[10] the football authorities have failed to prevent a series of clubs facing oblivion, only to be saved by their fans. However, the area in which the regulation debate has really come to the fore has been the commercial areas of the Football Task Force's remit.

Merchandising policies – and primarily the frequency and cost of new strips – appeared to be less of a concern for some fans, who regard access to the game as their priority, although the issue remained a staple in the media's diet of exposé and shock. When the matter was raised in the Task Force, either at the regional public meetings or in Task Force sessions, the football authorities clung to the line that they had absolutely no jurisdiction over what merchandising policies their clubs pursued. There was indeed scant regard for the poor image that such policies were giving the game and the problems which they posed for families in particular. Any recommendations on future merchandising policies are likely to be in the form of a voluntary code of conduct, which, without regulatory sanction, is likely to have only a minimal effect. Indeed, the vagaries of the market may have a bigger impact with many top clubs reporting that the 'merchandise bubble' has burst (Manchester United, for instance, suffered a 10% drop in revenue from shirt sales in 1998–99).[11]

Complaints about ticket policies topped the agenda for most fans giving evidence to the Task Force. By far the biggest concern was that prices were increasing so fast that some supporters could no longer afford to go to games. Indeed the Task Force's work showed that, on average, Premier League prices had risen 312% between 1989 and 1999, when the retail price index had increased just 54.8%. The dissatisfaction with pricing was confirmed by specially commissioned Task Force research by John Williams at Leicester University. His findings were that for those who used to go to football but no longer did, over 70% cited the price of tickets as the main reason for non-attendance, and amongst the unemployed this rose to over 80%.[12] Given that the Task Force had already stated that exclusion from the game on the grounds of race was in effect an exclusion from society, the ticket-price spiral has been nothing short of a form of social exclusion for the low-paid and unwaged, young and old.

There were other concerns with ticket policies. Many, especially outside the Premier League, complained that they suffered discrimination in pricing as away fans; others that they didn't get reasonable allocations of tickets for away games; and some that they even had to pay commission to their own club for administering away tickets. Given that the Premier League, FA and Football League have rules on provision for away fans – including a minimum of 10% or 3,000 to be given to away fans and that they should not be charged more for comparable accommodation – another supporting beam of the authorities' claims to be in charge of the game came tumbling down. Clubs responded by arguing that the inflation of prices was merely representative of the increased costs, especially wages, in football. Whilst a few demonstrated that they had schemes in place to tackle issues of exclusion, by far the majority saw little reason to alter their practices greatly, something particularly prevalent in the Premier League where stadiums have been operating on average at 90% capacity.

However, it was the response of the Football Association above all on this issue which convinced many that football's regulatory structure was inadequate. On numerous occasions, the FA representatives (Graham Kelly, David Davies or Nic Coward) stated that there was nothing that the FA could do to regulate the prices charged by clubs. They supported this by stating that each club was an individual private business and as such had to determine its own pricing structure. Whereas fans' groups and others argued that it was the responsibility of the English game's governing body to rein in the commercial voraciousness of the club chairmen and ensure that football remained a popularly accessible sport,[13] football's authorities argued that they were either unable or unwilling to protect access to watching the game for all. As with the ownership debates and the failure to uphold (then) existing rules on dividend payments and directors' pay,[14] the football authorities maintained their line that they could not intervene in the commercial operations of their clubs, whatever effect it might have on the long-term health of football.

Belatedly the authorities have begun to suggest a voluntary code of conduct on pricing, to include suggestions for 'stretching' price differentials (some people pay more, a lot of others pay less) and the segmented marketing of concessionary tickets. However, to date these have not been backed with any suggestions about forcing clubs to implement such policies, and the continuing failure of the Premier League even to uphold its existing rules on away-match allocations suggests that the authorities do not see their role as being one of a regulator in respect of such issues.

The approach of the authorities to this issue in particular has probably done more than anything else to generate interest in a football regulator. On one level it is because the issue is so fundamental – access to and the cost of tickets is a barrier to participation in the game as a supporter. However, whereas barriers of race and disability generated a broad consensus on action, barriers on economic grounds were met with statements such as 'we recognise that each club is an individual business and must be able to make balanced and sensible decisions on the right ticketing policy'.[15] Once the Task Force's work on increasing access to football suggested controlling the market to a degree, therefore, football's ruling bodies stepped back. In a rather ironic mirror of the approach of New Labour to big business, the free operation of the market in football was a holy cow which the football authorities (and the Premier League in particular, as the representative of the top 20 clubs), wanted left alone. Perhaps as important was that the centrality of the pricing issue to the regulator debate was underpinned by a theoretical comparison of football to other, regulated industries, which we shall return to.

The Football Task Force's remit on floated companies – to 'reconcile the potential conflict between shareholders, players and supporters' (*sic*) – was again a response to a public perception that quoted clubs were operating to the new, corporate agendas of the stockmarket which had less to do with football and more to do with making massive private fortunes. The very fact that clubs had been allowed to float in the first place, side-stepping the

FA's Rule 34 which restricted dividend payments and the payment of directors, was itself an illustration of the inability of the Football Association to govern effectively.[16] However, The football authorities' contention was that:

> The issue of whether or not to move to plc status has to be a matter for judgement of individual clubs based on their own sense of what is best for the longer-term development of the club . . . It would be wrong, in our view, for a new set of prescriptive rules to be devised either to prevent or encourage flotation. Each club must be free to choose its own path.[17]

This is an abdication of responsibility, lacking in any recognition of the fact that the way clubs, and particularly the richest clubs, are organised has implications which reverberate throughout football and which, ultimately, determine the structure and finances of the game. Such an approach also fails to recognise the reasons why Rule 34 was introduced in the first place – that football clubs should not be a source of profit for outside interests and should remain, primarily, sporting and not financial institutions – and fails to uphold the strong regulatory function which the FA has played historically.

Polarising the debate still further were the activities of some of those most closely involved in clubs' flotations. Manchester United's Martin Edwards managed to turn a share ownership worth £10 million in 1989, based on an investment of just £600,000 in 1979, into a personal fortune of around £100 million by 1999, through the flotation of the club. At Newcastle United, Freddy Shepherd and Douglas Hall, who between them own 65% of the club, mocked the club's supporters whilst in a Spanish brothel, in the infamous 'Toongate' affair. The control they hold over the plc also means that many small shareholders are effectively completely excluded from decision-making at the club. Thirdly, Keith Wiseman's role in Southampton's flotation has led to charges from the Southampton Independent Supporters Association of profiteering and has had a catastrophic effect on fans:

> In a bizarre twist, the large percentage of supporters who purchased shares in the plc now find themselves facing enormous season-ticket rises in order to ensure an operating profit for the parent company and the accompanying payment of their own minimal share dividends.[18]

Wiseman's new and short-lived role as FA chairman merely fanned the flames of the arguments of those who claimed that the authorities were letting the plc clubs run free and easy over fans' and shareholders' loyalties. Like their cousins in control of the former public utilities, football club chairmen appeared as fat cats waddling across the field of play, with the interests of fans and small shareholders coming a very poor second to increasing their own power and wealth.

That the authorities faltered in their regulatory function is epitomised by Rule 34. Whilst the Task Force debated the issue and some, including myself, pressured the authorities to admit at least that their own rules had been broken by flotations and that there was some need for the game's governing body to have a say over how their clubs were financed, the FA simply changed Rule 34. That this happened in May 1998 and only came to light in October 1999 suggests either a deliberate attempt to mislead or else an ignorance of the organisation's own rulebook.[19] The implication for the debate about the need for an independent force to make sure the game was being run properly was huge: 'If our rules are broken', the message went, 'we'll simply change them to fit the new circumstances.'

The final area of the Task Force's remit – the involvement of supporters in the running of clubs – similarly suggested that the FA was not even fulfilling its own undertakings. Although it had promised in its *Blueprint for the Future of Football* that a national supporter organisation would be funded and properly represented within the FA,[20] neither of these have been delivered. Piecemeal meetings with fans' organisations and the supporter panels now operating in both Leagues were less to do with 'involving supporters in the running of clubs' than the most superficial forms of consultation. In their submission to the Task Force, the contention of the authorities with regard to meaningful representation and to their own previous promise of funding was that 'the appointment of a supporter representative to the main board of each club as a right is unacceptable' and that 'it should not be the responsibility of clubs or the football authorities to finance groups of supporter-shareholders or national supporter organisations'.[21]

What the Football Task Force process exposed, therefore, was that through an examination of the issues of greatest public concern in football, the authorities were found wanting and unwilling to tackle the issues head on. At every turn in the 1990s, it seemed, the authorities became apologists for the worst of the clubs' commercial activities and, when rules and principles were broken, they simply ignored them or changed them to fit the new needs of the clubs. All these commercial areas of the Task Force's remit suggested that the existing regulatory structures were not coping with the demands of new corporate governance and the commercial priorities which dominated the decade. As 1999 unfolded, it appeared that the quasi-judicial bodies of government, such as the Office of Fair Trading (preventing the retail price-fixing of shirts), the Monopolies and Mergers Commission and the DTI (blocking BSkyB's takeover of Manchester United) and even the European Union (upholding UEFA's right to prevent dual ownership of clubs), were more effectively regulating the game in the interests of all stakeholders in football than the football authorities were able or willing to do themselves. For an organisation like the FA, which insists that football should be able to regulate itself, 1999 was not a good year.

However, as referred to above, underpinning this has been a more theoretical argument about regulation in football and a comparison with other sectors, most notably the privatised utilities, but also financial services, Lloyds and even the gaming industry. The basis of this is that football clubs occupy a local monopoly position given the peculiar nature of consumption in the football industry. Put simply, the argument is that football fans are not customers in the normal sense, but that their custom is based on a loyalty to a particular club which will remain unchanged whatever the success of the team and regardless of relative prices across clubs. This has been supported by a wide range of evidence – the Premier League fan surveys cite this loyalty as the dominant characteristic of football supporters; the Football Supporters Association defined 'support' to the Task Force as 'a lifelong and unchangeable commitment';[22] Sir John Smith's report on financial regulation in football claimed that 'the commitment of football supporters to their club is of a different order of magnitude to other kinds of 'brand loyalty';[23] and even the Salomon Brothers characterise football customers as 'exceptional in the sense that the customers do not need success. This target is desirable for them, but not a condition of their support'.[24]

Furthermore, the MMC's report recognised this 'local market power' and that clubs were in a position to exploit their customers, because of their loyalty. Backing even came from the Sports Minister for such a viewpoint, during the London regional Task Force meeting:

> You cannot treat football like any other product. It's a drug and clubs know that even if they continue to put up prices we will still go. Perhaps we should see it as a kind of national utility. As more clubs become public companies the whole area of financial accountability comes into play.

There were other similarities, too: the huge private wealth generated for a handful of individuals mirrored the outrage at the 'fat cats' of the utilities; and the behaviour of the Halls and Shepherds of the world seemed a neat comparison to the concern with the behaviour of public figures and the sleaze factor which caused disaffected voters to propel Labour to power. After all, abusing your own fans (and customers) is one thing: being caught doing so, on camera, in a Spanish brothel, is quite another. Although some pointed to the political economy of football in the 1990s as reflecting, belatedly, the Thatcherite revolution in the rest of the economy in the 1980s, there were fairly sound arguments that clubs were exploiting their market power and that consumers needed protection from this. Although there has never been an investigation into this under fair trading legislation, if the government wished to act to regulate football, there was no shortage of ammunition, justification or support.

Indeed, there was also mounting pressure for the government to intervene. Many felt that the football authorities had had their last chance and now was the time to take matters out of their control. In fact, Labour's own Charter for Football had called for the unification of the administration in the game before they were elected, to give it a new, strengthened administration,[25] yet such fundamental changes were airbrushed out in the Task Force's set-up. However, a combination of the populist appeal of such a stance and the genuine concern of both long-standing and 'new' football fan MPs should not be underestimated. Those MPs in inner-city constituencies had an electoral motive for being seen to be fan-friendly; it fitted with many of the concerns about social exclusion and the unfettered operation of the market; and in the summer of 1999 the new Sports Minister was announced as Kate Hoey, who had moved a private member's Bill for a football regulator back in 1995. On the other side of the equation was Labour's reluctance to regulate business and the lack of parliamentary time for any regulator legislation: if the Bill on fox hunting could not get through the Commons it was unlikely that one for a football regulator would do so before the end of the government's term. Furthermore, the government was keen for the Task Force to produce a consensus report, reflecting the interests of all parties, and it was clear that the football authorities would stand as one against an independent regulator.

The football authorities did respond to the mounting criticism and public and political pressure for an independent regulator for football and moved ground considerably. One element of this was that new personnel came into the top jobs in football's administration – the disgrace and sackings of Kelly and Wiseman at the FA and Quinton and Leaver at the

Premier League opened the way for a new approach, and in the FA's case the promise of a new structure for decision-making in the organisation. In a report to the Task Force which otherwise gave little comfort to fans and reformers, the authorities suggested an independent scrutiny panel for football, with terms and reference to be agreed with the Department of Culture, Media and Sport and to 'perform a function not unlike that of the British Standards Institute or the Audit Commission'.[26] Although some areas of this remain unclear – the BSI and Audit Commission are very different bodies, after all – for the authorities to be proposing an independent watchdog for football was a concession, albeit one forced on them by circumstance and pressure, including the political threat of a statutory regulator. At the time of writing it is still unclear whether an agreement can be reached in the Task Force about the form such an independent body might take, but some kind of arm's-length scrutiny body seems likely.

Also, it was evident that the government had little interest in imposing a regulator against the football authorities' wishes. Indeed, advice which the Task Force received – for instance from Howard Davies, head of the Financial Services Association – suggested that the most effective forms of regulation were ones which were voluntarily accepted by those being regulated. Delivering that in football means getting the support of the club chairmen, which even willing football authorities might struggle to achieve. It seems likely that there will be a proviso that if a scrutiny panel, or audit commission for football, is introduced and fails to implement change (and if clubs and authorities prove too resistant to its recommendations), a statutory regulator may be imposed.

The need for an effective regulatory package was given a late boost in the Task Force's work with the process of media investment in football clubs gaining pace. This is referred to elsewhere in this volume, but the implication for the 'regulator debate' as the Task Force was reaching its conclusions was that the authorities had to deal effectively with the dual-ownership question if they were to convince the rest of the Task Force membership that they were regulating the game according to their own rules properly. This is a real test, because, just as the Task Force process exposed a failure to protect fans' interests particularly in the corporate age of 1990s football, the dual-interest question goes to the heart of debates about regulation in football and the pressures of a new, TV-driven, commercial age.

It is the effectiveness of any new regulatory structure rather than the form which that takes which will count in the long term. Fans consulted during the Task Force process were unequivocal in their support for an independent regulator (the research undertaken by the Sir Norman Chester Centre, for instance, concluded that 63.7% of fans thought the game needed an independent regulator and only 24.3% thought that the FA were the body to do the job).[27] However, it is with supporters that the other half of the regulation equation lies. The importance of over-arching governance structures for football should not be underestimated, but will only be truly effective if there are adequate structures for 'regulation from below'.

Fans' organisations have played a crucial role in numerous instances in not only raising issues onto the public agenda and creating a 'culture of dissent' where authorities and clubs have to account for their actions,[28] but also increasingly by adopting positions with regard to ownership issues at clubs. The examples of Northampton Town, Bournemouth, Chester and elsewhere show how important fans can be in keeping clubs alive and how they can play meaningful roles in decision-making at club level. At the other end of the football hierarchy, Shareholders United at Manchester United are beginning to make inroads into the activities of the plc, including through resolutions submitted to the AGM and meetings with representatives of the plc board. What shareholding organisations can offer is scrutiny from ground level (they will have access to all company documentation and, under the law, should be treated the same as any other shareholder) and, in increasing instances, using their share power to influence decision-making.

It was therefore a signal that the government were beginning to take the Task Force's recommendations seriously when Culture Secretary Chris Smith announced at the 1999 Labour Party conference in Bournemouth that the government were to give practical support to the establishment of supporter-shareholder trusts at football clubs. The recommendation had been rather hidden in the body's third report on football's role in the community, but stated:

> New models of ownership, such as supporter trusts and community trusts, could provide a means of improving democracy and accountability whilst building strong community links for the long term'.[29]

Chris Smith's announcement was widely welcomed:

> 'Professional football is in danger of losing touch with its roots,' said the Minister for Culture, Media and Sport, in a surprisingly fierce denunciation of those running the game. Calling for a return to 'community values' and 'social responsibility', the

Minister announced the formation of a dedicated unit at the Football Trust to advise and provide administrative help to supporters to buy and hold shares collectively. The idea, promoted as part of the 'New Mutualism' movement by the Co-operative Party, is backed by preferential banking offered to supporters by the Co-op Bank . . . The new unit will offer supporters dedicated advice, forms of model constitutions they may wish to adopt, and 'modest' financial help with start up costs. 'We are not providing huge funds,' a spokesman said, 'and the onus is on supporters to work hard to take advantage of the help on offer. But this is the first time any government has practically assisted supporters to get properly involved in running their club and the game itself.'[30]

This has been well received by fans' groups, and rightly so. However, for this new unit to be as effective as possible it will need, in addition to the legal advice on constituting a shareholder organisation (which is under-way), adequate start-up funds: Shareholders United had to write to all 28,000 Manchester United shareholders during the campaign against the BSkyB takeover,[31] a burden of cost which normally would be beyond most fans' organisations. Making it financially possible for often overworked, voluntary and badly funded supporter organisations is the responsibility of football and the government, and an additional recommendation that fans' organisations need central funding is needed from the Task Force as it nears the end of its work. The new unit will also need firm political backing from above, away from the bright lights of the Party conference, so that attempts at representation through mutual associations are not sidelined by the 'forces of conservatism' referred to by Tony Blair, which seem so prevalent in football's boardrooms. Finally, it will also need to be flexible: fans must be able to take the leading role and decide for themselves how they wish to, or can be, involved in their club. For some, the supporter trusts road may not be appropriate – buying shares in a club wholly owned by one individual, like Blackburn, may not be possible – and alternative methods of representation will need to be found, at least in the short term.

Ultimately, the proper regulation of football will only be achieved with active, involved and well-run representative organisations of fans and shareholders at one level, and some form of independent scrutiny at the top (whether the FA, the proposed 'independent scrutiny panel', a statutory regulator, or a combination of these). The supporter-trust scheme (as with all the Task Force's recommendations) will need to be monitored, and targets set for its implementation. Although in many ways the scheme neatly fits with a Blairite mission for co-operation, inclusion and even share-ownership schemes, as one of the most radical departures from government's traditional hostility to any involvement in the running of football, it could provide one of the cornerstones of a properly regulated football industry. Also, crucially, the idea of trusts as espoused by Lomax and Michie[32] comes to the centre of debates about how to include fans in decisions. It provides one route through which an answer can be found to the problems of corporate control which excludes small shareholders from effectively having a say over key decisions, to 'clubs in crisis', and to the representation of fans throughout the levels of the game. Furthermore, it has the added benefit of bringing new investment into football clubs which, unlike the increased revenues from elsewhere, has a 'representation' condition attached, thus also enabling effective scrutiny from the grass-roots. Ultimately, a fan-ownership solution could be the hammer which gets the square peg of democratisation into the round hole of the structure and finance of the English game.

PART IX

DO WE NEED AN OFFOOT?

33. Why football needs an independent regulator
GERRY SUTCLIFFE MP

There is a growing debate within Westminster about football and football regulation. There is a thriving all-party football group and a thriving all-party sports group. Football has a very strong place within Westminster. And so it should, because as politicians we are there to represent our constituents. I was born in Salford and am a keen Manchester United supporter. I represent Bradford South and in the 1999–2000 season Bradford City were in the Premier League. This delighted me and many of my constituents even though Premier League status has brought problems for the club, which I will come to later. First I would like to explain why I presented a Bill to the House of Commons on 5 May 1999 calling for an independent regulator of football.

The Charter for Football was part of the Labour Party manifesto for the General Election in 1997, and we were pleased to see the establishment of the Football Task Force as fulfilling that manifesto pledge. Many of us in the Labour Party were happy with the Task Force's remit whilst recognising there would be some difficulties in bringing a diverse group of people together to try and formulate the reports. But even during the time that those discussions took place, before publication of the final report, the number of problems facing the game increased. Of particular concern in Westminster was rising ticket prices and the effects of this on the game right across the spectrum.

One of the procedures that we as politicians have to try to bring in legislation as private members is the ten-minute rule Bill. In order to submit a ten-minute rule Bill an MP must have a number of sponsors; this gives an MP the opportunity for ten minutes on an afternoon in Parliament to put the case for a particular piece of legislation. On 5 May 1999 I moved a Bill on football regulation and briefly the proposal I made and the arguments I put were as follows.

The regulator would have powers to establish a code of conduct for football clubs; to set performance targets for clubs on a variety of issues; to call clubs to account for alleged breach of the code; and to gain access to any evidence from clubs, including financial and ticket-sales records. The regulator would report to the appropriate government department, and would be independent of any vested interest.

Football is a part of the nation's identity: its roots in our communities and its developments are an integral part of our cultural heritage. Football is the source and topic of many conversations up and down the land, and it is no exaggeration to say that, occasionally, it affects the United Kingdom's productivity.

Football speaks a universal language, bringing nations and people of all races together – even in disagreement on the merits of a particular player or team, or even of a referee's decision. Football also plays a major role in the House of Commons, as witnessed by the excellent work of the all-party football group – which is expertly chaired by my honourable friend the Member for Bassetlaw (Mr Ashton) – not to mention the exploits of the parliamentary football team. As football is so embedded in our society, our paramount priority should be to protect and enhance its future. Recognising that priority, the government created the Football Task Force.

We cannot allow the ownership of and responsibility for professional football to be left in the hands of those who seek to exploit it financially or for some personal kudos at the expense of supporters. There is a clear need to address important issues such as ticket pricing, club ownership, plc status and merchandising policies. Clubs have every right to make a healthy profit, but not at the expense of fans. There is a difference between a surplus on the one hand, and profiteering on the other. Our big clubs in particular need to be seen to act in a more responsible and accountable way to ensure a greater and more equitable redistribution of wealth throughout the game, and proper financial regulation.

Many of our fine new stadiums, large and small, are the focal point of local communities and have received considerable investment from the public purse. There is an enormous vacuum of power in the game following recent sackings and financial irregularities. Members of Parliament on both sides who have the best interests of the game at heart agree that there are huge concerns about the governance of football.

Football is not just an industry. It has more in common with the National Gallery and St Paul's Cathderal than with BP and ICI. It is a national treasure, not a device for squeezing money out of customers who face a monopoly. If clubs raise prices too dramatically, the customer cannot just go somewhere else. Support is total and usually a legacy handed down from generation to generation. We have to be careful about who can own clubs and the motivation driving those who run the game. This is an issue of business interest versus public interest. Is it right that media or leisure interests should be allowed outright control of clubs?

Football's present direction towards prioritising the demands of shareholders rather than fans has created an uneasy climate in which a small number of rich clubs will get richer while poorer clubs go to the wall. Already this season we have seen many clubs in deep financial crisis, including Doncaster, Brighton and Hove Albion, Oxford, Crystal Palace, Hull City and Portsmouth. I pay tribute to the MP for Hove, Ivor Caplin, whose leadership has helped the community in the revitalisation of Brighton and Hove Albion FC.

Soaring wage bills – fuelled by an incredible 40% increase in players' wages – and extraordinary transfer fees have added to the immense pressure to succeed at all costs. There are many examples of good practice. A lot could be learned from what has happened at Northampton Town and Bournemouth, where supporter trusts have been set up to enable fans to be involved in the running and accountability of their clubs. I pay tribute to the MP for Northampton South, Tony Clarke, who is the elected director of Northampton Town (and another contributor to this book) – a club that was recently congratulated on having the best access and facilities in the country for people with disabilities, as well as an equal opportunities policy.

The football regulator would be charged with the responsibility of presiding over the financial integrity of clubs. It could also investigate genuine complaints about ticket-pricing policy and the cost and frequency of issue of replica kits. The regulator would also be involved in helping the game to clean up its image as regards transfer fees and the role of agents. That element of the game involves millions of pounds and many fans are concerned that the lack of transparency damages the well-being of football.

Those who argue against regulation and say that football should be left to put its own house in order must prove that they have all the game's interests at heart. Self-regulation has not kept pace with the modern game, hence the creation of the Task Force. It was left to the Popplewell and Taylor reports to make recommendations on ground safety after the Bradford City fire disaster and the Hillsborough tragedy. The 1990 Taylor Report was damning about the governance of the game.

We are developing all-seater stadiums, but the investment to achieve that has had to come through bodies such as the Football Trust, involving public funds. The massive revenues from television and media rights were not prioritised for the benefit of spectators. Without the Taylor recommendations, it is unlikely that ground improvements would ever have taken place.

The all-party football group has received representations from all aspects of football and there is a genuine desire to see the game progress. The group made representations on the Manchester United/BSkyB bid. Those representations showed that the receipts of one Manchester United home game were bigger than two years' income for smaller clubs such as Darlington or Hartlepool. That cannot be good for the game. While I wish Manchester United every success, their success must not come at the expense of smaller clubs who develop young players and keep football available for millions of match-going supporters across the country. There should be a more equitable redistribution of the plentiful resources at the top of the game for clubs throughout the Football League and beyond.

Football has tremendous power to do good in society and can be used to help reduce crime and promote positive education policies. If the game is to continue to thrive, football must be allowed to develop at grass-roots level in schools and junior teams. Figures show a reduction in the number of amateur teams, and schools football is running into difficulty. My own schools association in Bradford is in desperate need of financial support. It is from bodies such as those that the future footballing stars will emerge.

The balance of big and small is an integral part of football's attraction, and to upset that balance would threaten to damage the whole market. Football is more than just an industry but, like many other industries, there is a need for sensible regulation to prevent anti-competitive practices and the emergence of cartels. I am not alone in calling for action, as there have been many academic reports and press articles to that effect. Many organisations connected with football have recognised that self-regulation has not worked and that a regulator is now required.

The Football Association, through FIFA, is responsible for the rules of the game, but it has failed miserably to protect and act in the best interests of all who support the game. It is now time to separate the regulatory function. The FA, rightly, should be responsible for the rules of the game, setting the criteria for membership, running competitions, overseeing player discipline and running the national side. However, it should hand over the scrutiny of clubs' finances and codes of conduct to an independent regulator.

The regulator would seek the assistance of a football industry committee, made up of bodies including the Football Supporters Association, the FA, the Premier League, the Football League, the Football Trust and the PFA. The separate regulatory function would ensure that the regulation of the financial, legal and commercial activities of clubs was seen as independent from vested interests.

There are many good people in football, and many who spend their lives putting great effort into developing football. I congratulate my local club, Bradford City, its directors, management, staff and fans, who have worked together to improve the club's fortunes not only on the playing-field but also in the running of the club's community activities. The club's success has raised the morale of the city. It is involved in Football in the Community, and is working with young people and the unemployed. It has established positive role models within the community, developed educational support and helped to kick out racism. The same tests as apply to other industries can be applied to football – issues such as monopoly control and serving the customer – to ensure a healthy game from top to bottom. An independent regulator would seek to address those issues and many more affecting football at all levels.

In my constituency, Bradford, the local team was promoted into the Premier League in 1999. Total euphoria took hold of the town, and a great deal of support for the club emerged from people that perhaps had not supported them in the past. However, all over the summer break players at the club tried to renegotiate contracts. This of course caused the club a great number of problems in terms of its financial position. This should not be the case and we should be in a situation where there is a clear code of conduct in those types of situations. The Task Force was established to look at problems in the game including those arising from commercialism, such as those at Bradford, but has faced tremendous difficulties drawing conclusions on what should be done to prevent over-commercialisation.

The Labour government set the agenda of the Task Force to focus on the many issues that football faces but did not get a quick enough reaction to prevent the game running into all sorts of new difficulties.

I believe that the case for regulation is overwhelming. Government is already involved in football in terms of the funding through the Football Trust for ground improvements. Commercialisation of the Post Office provoked proposals for a regulator in a White Paper before the House of Commons in May 1999. A football regulator is overdue, and the support for it in Westminster is growing. The all-party football group put together a paper on regulation and submitted it to the Task Force and we believe that government should find time, in what is admittedly a heavy legislative programme, for the necessary debate and for introducing legislation. We will continue to monitor what happens, and look forward to the Task Force's final report but clearly we will be supporting the Football Supporters Association and all those individual clubs that are giving evidence to us, to try to ensure that government does indeed address the situation in the immediate future.

34. Uniting the fans

ALISON PILLING

It has been a common enough call over recent years: fans should speak with one voice, fans should unite. But before you can really address that issue, there has to be some understanding of how fans have organised themselves to date. As with almost any pressure group, the first fans' organisations were social groups – people brought together by the love of their team and the game, who perhaps met up during home matches and travelled together to away games. More than 70 years ago, some of these 'supporters' clubs' got together as the National Federation of Football Supporters Clubs. While the NatFed, as they are affectionately known, have had a role over the years in consultation with the clubs and football authorities, their membership has in the past largely concerned itself with issues of away tickets and travel, and social events for its members.

In 1985 a group of mostly Liverpool fans formed a national body, the Football Supporters Association, in response to the disastrous organisation and consequences of the Heysel Stadium disaster. At the time, they were unaware of the existence of the NatFed and so took a different path in giving fans' organisation a more campaigning edge.

Since then a number of club-based Independent Supporters Associations (ISAs) have formed. Initially these were formed in response to a number of ill-conceived 'bond schemes' such as at Arsenal and West Ham. There are now ISAs at perhaps half the professional league clubs. With increasing politicisation of fans over the last decade, the distinction between ISAs and traditional supporters' clubs has become a little hazy. Alongside these developments there has also been the rise of the fanzine movement. In addition, thousands of football supporters subscribe to e-mail lists. There are also regional groups, more obviously 'political' groups, such as Football Fans Against the Criminal Justice Act, and Libero, so there is now a variety of ways and means of getting together.

This is a very sketchy picture, but it does give some sense of why demands for one supporters' voice are over-simplistic. With perhaps half a million people watching live football every weekend, there is of course a remarkable degree of agreement amongst fans. Whilst different organisations, publications and e-mail lists may have different roles and functions, there is an increasing convergence of views both on what the main issues are and how we feel about them.

During the 1980s, it was fairly clear that our concerns were about policing and safety. That came to a head with the Hillsborough disaster and the subsequent Taylor Report. Yet since then the focus for most fans has changed. Since Taylor, stadiums are safer and policing and stewarding have improved, though they are still far from perfect. But alongside these improvements has been the creation of the Premier League, a 400% increase in ticket prices at the top end and the massive impact of broadcasting on the live game, leading to a spiralling of players' wages and talk of a European super league. These developments have prompted new responses to the big issues as we enter the new millennium.

While the Premier League has apparently 'never had it so good', increasingly large numbers of football clubs are finding it hard to survive. And many of the fans of those clubs are deciding that the only way to be really sure that their club doesn't go under is to acquire a financial stake in the club themselves. The current focus on ownership is thus very apt, although it has to be made clear that this is a strategy of despair for many, not a genuine desire to own a club.

But how would fans uniting address any of these issues? It's our feeling that if there is a common agenda, it is important that fans speak with one voice wherever possible. It has been relatively easy for our detractors in the past to claim that individual supporters' groups are unrepresentative of the general opinion of the mass of football-goers, particularly if different groups are sending out different messages. The Premier League regularly airs this view alongside praise of its own 'supporter panels'. The fact that individuals are selected for their panels and asked set questions often with a clear market research agenda, as opposed to joining an organisation of their own free will, seems largely to have escaped notice. In any case, it is evident that reinforcing the message of unity around major issues would be a positive step.

Secondly, a united fans' movement could offer support to local campaigns. Whilst fans at Brighton, Chester and Doncaster have effectively fought their own battles, the Fans United events at each of these venues was a solid demonstration that football supporters can see beyond their own club loyalties to the greater good of the game.

Uniting the fans would also mean the opportunity to exchange experiences. One of the saddest indictments of the current situation in which football finds itself was the comment made by Crystal Palace fans to me recently: 'It's important that fans know the difference between going into administration and receivership.' I hadn't anticipated that supporters would need to exchange phone numbers of good accountants, but it demonstrates a need for information and support. Given that one of the greatest crises facing any football supporter is the threat to their club's very existence, the expertise of those involved in supporter trusts at Bournemouth and Northampton, for instance, is crucial. Finally, fans' unity means big national campaigns and the opportunity to be proactive in setting a new agenda. This is the gap that the Coalition of Football Supporters seeks to address.

The Coalition began, as with so many other supporter initiatives, by a group of fans sitting down together in a pub and talking. The FSA has several affiliated ISAs but these ISAs were rightly seeking a more equal relationship with the national body given the obvious strengths of their campaigning activities. A unanimous motion from the FSA's 1998 national conference strengthened this feeling of working together. There had recently been a thawing of previously tense relations between the FSA and the National Federation. Eventually a group of around 12 people emerged representing the two national fans' organisations plus the Disabled Supporters Association and representatives from four ISAs.

The 'steering group', as it grandly and ironically called itself, sent out questionnaires to all ISAs, supporters' clubs and fanzines for whom we had any contact details. We also organised a number of regional roadshows, inviting along all local supporter groups and advertising in the local press and club programmes. The level of consensus astonished us, despite our belief that most fans agreed about the major issues facing the game. If anything, there were two main responses to our questions (a) about problems in the game and (b) what to do about it, which were:

(a) variations on the wealth gap, ticket prices, big business controlling the game, television money, and

(b) don't talk about it any more – get campaigning!

The Coalition held its inaugural conference on 27 June 1999. An interim federal structure was agreed with any organisations with the ability to forward democratic representatives eligible to join. We recognise that this is an interim structure and debates continue about a more permanent, entrenched and democratic structure. It was also agreed that initially only those points on which we could achieve consensus would be pursued. By way of the focus on campaigning, a Fans' Charter was placed before conference. The Charter was unanimously agreed and is reproduced below.

For the establishment of independent regulation of football, to ensure the implementation of the following:

- the redistribution of wealth, including TV income, within football;
- controls over the type of people who are allowed to own football clubs;

- controls over the activities of plcs running football clubs;
- ticket prices to be pegged at levels which keep the game accessible to all fans;
- the democratisation of football to give supporters a voice.

At the time of writing 105 organisations have signed up to the Charter. The only organisations to date that have not signed when asked (perhaps four or five) have done so on the entirely legitimate grounds that they haven't yet had the opportunity to consult their membership fully. The Charter was presented to the government's Football Task Force in August 1999 in an effort to remind the Task Force members of the strength of feeling from a variety of groups and clubs across the country.

How far the Task Force or the football authorities are able to respond is debatable. There is a clear message, however. Football has always been the people's game but, for increasing numbers of people, it is no longer accessible. The ownership issue is one means of addressing the problems. At struggling clubs such as Northampton and Bournemouth, supporter trusts were their salvation. But to use a sadly old-fashioned phrase, working-class fans need other answers. If you can't afford a ticket, you are unlikely to be able to afford shares. In addition, those clubs with the worst practices regarding ticket pricing and exclusion are not making shares available on the market to groups of organised fans. In any case any combined stake of less than 10% is at risk of takeover by media conglomerates and other big-business interests.

It is the Coalition's view that each of the elements of the Charter relies on the others. Accessibility and financial controls rely on effective regulation. They also rely on further democratisation of the game with effective consultation on all major decisions. But underpinning the whole must be redistribution of wealth. There is plenty of money in the game for the present. It could leak away into the hands of a few club chairmen, media executives and the odd player and his agent, or it could be invested in the health of our national game well into the next century.

35. Self-regulation or regulation?

BRIAN LOMAX

As we look towards the future governance of professional football in the new millennium, 1999 will be remembered for two famous decisions, both involving BSkyB. The two decisions may at first sight appear mutually contradictory in their attitude to monopoly, but both were undeniably correct as far as the best interests of the public and the football industry are concerned.

The bid by BSkyB for Manchester United would have placed the broadcaster in pole position to negotiate an optimum contract for football broadcasting rights whatever the outcome of the OFT case in the Restrictive Practices Court. It was a fine each-way bet, but thankfully it failed. Yet the same people who rejoiced in that outcome were also found rejoicing on 28 July when the RPC found in favour of the FA Premier League and therefore BSkyB.

The reason for this apparent contradiction is simple: both decisions upheld the right of the footballing public not to be dominated by a handful of major clubs to the detriment of all the rest. They preserved a reasonably equitable distribution of broadcasting income between the 20 Premier League clubs, and at the same time ensured that the Premier League's undertaking to the Football Task Force over the redistribution of monies to the lower levels of the game would be binding.

We must not, however, be deceived into thinking that these decisions have saved football from the crisis of new commercialism so eloquently described and analysed by David Conn.[1] They have merely avoided making the situation worse.

One of the best outcomes of the February 1999 and July 1999 Birkbeck College Conferences[2] was to show that David Conn's analysis, considered subversive and extreme when first published just two years previously, is now accepted as conventional wisdom by the vast majority of thinking observers. At the risk of being repetitious, it is briefly this: that the FA historically had the role of protecting the whole of football from the dominance of the rich and powerful. Its byzantine structures and consequent resistance to change, which are now so widely criticised and ridiculed, were its greatest strength when performing that role. However, since it abandoned those responsibilities by christening and anointing the

Premier League breakaway, and has now degraded even its own cup competition by exempting the holders in pursuit of its international wheeler-dealing, it can safely be said that the referee has unfortunately become one of the players.

The question now facing us is whether the FA, as a player in the game, can ever again be trusted with football's regulation. That regulation of some sort is required can scarcely be doubted, if the game is not to be strangled by the wages spiral on the one hand and a plethora of club bankruptcies on the other.

In my younger days I used to be a probation officer, and if I were sitting in court for this one, I would be expecting the bench to find the defendant guilty as charged, but I would ask for a two-year probation order. The defendant was of previous good character, if somewhat pompous and stuffy, for most of this century, and only in the last seven years has become easily led by a bunch of spivs and entrepreneurs. Perhaps he deserves one last chance before being condemned to historical ignominy.

In recent years, my daily work has been to run a charity, and in my seven years as a director of a lower-division football club I have seen many similarities between the two. Charities do not make a profit; while they may sometimes make a surplus, this is purely for reinvestment in the organisation's work and not for distribution to shareholders. Charities are not there to make money, but they are not there to lose money either, or the public will lose confidence in them and their managers. The trustees are there to administer the funds honestly and beneficially, providing the best possible product or service to ensure solvency and rectitude.

The analogy should by now be clear. The idea of a lower-division football club making an operating profit, and its shareholders reaping a dividend, is ridiculous to most of us who have been practitioners. Only an immensely wealthy patron, or the windfall of a large transfer fee or an unforeseen cup run, can change the picture; and the effect of these is normally quite temporary and any profit absorbed by the consequences of success. Few benefactors stay for any length of time, and even if they do, their largesse merely masks an operating deficit by helping to fund it.

So if trading profits are impossible to sustain, why not give up the pretence, and declare in public that a football club is a not-for-profit company? This would make little change to its organisation or finances, but would have the effect of proclaiming its probity and deterring potential predators. It would also make co-operation with the local authority, and with the community in general, much more practicable and likely. This is one possible model of future governance, and while the plcs will never adopt it, the majority of the rest might usefully consider it. Remember FA Rule 34![3]

Returning to our question of regulation, any form of regulation must be universally applicable if it is to be seen as fair. Those who make or seek a profit from the game must accept the restraints imposed on others if the game is not to implode financially. Big business, in the form of the Premier League via BSkyB, has extracted a disproportionate amount of the game's income for profit over the last seven years, and in doing so has forced many of the smaller local clubs into the red.

The whole thrust of the work of the Football Task Force has been to produce a code of good practice, and to rectify as far as possible the imbalance that has come into the game in the 1990s. Clearly, the profit-making vested interests will resist these changes. The FA should be given two years to prove that it is not just one of those vested interests, and that it is capable of reassuming, in effect, the role of the Charity Commission, regulating impartially for everyone's benefit. Two years' probation – but with the sanction of being brought back before the Court for breach. If this happens, it will be time for a statutory regulatory body for the game.

The Task Force is expected shortly to publish its final report on the commercial aspects of the game. I would expect such a report to address how its recommendations are to be implemented through a new regulatory structure. If the FA is to be given a final chance to put its house in order, it must recognise that any new regulatory régime should protect consumers against vested interests. The key here is to create a balanced structure that cannot be dominated by the game's major players. The FA could do a lot worse than consider involving people from outside the game, but with relevant knowledge and experience, as well as a supporters' representative. As the Task Force itself has shown, both these groups can have a crucial input into the game's development. In effect, this would also be a good model for a local club board of directors. As one who has served for seven years as a supporters' representative on a board, I will close by seeking to define what I see as the role of the supporters' representative on the regulatory body, over the initial two-year period:

1) To negotiate the unification of the Football Supporters Association (FSA) and the National Federation of Football Supporters Clubs (NFFSC). Given the emergence of the Coalition of Football Supporters in 1999, there would appear to be sufficient goodwill around to achieve this, but I believe the initial appointee should not be chosen from the FSA or the NFFSC if he or she is to be seen to be impartial. Each organisation has a different basis of membership, and this issue needs to be handled carefully in order not to be seen as a takeover of one body by the other.

2) To establish an agreed electoral system, and procedures for the election of supporters' representatives to club boards of directors. Our

system at Northampton Town FC, the single transferable vote by an electorate based on a minimal membership subscription, is a good one, but would be improved by the inclusion of all season-ticket-holders, and members of all accredited supporters' organisations, of which many clubs have several. The wider the electorate, the more democratic the system, but it must be confined to committed supporters.

3) Finally, to establish a national supporters' electorate from all clubs and recognised bodies, for the election of future supporters' representatives to the regulatory body: in effect, a supporters' 'general election' every two or three years. This would not only generate considerable media interest, but it would make the concept of a 'supporters' representative' real and true, and give every encouragement to local boards to accept the principle of democratic representation within their own ranks.

These three tasks would, of course, be in addition to playing a full part in the day-to-day work of the regulatory body. It would be a key activist role for whoever was appointed, and by virtue of the workload it should ideally have support services provided. But for a minimal outlay, so much could be achieved. Look at what the Task Force has achieved with just £130,000 of public money. If their work is to bear fruit, we must have a regulatory body to carry it on. And if after two years the FA has shown itself unable or unwilling to do it, the Secretary of State must intervene. To borrow an analogy from our summer game, if the wicketkeeper misses the ball, we need the deep fine leg.

Notes on the contributors

ALASDAIR BELL
Legal Adviser on European Union Affairs to UEFA, White & Case Solicitors

GERRY BOON
Head of Deloitte & Touche Football Industry Team

DR ADAM BROWN
Institute of Popular Culture, Manchester Metropolitan University, and a member of the Football Task Force

ANDY BURNHAM
Special Adviser at the Department of Culture, Media and Sport

PROFESSOR TOM CANNON
Chief Executive, Management Charter Initiative

ARMAND CARABÉN
L'Elefant Blau (FC Barcelona Independent Supporters Group). Currently a consultant to several Spanish and international companies. From 1970–75 he was the general manager of FC Barcelona, when he famously signed Johan Cruyff

PROFESSOR MARTIN CAVE
Department of Economics, Brunel University, and a member of the Competition Commission. He was an expert witness for the director-general of Fair Trading in the Premier League case before the RPC

TONY CLARKE MP
Member of Parliament for Northampton South and the elected director of Northampton Town FC

NIC COWARD
Company Secretary, the Football Association

DR PETER CROWTHER
Consultant to Rosenblatt Solicitors

JOHAN CRUYFF
Former player and coach at FC Barcelona. Three times winner of the European Cup with Ajax (1971, 1972, 1973). Three times European Footballer of the Year (1971, 1972, 1974)

TONY DART
Director of Technical Services, Chartered Institute of Management Accountants (CIMA)

STUART DYKES
Schalke 04 Fan Initiative

NICHOLAS FINNEY OBE
Monopolies & Mergers Commission Panel Member for BSkyB/Manchester United case and managing director of the Waterfront Partnership

ALFONS GODALL
L'Elefant Blau (FC Barcelona Independent Supporters Group)

MARK GOYDER
Managing Director, Tomorrow's Company

SEAN HAMIL
School of Management and Organisational Psychology, Birkbeck College

NIGEL HAWKINS
Utilities and football analyst at Williams de Bröe

CHRIS HEINITZ
Chair, Leisure & Tourism Committee, Local
Government Association

KEVIN JAQUISS
Cobbetts Solicitors

JOAN LAPORTA
President, L'Elefant Blau (FC Barcelona
Independent Supporters Group)

MIKE LEE
Spokesman for the FA Premier League

L'ELEFANT BLAU
FC Barcelona Independent Supporters Group

BRIAN LOMAX
Chairman of Northampton Town Supporter
Trust and elected director of Northampton
Town FC, 1992–99

LEE MANNING
Buchler Phillips & Co.

ROBERT MATUSIEWICZ
Ambition Management, licensed FIFA agent
and specialist sports consultant

PROFESSOR JONATHAN MICHIE
School of Management and Organisational
Psychology, Birkbeck College

STEPHEN MORROW
School of Management, Heriot-Watt
University

DR CHRISTINE OUGHTON
Reader in Management, School of Manage-
ment and Organisational Psychology,
Birkbeck College

TOM PENDRY MP
Chairman, Football Trust

ALISON PILLING
Chair of the Football Supporters Association
and a committee member of the Coalition of
Football Supporters

PIARA POWER
Kick Racism Out Of Football

RICHARD SCUDAMORE
Chief Executive of the Premier League

PROFESSOR PETER SLOANE
Department of Economics, University of
Aberdeen

GERRY SUTCLIFFE MP
MP for Bradford South

DR STEFAN SZYMANSKI
Department of Economics, Imperial College

GORDON TAYLOR
Chief Executive, Professional Footballers
Association (PFA)

DR ROGAN TAYLOR,
Director, Football Research Unit, University
of Liverpool

ANDY WALSH
Chair, Independent Manchester United
Supporters Association (IMUSA)

STEVEN WARBY
School of Management and Organisational
Psychology, Birkbeck College

JOHN WILLIAMS
Sir Norman Chester Centre for Football
Research

Notes

Preface

1. S. Hamil, J. Michie and C. Oughton (eds), *A Game of Two Halves? The Business of Football* (Mainstream, 1999).

Chapter 1

1. Now the Competition Commission.
2. For example with the ruling against ENIC's attempts to own more than one club in the same competition (in this case the UEFA cup), on which see chapter 8 below.
3. Or whatever body will replace the Football Trust when it is reconstituted from April 2000.
4. For more information on Shareholders United, see www.shareholdersunited.org or write to PO Box 26034, London SW10 9GN.
5. And the continued failure of *The Observer* newspaper in particular to understand or even accept the decision.
6. Gerry Boon edits this series.
7. However, NTL have held on to their shareholding which they admit was bought in order to get a seat at the table for the Premier TV rights decision (see Chapter 8).
8. On 23 November 1999 BSkyB were forced by the Premier League to reduce their shareholding in Manchester United from 11.1% to under 10%. They therefore cut their holding to 9.9% which is still by far the largest shareholding, the next largest being the 6.5% owned by Martin Edwards.
9. Indeed, the Task Force played an important role in giving evidence in the RPC case, with the judge citing that evidence favourably, and although the Task Force were prevented from giving evidence against the BSkyB attempt to take over Manchester United, Adam Brown did organise for Task Force members to make a joint submission (as individuals) to the Office of Fair Trading against the takeover and Dr Brown also gave evidence to the MMC panel.

Chapter 2

1. On the pitch we are not so good but we are getting better, thanks mainly to Manchester United.
2. G. Boon (ed.), Deloitte & Touche *Annual Review of Football Finance*, Deloitte & Touche Sport, August 1999, p.26; and G. Boon (ed.), *England's Premier Clubs: A Review of 1998 Results*, Deloitte & Touche Sport, April 1999.

Chapter 3

1. In December 1999 it was announced that music impresario Ken Kenwright had bought Peter Johnson's 68% controlling stake in Everton.
2. See Chapter 10 by Mark Goyder for a discussion of what a stakeholder firm would look like.
3. See Chapter 2 in this volume.

Chapter 5

1. See Chapter 27 by Tony Clarke in this volume.
2. Perhaps the same will be true of New Labour voters as well . . .

Chapter 6

1. *British Sky Broadcasting Group plc and Manchester United plc: A Report on the Proposed Merger*, April 1999 (Cm 4305) ('the MMC Report'). The MMC has now been renamed the Competition Commission, but 'MMC' is used for the purposes of this chapter.
2. A brief summary of SUAM's submissions can be found in the MMC Report, at 6.191–6.209.
3. In its summary, the MMC stated (para 1.6): 'In considering the public interest consequences of the merger, *we looked primarily at its effects on competition among broadcasters for live Premier League rights*' (emphasis added).

4. *The Director-General's Review of BSkyB's Position in the Wholesale Pay TV Market,* OFT, 1996.

Chapter 8

1. For further discussion, see also Chapter 7 in this book by Nicholas Finney, an MMC panel member at the time of the BSkyB/Manchester United judgement.
2. Patrick Harverson, *Financial Times*, 4 November 1999.
3. *The Guardian*, 14 July 1999.
4. In December 1999 it was announced that BSkyB had taken a 5% share of Sunderland FC, making it the exclusive media and commercial agent of the club.
5. On 23 November BSkyB reduced their holding in Manchester United to 9.9%. This still leaves them as by far the largest shareholder, with Martin Edwards the second largest shareholder, holding 6.5%. While some points in the chapter refer to the specific issue of BSkyB having had more than 10% of Manchester United's shares, and while it is to be welcomed that this particular breach of the rules has been dealt with, as is detailed in the text, BSkyB are still in breach of Premiership, FA and UEFA rules, and are still in effect circumventing the Government decision following the MMC ruling against BSkyB's ownership of Manchester United.

Chapter 9

1. C. Shindler, *Manchester United Ruined My Life*, Hodder, 1998.
2. I. Taylor, 'English football in the 1990s: Taking Hillsborough seriously', in J. Williams and S. Wagg (eds), *British Football and Social Change*, Leicester University Press, 1991.
3. S. Lash and J. Urry, *Economies of Signs and Space*, Routledge, 1994.
4. O. James, *Juvenile Violence in A Winner-Loser Culture*, Free Association Books, 1995.
5. J. Williams, *Is It All Over? Can Football Survive the Premier League?*, South Street Press, 1999.
6. G. Whannel, *Fields in Vision*, Routledge, 1992.
7. J. Williams, 'The local and the global in English soccer and the rise of satellite television', *Sociology of Sport Journal*, 1994,

Vol. 11, No. 4, pp.376–97.
8. J. Williams and S. Perkins, 'Ticket pricing, football business and "excluded" football fans' in *A Report to the Football Task Force*, University of Leicester, 1999.
9. *The Guardian*, 17 August 1999.
10. I. Taylor, *Crime in Context*, Polity, 1999.
11. J. Sugden and A. Tomlinson, *FIFA and the Contest for World Football*, Polity, 1998.
12. S. Morrow, *The New Business of Football*, Macmillan, 1999.
13. A, Brown, 'Thinking the unthinkable, or playing the game?' in S. Hamil et al. (eds), *A Game of Two Halves? The Business of Football*, Mainstream, 1999; D. Conn, *The Football Business*, Mainstream, 1997; S. Hamil, 'A whole new ball game?' in S. Hamil et al. (eds), A *Game of Two Halves?* op. cit.; E. Horton, *Moving the Goalposts*, Mainstream, 1997.
14. R. Giulianotti, *Football: a Sociology of the Global Game*, Polity, 1999.
15. J. Sugden and A. Tomlinson, op. cit.
16. I. Taylor, 'It's a whole new ball game: sports television, the cultural industries and the condition of football in England in 1993', 1994 (revised version of paper presented at the University of Leicester, 18 June, 1993).
17. Ibid., p.29.
18. U. Beck, *Risk Society: Towards a New Modernity*, Sage, 1992.
19. J. Gray, *False Dawn: The Delusions of Global Capitalism*, Granta, 1998.
20. *The Observer*, 20 June 1999.
21. M. Jacques, 'The age of sport', *The Observer*, 13 July 1997.
22. J. Williams and S. Perkins, op. cit.
23. J. Michie and A. Walsh, 'What future for football?' in S. Hamil et al. (eds) *A Game of Two Halves?*, op. cit.
24. R. Levitas, *The Inclusive Society?*, Macmillan, 1998; I. Taylor, *Crime in Context*, Polity, 1999.
25. I. Taylor, op. cit.
26. A. King, 'The lads, masculinity and the new consumption of football', *Sociology*, Vol. 31, No. 2, May 1997; A. King, *The End of the Terraces?*, Routledge, 1998.
27. A. Giddens, *Modernity and Self-Identity*, Polity, 1991.
28. T. Watkins, *Cherries in the Red*, Headline, 1999.

Chapter 10

1. For example, see the chapters by Gordon Taylor of the PFA and by the FC Barcelona supporters group, L'Elefant Blau.
2. For more details on Schalke 04 and the German perspective on commercialisation of football, see Chapter 14 by Stuart Dykes in this book.

Chapter 12

1. On which, see A. Brown and A. Walsh, *Not For Sale: Manchester United, Murdoch and the Defeat of BSkyB*, Mainstream, 1999.
2. For further detail of the FC Barcelona supporters group L'Elefant Blau, see 'The Struggle for Democracy at Barcelona FC' written by the group, in S. Hamil, J. Michie and C. Oughton (eds), *A Game of Two Halves? The Business of Football*, Mainstream, 1999.
3. See Chapter 4, this volume.
4. On which, see Chapter 8 by Adam Brown, this volume.

Chapter 13

1. For a discussion of these rules, see Chapter 8 in this volume.
2. See Chapter 4 of this volume.

Chapter 15

1. A fuller description of the work of the organisation can be found in S. Hamil, J. Michie and C. Oughton (eds), *A Game of Two Halves? The Business of Football*, Mainstream, 1999, pp.202–8.

Chapter 16

1. For a discussion of the situation in Germany, see Chapter 14 by Stuart Dykes, this volume.

Chapter 17

1. Arguably these assets include the expected future earnings from the sale of broadcasting rights, which may be viewed as a form of intellectual capital or property right.

Chapter 18

1. Administration is a procedure designed to give a company protection from its creditors in order to secure sufficient time to put a business plan together which incorporates a financial reorganisation to provide a viable future for the business and incorporates sensible proposals to deal with the existing debts which have been temporarily frozen in the administrative process. In most cases creditors will only expect to be repaid a proportion of their new debt, which could be over a number of years.

Chapter 20

1. An illiquid market in a company's shares occurs where there are only a small number of potential buyers or sellers of those shares, resulting in limited or 'thin' trading.
2. *The New Business of Football: Accountability and Finance in Football*, Macmillan, 1999.

Chapter 21

1. M. Bainbridge, S. Cameron and P. Dawson, 'Satellite Television and the Demand for Football: A Whole New Ball Game?' in *Scottish Journal of Political Economy*, Vol. 43, No. 3, August 1996, pp.317–33.
2. R. Fort and J. Quirk, 'Cross-subsidisation, Incentives and Outcomes in Professional Team Sports Leagues' in *Journal of Economic Literature*, Vol. 33, September 1995, pp.1265–99.

Chapter 22

1. Any new agreements will, however, be subject to the Competition Act, 1998.
2. R. Fort and J. Quirk, *Paydirt: The Business of Professional Team Sports*, Princeton University Press, 1992.
3. Recent government proposals to modify this criterion would have the effect of bringing more Premier League clubs (than the current three) into the merger reference net (DTI, *Mergers: A Consultation Document on Proposals for Reform*, DTI, August 1999).
4. Because uncertainty of the results of any match, or of the competition as a whole, generates spectator interest.
5. A possible analogy is the approach taken in competition law to collaboration among firms in pre-competitive R&D, which may be justified, but is followed by competition in production and selling.
6. In August 1999, the OFT found that some Premier League clubs had, in fact, been fixing the prices of replica shirts.
7. This test is endorsed by the US Depart-

ment of Justice, the European Commission and the Office of Fair Trading (in its Guidelines for the Competition Act, 1998).

8. Thus if Premier League rights satisfied this criterion, then so would all football rights, as anyone cornering this larger set of rights could clearly raise prices. But Premier League rights alone would constitute a market.

9. See MMC, *British Sky Broadcasting Group plc and Manchester United plc: A Report on the Proposed Merger* Cm. 4395, Competition Commission, April 1999, paras 2.25-2.51 and 4.52-4.165.

10. For further development of this point, see Stefan Szymanski's chapter in this volume.

Chapter 23

1. Richard Scudamore was subsequently appointed chief executive of the Premier League.

2. A. Brown, 'Thinking the Unthinkable or Playing the Game?' in S. Hamil et al, *A Game of Two Halves? The Business of Football*, Mainstream, 1999.

3. S. Inglis, *League Football and the Men who Made It*, Collins Willow, 1998.

4. J. Ferris, Restrictive Practices Court Judgement, 28 July 1999.

Chapter 24

1. The case was heard in the Restrictive Practices Court between January 1999 and April 1999.

2. This charge was not upheld by the RPC and the OFT lost the case.

3. The effects of TV overkill should not be underestimated. For example, falling audiences for snooker are often attributed to the explosion in TV coverage that the game experienced.

Chapter 26

1. David Conn, *The Football Business: Fair Game in the 1990s?*, Mainstream, 1997.

2. See Adam Brown's chapter in this volume on the work of the Football Task Force.

Chapter 29

1. For further discussion, see Chapter 26 by Piara Power in this book

2. See David Conn, *The Football Business: Fair Game in the 1990s?*, Mainstream, 1997; S. Hamil et al, *A Game of Two Halves? The Business of Football*, Mainstream, 1999.

3. For a full discussion of this rule, see D. Conn, op. cit., 1997, and D. Conn in S. Hamil et al, op. cit.

4. J. Michie, *New Mutualism – A Golden Goal?*, The Co-operative Party, 1999.

5. See Brian Lomax in S. Hamil et al, op. cit., and Chapter 35 in this volume.

6. For further details contact Alister Bennett at The Football Trust, AlastairB@football-trust.org.uk

Chapter 30

1. On which, see Chapter 26 by Piara Power in this volume.

Chapter 32

1. I was a member of the Football Task Force Core Working Group from August 1997 and a full member of the Task Force from February 1999. For a full description of the body's formation and work, see A. Brown, 'Thinking the Unthinkable or Playing the Game: The Football Task Force, New Labour and the reform of English Football' in S. Hamil et al, *A Game of Two Halves? The Business of Football*, Mainstream, 1999.

2. Ibid.

3. G. Boon (ed.), *Annual Review of Football Finance*, Deloitte & Touche, 1999.

4. A. Brown and A. Walsh, *Not For Sale: Manchester United, Murdoch and the Defeat of BSkyB*, Mainstream, 1999.

5. DCMS (1998a), *Eliminating Racism From Football*, DCMS.

6. For details of the 'Kick It Out' campaign, see Chapter 26 by Piara Power in this volume.

7. DCMS (1998b), *Improving Disabled Access*, DCMS.

8. DCMS (1999), *Investing in the Community*, DCMS.

9. B. Lomax, 'Supporter Representation on the Board: The Case of Northampton Town FC' in S. Hamil et al, op. cit.; J. Michie, *The New Mutualism: A Golden Goal?*, Co-operative Party, 1999.

10. J. Smith, *Football, Its Values, Finances and Reputation*, FA, 1998.

11. *Financial Times*, 5 October 1999.

12. J. Williams and S. Perkins, 'Ticket pricing,

football business and "excluded" football fans' in *A Report to the Football Task Force*, University of Leicester, 1998.

13. Football Supporters Association, *Submission to the Football Task Force* (unpublished paper), 1998; T. Crabbe, *The Price Ain't Right*, FSA, 1995.

14. D. Conn, *The Football Business*, op. cit.; D. Conn, 'The New Commercialism', op. cit.

15. Football Association, Premier League, Football League, *Football's Report to the Football Task Force* (unpublished paper), 1999.

16. D. Conn, *The Football Business*, op. cit.

17. Football Association et al, *Football's Report to the Football Task Force*, op. cit.

18. R. Chorley, *Submission to the Football Task Force* (unpublished paper), 1999.

19. *The Independent*, 28 October 1999.

20. Football Association, *Blueprint for the Future of Football*, FA, 1991.

21. Football Association et al, *Football's Report to the Football Task Force*, op. cit., pp.64–5.

22. Football Supporters Association, *Second Submission to the Football Task Force* (unpublished paper), 1999.

23. FA, *Football, Its Values, Finances and Reputation*, 1998.

24. Salomon Brothers, *UK Football Clubs: Valuable Assets?*, Salomon Brothers, 1997.

25. Labour Party, *Charter for Football*, Labour Party, 1996.

26. Football Association et al, *Football's Report to the Football Task Force*, op. cit., p.132.

27. J. Williams and S. Perkins, 'Ticket Pricing', op. cit.

28. A. Brown, 'Let's All have A Disco: Football, Popular Music and Democratisation' in S. Redhead, D. Wynne and J. O'Connor, *The Clubcultures Reader: Readings in Popular Cultural Studies*, Blackwells, 1997.

29. DCMS, *Investing in the Community*, DCMS, 1999, 5(d).8.

30. *The Independent*, 8 October 1999.

31. Brown and Walsh, op. cit., 1999, pp.77–81

32. B. Lomax, 'Supporter Representation on the Board: The Case of Northampton Town FC' in S. Hamil et al, op. cit.; J. Michie, *The New Mutualism: A Golden Goal?*, Co-operative Party, 1999.

Chapter 35

1. David Conn, *The Football Business: Fair Game in the '90s?*, Mainstream, 1997; David Conn, 'The New Commercialism' in S. Hamil et al, *A Game of Two Halves? The Business of Football*, Mainstream, 1999.

2. Conferences held at the Department of Management, Birkbeck College, 3 February 1999 and 8 July 1999. See http://www.bbk.ac.uk/manop/man/Football.htm for more details.

3. Rule 34 of the FA rulebook states that nobody should draw a salary for acting as a director of a football club; that nobody should derive major income from owning football company shares; and that a football club company is protected against asset-stripping. For more details, see Conn (1997), pp.35. For more details see http://www.cofs.co.uk

Index